It b

methyl-alcohol cocktail

It was with this stuff—basically, paint thinner—the gang planned to do Malloy in. They thought it was a brilliant idea. Instead of using deadly force and risking some kind of direct confrontation with their prey, they would actively encourage Malloy to bring about his own demise. His ravenous thirst would prove to be his undoing. . . .

While Marino and Pasqua were sure Malloy would easily succumb to the vast amounts of alcohol that would be thrust upon him, they decided to set up the foundation as a backup plan just in case.

It would be called "the most grotesque chain of events in New York criminal history". . .

On the House

THE BIZARRE KILLING
OF MICHAEL MALLOY

SIMON READ

BERKLEY BOOKS, NEW YORK

THE BERKLEY PUBLISHING GROUP
Published by the Penguin Group
Penguin Group (USA) Inc.
375 Hudson Street, New York, New York 10014, USA
Penguin Group (Canada), 90 Eglinton Avenue East, Suite 700, Toronto, Ontario M4P 2Y3, Canada
(a division of Pearson Penguin Canada Inc.)
Penguin Books Ltd., 80 Strand, London WC2R 0RL, England
Penguin Group Ireland, 25 St. Stephen's Green, Dublin 2, Ireland (a division of Penguin Books Ltd.)
Penguin Group (Australia), 250 Camberwell Road, Camberwell, Victoria 3124, Australia
(a division of Pearson Australia Group Pty. Ltd.)
Penguin Books India Pvt. Ltd., 11 Community Centre, Panchsheel Park, New Delhi—110 017, India
Penguin Group (NZ), Cnr. Airborne and Rosedale Roads, Albany, Auckland 1310, New Zealand
(a division of Pearson New Zealand Ltd.)
Penguin Books (South Africa) (Pty.) Ltd., 24 Sturdee Avenue, Rosebank, Johannesburg 2196,
South Africa

Penguin Books Ltd., Registered Offices: 80 Strand, London WC2R 0RL, England

ON THE HOUSE

A Berkley Book / published by arrangement with the author

PRINTING HISTORY
Berkley mass-market edition / October 2005

ISBN: 0-425-20678-5

BERKLEY®
Berkley Books are published by The Berkley Publishing Group,
a division of Penguin Group (USA) Inc.,
375 Hudson Street, New York, New York 10014.
BERKLEY is a registered trademark of Penguin Group (USA) Inc.
The "B" design is a trademark belonging to Penguin Group (USA) Inc.

PRINTED IN THE UNITED STATES OF AMERICA

10 9 8 7 6 5 4 3 2 1

To my parents, Bill and Susan,
who always encouraged and believed.

ACKNOWLEDGMENTS

Writing a book is a somewhat lonesome undertaking, but there are people who help along the way—in this case, quite a few people. For their friendship and support, I thank Danny, Brian, Ryan and Mike R. Many thanks go to Simon B. and Jessica for the web design, dinners and frequent trips to the movies. To the chain gang—Dave, Randy, Matt, Mike, Jeanine, Lea, Sajid, Rebecca, Dean, Ben, Scott, Tammie, Tara and Angileé—thanks for putting up with my politically incorrect behavior. Australian Jack, thanks for being more politically incorrect than I am. A special thanks to Ben for the scotch and Chris W. for the appetizers. To my agent, Ed Knappman, I want to extend heartfelt thanks for your dedication and hard work on my behalf. This being my first book, I was very fortunate to have a fantastic editor in Samantha Mandor, who gently shepherded me through the whole process. In the Bronx, I am forever in the debt of Mark Nusenbaum, who oversees the archives at the Bronx County Courthouse. He presides over an amazing wealth of history and did a wonderful job tracking down ancient case files for me. With kindness and patience, he put up with countless phone calls from me, too. Love and thanks go to Mike and Debbie for always making me feel at home and fighting the brave fight. To Tony, Phil and Mike—thanks for the music. Finally, to all my family, love and thanks for all the years of support and for never doubting the dream.

"Everybody should believe
          in something.

I believe I'll have
          another drink."

—UNKNOWN

CONTENTS

PROLOGUE
Digging in the Dirt

This story is true. Names have not been changed to protect the innocent, for nearly all the participants were perpetrators of nefarious schemes and bodily harm. They were low-rent thugs and booze-addled crooks surprisingly incompetent in their criminal undertakings. This is not a tale of smooth operators in silk suits. It is, instead, a story of bungling ineptitude, of a crime so convoluted, authorities were "admittedly skeptical" as to its veracity when it first came to light. Once the facts were established, Bronx District Attorney Samuel J. Foley declared the scheme to be "the most grotesque chain of events in New York criminal history."

On Saturday, May 13, 1933, a headline in the *New York Times* declared:

INSURANCE MURDER CHARGED TO FIVE
TALE OF HORROR IS TOLD

Five men were charged with murder and two others were detained as material witnesses yesterday after an inquiry into charges that a derelict man had been murdered to collect $1,788 for which the defendants had him insured.

A story of horror was unfolded by the police and District Attorney Samuel J. Foley of the Bronx. It concerned a man who proved so hardy of life that another man, with a false identification card, almost was done to death as a substitute. The authorities were admittedly skeptical two weeks ago when they were informed of the plot, but their first search for proof not only uncovered the murder of Michael Malloy, a former stationary fireman, but led them on to clues that indicated a woman also may have been a victim . . .

It was a Thursday when Detective Edward Leonard of the New York City Police Department's Homicide Squad dropped by Ferncliff Cemetery in Westchester County, New York. Accompanying him was Assistant District Attorney Arthur Carney and Dr. Charles E. Hochman, assistant medical examiner for the Bronx. The date was May 11, 1933. With a flash of his badge, Leonard introduced himself and his entourage to Alex Medovich, the grave superintendent on duty that afternoon. Motioning to Carney, Leonard explained they had a court order authorizing the exhumation of grave No. 2070. Medovich nodded and led the way, taking the men on a brief tour past grand mausoleums and ornate angels carved in stone.

Buried in grave No. 2070 was a man who—up until his violent end—had distinguished himself as a marvel of resilience. He was a tragic figure and extraordinary fellow if only because the circumstances of his death had been so outrageous. Those who pursued his demise had invested much sweat and toil in realizing their ambition. In life, he was a worthy adversary—though it seemed he was unaware of the forces plotting against him.

Leonard pulled his notebook from an inside jacket pocket. He flipped through its pages and briefly reviewed the case's particulars. There were five suspects: a swarthy speakeasy owner, a paralytic drunk of a bartender, a psychotic cabbie, a crooked undertaker and a greengrocer. Three of them were already in the Bronx County Jail for unrelated crimes. Suspect number six was a well-known—and now dead—Bronx thug named Anthony "Tough Tony" Bastone, a gentleman cut down in a hail of gunfire only two months prior. No sooner had Tough Tony claimed a cold slab in the Bronx morgue, than police began hearing rumors of a sinister conspiracy. It was a story of shocking degradation and cold-blooded desperation. The information investigators received paved a twisted path to Ferncliff Cemetery. It was here, after two weeks of wading through the lower dregs of humanity, that Leonard was sent by Inspector Henry Bruckman—head of the Homicide Squad—to dig for answers.

"This is it."

Medovich's words derailed Leonard's train of thought. They were in the St. Francis section of the cemetery, an area set aside for charity graves. In front of them was a single stone. The name on it was Nicholas Mellory. He'd been laid to rest on February 24, just two days following his death on George Washington's Birthday. The grave was devoid of flowers or any other offering to indicate he was missed. Nope, he was dead; gone and—until now—forgotten.

"Dig it up," Leonard said.

The lawmen and the medical examiner watched as two laborers, supervised by Medovich, began their arduous task. Eight feet down, their shovels hit wood. Leonard ordered them to bring the coffin up. It was a cheap pine box. The lid had caved in under the weight of the earth. The lining was soaked through. Inside was a corpse covered in filth and wearing an undershirt, pants, drawers, shoes and stockings. Blood, still moist, was visible on the deceased's face. Dr. Hochman bent down to get a closer look and noticed that the face and neck were "pinkish red or cherry red in color."

The body was loaded into the city's mortuary wagon and taken to the morgue at Fordham Hospital. There it was stripped and cleaned, then photographed for the record. The time was 6:30 P.M. Hochman noted that the body was "in a fairly good state of preservation." The pinkish discoloration he had first noted at the cemetery was in greater evidence now on the face, neck and back, as well as on the back of the arms and legs. Notes were made and additional photographs were taken for evidence. At 7:45 P.M., Detective Leonard brought a man named John McNally into the morgue.

"Do you know the man on the table?" Leonard asked.

McNally nodded.

"Is that the man you knew to be insured and buried under the name Nicholas Mellory?"

"That's him," McNally replied.

"Did you know him by any other name?"

"I knew him by his real name."

"Which is?"

"Michael Malloy," McNally said.

McNally, twenty-six, a petty crook with multiple convictions behind him, was being held as a material witness in the case. Not long after police picked up on the rumors of Malloy's death, McNally was busted on an unrelated charge of carrying a concealed weapon. Little did authorities know at the time that they had nabbed a small cog in a vast machine. While he sat in the Bronx County Jail, word reached McNally through the "inmate grapevine" that police were investigating the possible demise of one Michael Malloy, a man with whom McNally had been acquainted through violent circumstance.

Realizing that his prior record made him eligible for a lengthy sentence, McNally approached the district attorney and said he'd been offered $200 to do something quite nasty to Malloy. Larceny and burglary were his things, not murder. Thus, he ultimately passed on the unscrupulous offer. The information he provided was now helping investigators assemble the jumbled pieces of a complex puzzle. Having identified the body, McNally was hauled back to his cell.

By 9 P.M., Hochman was ready to start the autopsy. "The body is that of a male white adult, six foot high or tall," Hochman noted. "His approximate weight is 180 pounds. The hair was brown. Brown eyelids. The iris was brown. No rigor mortis present." There were early signs of decomposition, evident by the skin slip, or the ease with which the skin slipped off when touched. There was green discoloration to the abdomen and the front of both thighs. Both the upper and lower right eyelids were tinged blue, as was the lower left eyelid. There was no hint of embalming. Having concluded his external examination, Hochman applied scalpel to skin and opened the body with incisions stretching down from the shoulders. Peeling back flesh and muscle, he saw that the insides were "cherry red in color; intensely so." After sawing through the rib cage, he removed the sternum and lungs. The heart was of natural size, though Hochman noted that there "was a moderate amount of epicardial fat." Again, the cherry red discoloration was evident on the inner lining of the heart cavity and the bronchial membrane of the lungs.

The stomach was empty. The intestines and bladder were collapsed. The neck was dissected and the larynx and trachea were removed. Neither showed signs of trauma. Replacing scalpel with bone saw, Hochman got to work on the cranium. The musculature covering the scalp was discolored cherry red. Removing the skullcap, Hochman saw the same discoloration on the top part of the skull. With an eyedropper, he took blood samples from the heart, specifically the aorta. He placed the samples in a test tube, adding an equal amount of sodium hydroxide. The death certificate filed at the time of the body's interment listed the cause of death as "lobar pneumonia." The certificate was signed by Dr. Frank A. Manzella, former Republican alderman from the Twentieth District in Harlem. Hochman knew lobar pneumonia had nothing to do with this death. Several days earlier, detectives had paid Hochman a visit. Was it possible, they asked him, to detect carbon monoxide poisoning in a body buried for three months? Hochman answered in the affirmative.

He eyed the contents of the test tube. If carbon monoxide was not present, the blood—mixed with sodium hydroxide—would turn a greenish brown, or black. Traces of carbon monoxide would result in the blood staying red. "The result of that test," Hochman noted, "was strongly positive. The cause of death was asphyxiation by carbon monoxide."

It was a crude manner of extermination, but one that had been broached only after every alternative had been exhausted.

CHAPTER 1

The Murder Trust

Tony Marino's joint at 3775 Third Avenue in the Bronx was not an establishment one would call classy. It was, in fact, a rather squalid affair, consisting of four round tables, several chairs, a mangy three-cushioned sofa propped against one wall and a makeshift bar measuring about twelve feet in length. There was a cramped lavatory in the back. All this was kept from view by a partition. Observing the building, the casual passerby would notice nothing more than an empty storefront. The few regulars Marino's establishment boasted were of unsavory character, perpetrators of mischief and violence. Most were unemployed, more interested in a sip of drink than looking for a day's work. Granted, there was little of the latter. The glitz and glamour of the 1920s had succumbed to the desperation of the 1930s. Shoulders were slumped under the heavy burden of economic depression.

At twenty-seven, Marino was a mess of a man, being

not only a shabby dresser, but also syphilitic. By his own account, he was harangued by frequent bouts of the "clap and blue balls." He was not a man who sensed any urgency in receiving treatment for such nagging conditions. He allowed the syphilis to reach "a pretty well-advanced" stage before he sought medical attention and had "the marks to prove it." After coming down with the clap in his teens, he paid a visit to the Board of Health on Pearl Street. A doctor there "wanted to ship me over to the Island" for treatment at Metropolitan Hospital. Having no desire to be shipped anywhere, he simply "ran away" and failed to follow up on any treatment.

Consequently, this did not bode well for his young wife, who claimed Marino passed on to her his "venereal issues." She was unaware of her afflictions until she became pregnant with their child. "I went to see a doctor, and a blood test was taken," she said. They lived in less than harmonious matrimony at 1918 Pilgrim Avenue in the Bronx. Marino described himself as having quite a nasty temper and was prone to violent tantrums, during which he smashed furniture. According to his wife, Elinor, whom he married on August 13, 1928, Marino "once put the stove into the hall and proceeded to smash the furniture with an ax and then ran into the street with the ax in his hand. On numerous occasions, he became so violent that it was with difficulty that we were able to restrain him. On several occasions, he threatened to turn the gas on in our room and kill the baby and myself."

He attributed such behavior to a childhood accident. As a boy, Marino lived with his family at 186 Lincoln Avenue. When he was twelve, he fell down four flights of stairs at the residence. The fall left him concussed and with a permanent scar on his left temple. It was not long after he recovered from his wounds that his family alleged he began acting "queer." He made weird noises and stayed out all night. He cut classes and randomly slugged people. He would coerce his younger brother, John, into shoplifting for him, beating him up when he refused. "We'd walk past a bakery or something," his brother said, "and he'd see a cake and say something like, 'Gee, that cake sure looks nice.' If I didn't grab it for him, he'd deck me." When he wasn't punching people, he was pulling odd faces at them. "He'd do funny things with his eyes, or stick his tongue out at people," his sister, Rose, said.

He was, according to his brother, a constant smart-ass. "He was troublesome and gave the most peculiar and queer answers to simple questions. On one occasion, I recollect a teacher asked him if he had a piano at home. He said that he did, and the teacher asked him whether he played it. He answered that he did, with his 'feets.' " Other family members thought there was something "radically wrong" with young Tony. Some relatives he visited in Philadelphia "felt from his conduct, behavior and talk, that he was crazy." His behavior and penchant for ditching classes eventually got him kicked out of school in the sixth grade. Things only seemed to deteriorate from there. Following the death of his mother when Marino was nine, he tried to kill himself on at least two occasions. "When my mother died, he became very violent and tried to throw himself out of a five-story window," his brother said. "It was with considerable difficulty and trouble that we prevented him from committing suicide."

His second attempt was an unsuccessful go at hanging.

When Marino turned sixteen, "he came in contact with women of ill repute and, by reason of his friendships, he contracted syphilis and also suffered from 'blue balls,' which necessitated an operation." This did nothing to enhance his temperament. He took great pleasure in putting "money in front of a person and when one attempted to pick it up, he would violently push them away, causing them to fall, or he would step on their hands." He staggered through life with minimal direction, staying away from home night after night and "never followed any steady employment." Throughout his adolescence and most of his twenties, he ventured from one dead-end job to another.

Then, sometime in the late 1920s, he ventured into the speakeasy trade. He went into business with a nameless associate and opened a no-name establishment in Harlem, on Park Avenue at 128th Street. It was not, however, an amicable partnership, and eventually—for reasons unknown—the partner "got disgusted with him and left the place." It was this partner who fronted the operation's money. After the business was left in Marino's sole charge, it promptly went under. But he was soon at it again and somehow managed to open a dive at 3775 Third Avenue in the Bronx. Unlike some flashier joints, there was no pink champagne bubbling into chilled glasses at Marino's. Nor did the sound of hot jazz pervade the premises. There was, however, the occasional game of pinochle accompanied by the sound of someone hitting the floor in a drunken stupor.

And still his "venereal issues" festered, inflicting an increasingly heavy toll on his marriage. Elinor was convinced her husband was suffering from a number of mental maladies brought on by his afflictions. She noticed things other family members had pointed out. "He made funny faces while I was talking to people," she said. He would stand "behind them making faces. Of course, the people wouldn't see him, but I would see him doing it." In 1931, she left him, moved in with her father and took a three-month sabbatical from the combative marriage. "I told him to go to the hospital and get treatments," she said. "That is why I left him and that is why I kept arguing with him, telling him to go. He would tell me he was his own doctor. That was what the arguments were about."

A rather nasty medical development involving his nether region finally persuaded him to do what his wife's constant pleading and harassment had failed to. He sought treatment with Dr. Alphonse Ziviello, a licensed physician and surgeon with an office at 2583 Marion Avenue. The good doctor treated Marino for syphilis, operating on abscesses that had formed on the lymph glands on both sides of his groin. Between the end of August and the end of September 1932, Marino sought treatment with Dr. Ziviello half a dozen times, during which the good doctor formed his own opinion of Marino. "He is not the type that the average layman is," he noted. "Very peculiar in his mode of action, in his mode of speech. His speech was not that of a man of his age. More or less simple. That of a child."

Thus it was the doctor's opinion that Marino belonged penned up in a sanitarium for "observation and treatment."

Instead, Marino returned to his speakeasy. It was an operation he basically ran on his own, though he did employ "bartender" Joseph Murphy—known as "Red" to the few patrons who frequented the joint. He was hired to pour drinks for a dollar-a-day wage that Marino paid sporadically. But as a bartender, Murphy spent more time sampling the inventory than pouring it into customers' glasses. He consumed vast quantities of whiskey, often drinking from the moment he woke up to the time he went to bed. The bottle took priority over all aspects of his life. He drank more than he ate and he rarely bathed. Being homeless, Murphy spent all his time at the speakeasy, sleeping on its mangy sofa at night with a single blanket to keep himself warm. It was luxurious compared to the lifestyle to which he had become accustomed. He had spent many nights sleeping on subway platforms, or on a grungy mattress in one of the quarter-a-night motels he frequented in Harlem.

Life had never been easy for Murphy. He was born Archie Mott on May 24, 1906, in New York City. He was an unruly youngster, a runaway who spent his childhood being

bounced from one foster home to another. At the age of
ten, he was taken off the streets by the Children's Aid Society of America and placed in the care of a Reverend
Greene, an "elderly and retired" clergyman who lived by
himself on a farm in rural Delaware. Mott's penchant for
general misbehavior proved too taxing for the reverend
who—after one year as Mott's legal guardian—was forced
to place the boy in another home. He was left in the care of
a Mr. William J. Bryan, of Barrington, Delaware. According to a report on Mott's history put together by the Children's Aid Society, "This was a most excellent home and
Mr. Greene took a deep interest in the boy, apparently
greatly disliking the idea of having to admit his failures of
making something of him."

Mott remained immune to the calming qualities of his
stable environment. "In this home," states the report, "the
complaints were that he frequently ran away, was always
making plans to get tobacco and cigarettes, was constantly
doing things he was told over and over not to do both in
school and at home, and 'the truth was not him.'" At one
point, he received "a good spanking" for his "outrageous
behavior and disobedience." So it was that Mott was placed
in a new home after no more than a month.

On August 4, 1917, he took up residence with Mr. and
Mrs. Harry Lane, of Federalsburg, Maryland. The Lanes
had two young daughters—described as "nice and
refined"—aged eleven and thirteen. It was hoped that the
young female presence would have a somewhat soothing
effect on the bristling young man. Apparently, it had "none
whatever." In fact, having the girls around only seemed to
exacerbate matters. He cared not for the delicate sensitivi-
ties of the female species and would use language of the
most vile kind in their presence. He was dragged to Sunday
school every week, much to his chagrin. He let his lack of
enthusiasm for the theological ramblings of others be

known by stamping through mud and kicking up puddles "like a child of five" on the way to and from classes.

The end of his association with the Lane family came when Mrs. Lane's gold watch mysteriously disappeared one evening. It was no mystery where the timepiece had gone. Young Archie quickly found himself besieged by the accusations from both Mrs. Lane and her husband. Although he denied any knowledge of the watch's whereabouts, his claims of innocence fell on deaf ears. The watch's disappearance, coupled with his habitual refusal to obey Mrs. Lane or "do anything for her," wore out his welcome with yet another family. This time it had taken a mere six weeks.

His knack for exhausting the patience of others led to severe beatings in the next home in which he was placed. Arthur Rosser was a young farmer with a spread just outside Federalsburg. Mrs. Rosser was a former schoolteacher, and it was hoped that her guidance and enthusiasm for education would turn Mott around. When he was placed in the Rossers' care, the Children's Aid Society cautioned "one or two 'good' whippings" might be necessary to keep the boy in line. However, "if these did not suffice to bring him to an understanding, it would be useless to continue." During his eight-month stay with the Rossers, he ran away no fewer than four times, lied repeatedly and was a general nuisance. He was removed from their care after an anonymous letter was sent to the society alleging that Mott was being "cruelly treated." A subsequent investigation proved the allegations to be true, and the Rossers were relieved of their foster duties.

With little hope left, the society placed Mott with another family in a last feeble effort to give the boy a proper home. On May 18, 1918, Mott took up residence with Mr. George Seymour and his family in Breston, Maryland. Things progressed in a manner similar to Mott's past experiences. There were the usual reports of lying, foul language and unruliness. But to this list of misdeeds, he now added bed-wetting. On October 26, he ran away from the home after receiving "a good whipping for having dirtied . . . and wet his bed." Despite there being a chamber pot in his room, this was Mott's third such offense. He was missing for two days before he was found hiding in the woods, where he had made the acquaintance of a homeless man.

Now realizing it was quite impossible to straighten the young boy out, the Children's Aid Society shipped him off to Connecticut, where he was committed to the Connecticut School for Boys in Meridan on February 15, 1919, for "incorrigibility." It was not the sort of place where one of Mott's temperament was destined to excel. He couldn't read or write, and played truant with grating regularity. Not long after Archie's arrival, the school's superintendent began to suspect the boy's problems were symptoms of a more complex issue. He called the boy to his office one afternoon and sat him down for a heart-to-heart. His conclusions were thus: "The boy is non compus [sic] mentis. Knows nothing about his parents . . . Doesn't know where he went to school, nor how long he was there. The committing judge had full knowledge of this boy's mental condition."

Exactly one month after entering the boys' school, he was shipped off to the Mansfield State Training School and Hospital, where he remained a patient for the next ten years. There he began to display a moderate interest in his studies, and even took to practicing the trombone and violin. His musical abilities were described as "fairly good." He often leant a hand in the dining room and bakery. "His conduct," according to hospital records, "was usually very good but occasionally he became moody and sulky." He once stole money from a hospital worker, was often untruthful and "could not be relied upon." Nevertheless, there was a noticeable improvement in his behavior. This, however, did not prevent doctors from classifying him as "feeble-minded . . . a subnormal individual unable to get along without supervision and usually unable to make a living on their own without supervision, and who may or may not be a menace to society."

An evaluation by a hospital psychiatrist in 1924, when he was eighteen, determined Mott's mental age to be "9 years, 6 months." He had an IQ of 56. He took a liking to sports and often partook in various games and physical activities. Movies enthralled him, and he enjoyed dancing. Then, on July 31, 1929, he somehow slipped away from his ward, snuck off the grounds and made his way for the real world. Noted a hospital report: "Information was received that in all probability he was in New York."

On the streets, he cared for himself. He would "sleep in hallways, eat from garbage cans and the like and would occasionally be given a meal by some friendly or good-hearted housewife." He floundered his way from one odd job to another, making just enough to support his ongoing relationship with the bottle. Some reports indicate he found work at one point as a chemist. By the time he stumbled into Marino's one evening in mid-1932, he had a job cleaning and repairing awnings. His sole possessions were the overcoat and worn workman's clothes he had on his back. While it seemed he could afford to down considerable amounts of whiskey, he would later say that owning underwear was beyond his financial means.

For whatever reason, Marino took pity on Murphy and offered him a chance to work behind the bar. For a man who later confessed to drinking heavily "morning, day and night," it was a swell opportunity. If Marino was perturbed by Murphy's constant thirst, he did little to express it. It was a dangerous attitude to take for one whose business was teetering on the precipice of financial disaster. In 1930s New York, speakeasies were as common as illicit martinis. A price war was being waged among the city's

drinking dens to draw in clientele. Marino's drab hutch—
one of the more lower-class establishments around—had
little chance of competing with the big boys in Harlem and
Greenwich Village. But for the man blessed with a conniving entrepreneurial spirit, there was always a way to
generate easy cash. In early 1932, Marino's was twenty-
seven-year-old Mabelle Carlson.

A blonde hairdresser originally hailing from Washington,
D.C., Mabelle—described as the "black sheep" of a once
wealthy family—moved to New York in December 1931.
Distraught over the death of her mother and a failed marriage to a D.C. businessman, she had made her way to the
Big Apple in the hopes of starting a new life. Unfortunately, she picked the wrong city. No one knows what cos-
mic alignment brought her into contact with Anthony
Marino—but of all the crummy gin joints, she had to walk
into his. The story Marino would later tell was one of kind-
heartedness and pity. She was, he said, a habitué of his
drinking establishment. As she appeared destitute and had
no place to lay her head, he extended to her the comforts of
his home. By this time, Marino's wife had moved back in
with her husband, only to discover that he was bringing another woman home "sometimes every night." At this point,
they were living at 3806 Third Avenue, just several doors
removed from Marino's place of business.

Elinor did not take kindly to the intrusion into her marriage, but she was "chased all over the house" by a raving
Marino whenever she voiced her protestations. Again she
moved out with their one-year-old son, this time taking up
residence with her sister-in-law and Marino's father, An-
gelo, at 1918 Pilgrim Avenue. Thus, Marino was left alone
to pursue his own insidious designs. At 10:30 A.M. on
March 17, 1932, police were summoned to the Third Avenue address. There they found poor Mabelle dead in bed.

She was carted away to Fordham Morgue, where Dr. David H. Smith, assistant medical examiner for the County of the Bronx, performed the autopsy. His verdict: "Bronchial-pneumonia, terminal. Acute and chronic alcoholism." His report included a note based on information provided by Marino: "History of drinking for the past three weeks. Refused to stop, go to hospital or see a doctor."

Marino told the authorities he had come home the night before and found the girl lying on her bed. He said he thought she was merely sleeping. Although Dr. Smith concluded that Mabelle's death was free of "suspicious circumstances," he did note an "old hematoma of the left lower [eye]lid, somewhat masked by the application of some flesh powder." Other contusions were found on her body. For Marino, this "tragedy" was offset by the fact that he had been made beneficiary of a $2,000 life insurance policy that Mabelle had secured from Prudential. Less than a week after she died, Marino showed up at Dr. Smith's East 94th Street office with insurance papers completed and signed. "There was nothing concerned with the death to arouse suspicion," Dr. Smith said. "The autopsy confirmed a great deal of Marino's story and it appeared to be just another one of those natural deaths brought on by alcoholism."

For at least five days before her death, Mabelle had fought a losing battle with pneumonia, Dr. Smith said. Not until the following year—and the ordeal of Michael Malloy—would the morbid truth behind Mabelle's death come to light. The night she died had been particularly brisk for spring. There was a hard edge to the air that brought with it the promise of a morning frost—but there was warmth to be found in a bottle. Marino plied Mabelle with whiskey until she was babbling incoherently. Then he gave her some more, pouring drinks down her throat until she was properly pickled. It was Dr. Smith's later assessment that Mabelle was probably force-fed the alcohol, as she would have been too weak from illness to serve herself. Satisfied that Mabelle was severely sauced, Marino helped her to bed. But before doing so, he moved the bed under an open window and poured ice water over the sheets and mattress. He then stripped her naked and wrapped her in the sodden bedclothes. It did the trick.

At the request of Mabelle's elderly aunt, Ellen Waters, the hairdresser's body was shipped back to Washington, D.C., for burial. On Mabelle's death certificate, her occupation was listed as Marino's housekeeper. With Mabelle gone, Marino continued his shabby existence. Whatever he spent the insurance money on, it's clear he didn't splurge on classing up his business. By the end of 1932, he was again strapped for cash. The authorities, meanwhile, remained clueless. As far as Marino was concerned, Mabelle's murder remained a masterstroke of cunning. In the meantime, he moved in with his wife, sister and father. The paternal presence did nothing to ease his demeanor. According to his wife, "he beat me and his sister every morning."

He would soon exercise his violent impulses on a new target.

"I cannot prove much to you about Michael Malloy, who he was or where he came from," District Attorney Samuel J. Foley would later say in court. "Malloy is to me an unknown. The proof will develop that during the time through which we trace his movements, he was a derelict hanging out in speakeasies, working, doing odd jobs for a bit of food or shelter, probably never on salary, and always working for drinks when he could get them." Newspaper articles of the day simply referred to Malloy as a "speakeasy derelict."

It seems he hailed from County Donegal, Ireland, and was probably swept across the Atlantic in one of the many tides of European immigration that came ashore in the late nineteenth and early twentieth centuries. He arrived in obscurity and lived in anonymity, but through death he would achieve cult immortality. By all accounts—including his own—he was a loner, a man bereft of friends or family. A staggering drunk, his only acquaintances were those he nudged elbows with at the bar. Newspapers put his age at sixty years old. Malloy, wrote the *Daily Mirror,* was just one of many pieces of "flotsam and jetsam in the swift current of underworld speakeasy life; those no-longer responsible derelicts who stumble through the last days of their lives in a continual haze of 'Bowery Smoke.'" He worked numerous slum jobs, sweeping alleyways and collecting garbage. During a certain high point, he was employed as a stationary fireman. But when that job fell through—sometime in mid-1932—he returned to street cleaning.

Occasionally, he did work for Pasqua's Burial Service at 246 East 116th Street, in Harlem. On days when he wasn't stupefied with drink, he swept the place out and polished the coffins. Sometimes he would help make a corpse look dapper for its open-casket send-off. In exchange for his sporadic labor, Malloy received a few scant dollars and was allowed to sometimes sleep in the mortuary at night—such was the beneficent manner of Malloy's boss, Frank Pasqua. At twenty-four, Pasqua was married with a newborn son to care for. He had never graduated high school, opting at the age of seventeen to go to work for his father, Ralph, in the family business. But working around dead people rarely provided Pasqua the chance to engage in meaningful conversation. So it was that he often grabbed a drink after work—with Malloy in tow—stopping by the little watering hole at 3775 Third Avenue.

Pasqua was on friendly terms with the establishment's owner. Both were married with young kids and found camaraderie in their tales of husbandly hardship. Often, the two men conversed in their families' native Italian, as if concealing a dark secret. In fact, they were. In his duties as undertaker, Pasqua was frequently in contact with insurance agents. On many occasions, he accompanied beneficiaries to the offices of insurance companies to collect the amount of the policy. This ensured he received payment for his undertaking duties. Pasqua's contacts proved useful when Mabelle Carlson sought life insurance at Marino's urging. Grateful for his assistance, Marino had paid Pasqua a small fee following Mabelle's untimely demise.

Unless he was passed out somewhere, Malloy could be found most nights hunched over Marino's bar with his hands lovingly cupped around a glass of precious liquid amber. The odiferous lure of sardines on the free lunch tray would occasionally pry him away from the bar, for nothing complemented a glass of whiskey better than a sardine sandwich—or another glass of whiskey. Alcohol brought out Malloy's Irish brogue, and he used what Emerald Isle charm he could muster to engage others while he munched on his somewhat unsavory choice of cuisine.

He was, to begin with, a good-paying customer, welcomed by Marino whenever he sidled up to the bar. Such open-armed hospitality only encouraged Malloy to partake of the bottle with increasing regularity. Soon, he was spending more time in Marino's than he was at the occasional odd job that paid his way. His tab began to mount. The charming anecdotes he imparted between swigs of drink were not as charming as hard cash. When Marino made this clear, Malloy hit the streets with his broom. His tab, however, continued to stretch beyond his meager financial means and eventually led to a grim inevitability. It was one evening in November 1931 that Marino broke the hard news to Malloy: His line of credit had been canceled. Malloy was shattered. His pleading eyes and promise of future payments carried no weight. Denied his panacea and feeling dejected, he staggered out into the cold night of a Depression winter. But he returned the following evening and began his nightly ritual of appealing to the charitable nature of Marino's few other customers. Malloy deemed it a humanitarian effort. Marino simply considered it begging.

Malloy spent most of his time in an alcohol-induced daze and lived what many considered to be a wasted existence. Little did anyone know he was on the brink of securing his legacy. Sixty years of anonymity were about to give way to a tale of a hardy soul, a man who would prove a marvel of near-indestructibility. Oblivious to the schemes swirling around him, he would simply stumble from one episode to another and defy the treacherous path journeyed by Mabelle Carlson before him.

And it all began with a simple complaint.

"Business," Marino said, twirling the drink in his glass, "is bad."

He was sitting at a table with Pasqua in the cramped proprietor's room in the back of the speakeasy. Also with them was Marino regular Daniel Kriesberg, a twenty-nine-year-old wholesale greengrocer and father of three. It was July 1932, and all three men were feeling light in the wallet. Marino stared through the beaded curtain that separated the small room from the rest of the speakeasy. A few shabby denizens were leaning on the bar, sipping drinks. Another guy was standing at the lunch tray, eating off it with his fingers. Barflies and derelicts, Marino thought. "What? They don't think none of this stuff costs anything?" he said to no one in particular. "Half of them don't pay nothing when they leave here."

Murphy and Malloy were behind the bar, stealing swigs from a bottle. Malloy, taking advantage of Marino's loose criteria for employment, was now occasionally working as a "bartender" to cover his drinking expenses. Sometimes, he slept in the speakeasy overnight, taking a spot on the floor near Murphy's sofa. Pasqua eyed Malloy's teetering figure, the head back, a bottle jutting upward from the mouth. Surely, the man was no more than a few sips from the grave. Death was never far removed from Pasqua's thinking. It was part of his job. But at that moment, something in the undertaker clicked. Spurred by this random—and seemingly innocent thought—an old idea resurfaced, aglow with new vitality.

"Why don't you take out insurance on Malloy?" Pasqua asked. "I can take care of the rest."

There followed a moment of contemplative silence. It occurred to Marino that Malloy did indeed present an ideal opportunity for financial betterment. He was a raging drunk. He had no friends and no family. Should some unfortunate mishap relieve Malloy of his mortal obligation, there would be no one to miss him. His physical condition—or so it seemed—left much to be desired. Marino assumed that years of hard living had left Malloy battered and feeble. It would take little to put him in the ground, and the money would certainly be nice. He looked at Kriesberg, who stared back at him with hopeful expectation. Apparently, the grocery business was not what it once was.

Like his drinking partners, Kriesberg was a family man. He had a wife and three kids waiting for him at home at 653 Cauldwell Avenue, near Westchester Avenue, in the Bronx. Unlike Marino, however, his marriage appears to have been a cordial affair. Kriesberg often professed his love for his family and was eager to provide for them. That eagerness led him down a dark path.

Now, under Kriesberg's expectant stare, it took Marino little time to convince himself that the plan was a good one. Looking at Pasqua, Marino said, "Sure."

The three men chuckled and raised their glasses. On its face, the moment was a lackluster microcosm in the grand sweep of time, missing the weight of those historic moments that signify the commencement of some great struggle. At that moment—though Marino, Pasqua and Kriesberg failed to realize it—life was very simple. They were simply three guys looking to make a quick-and-ungodly buck. But the clinking of glasses and the consecration of their deal forever cast simplicity aside.

Later, the tabloids would dub the conspirators "The Murder Trust." The name implied slick precision and deadly skill. Such an implication could not have been further from the truth.

CHAPTER 2
Rejected

Michael Malloy emerged uneasily from the comfortable oblivion of unconsciousness. Behind heavy lids, his eyeballs throbbed in haphazard time to the arrhythmic beat in his skull. His brain pounded out an uneasy cadence between aching temples. His mouth was dry and his tongue felt as though it were garbed in a fur coat. His lips felt thick and slimy, like two Polish sausages slapped together. He lay motionless, his eyes still closed, mustering the determination to face yet another day. He moaned softly and slowly opened one eye to the swirling blur of his surroundings. It was as if the room had a kaleidoscopic quality to it. Nothing at first was clearly defined. There were no straight angles or sharp edges. Everything was wavy as if he were viewing it from underwater. Floating dots—the kind you see after staring directly at the sun—drifted before him in the harsh light of this unkind morning. God almighty, he had yet to open the other eye!

His stomach churned and rumbled in protest, bringing to the back of his throat the bitter taste of something he may have eaten the night before. He pushed his tongue between his lips and felt his top lip unglue itself from the bottom one. He took a deep breath. Opening the other eye was just as traumatic. Instead of everything coalescing into one cohesive image, he saw blurry twin visions of everything. This was not as bad as some mornings, when the world would appear to him in triplicate. It was this realization that suddenly spawned in him a mild curiosity. Where the hell was he? He stared nauseously at the ceiling and tried to think back to the night before. As on most mornings, the memory was fragmented and disjointed, like the scattered pieces of a jigsaw puzzle. Sleeping in different places on most nights, it was often hard for him to keep track of his surroundings. A lot of these ceilings looked the same—as did the toilets (and gutters) he spent many a morning bent over.

Through the fog he remembered the melodious trickle of liquor being poured from bottles the night before. There had been light conversation and the occasional toast. Perhaps he'd even belted out a traditional melody native to his homeland:

> Of all the money that e'er I spent
> I've spent it in good company
> And all the harm that ever I did
> Alas it was to none but me
> And all I've done for want of wit
> To memory now I can't recall
> So fill to me the parting glass
> Good night and joy be with you all

The memory was not unique unto itself—it was merely a playback of numerous evenings spent in the embrace of Lady Hooch. In the dreary early hours of countless mornings after, recollections of nights before never reached a graceful conclusion with him, say, climbing into a nice, soft bed and sleeping the sleep of the clean and righteous. Instead, they concluded in an abrupt manner with an impenetrable wall of darkness that descended on his memory like a jackhammer. Perhaps this was because on most evenings he drank himself unconscious. He would assault his body with the hardest of liquors until it could take no more. On more than one occasion, he'd been left to sleep where he fell. To those who witnessed such episodes, it was a form of entertainment—a source of much-needed merriment during that dismal Depression winter.

Wincing, he felt the cold, hard floor beneath him. There was no pillow under his head, just the rough grain of wood. He achingly cast his gaze down the length of his body, which made its discontent known with even the slightest movement. There was a thin, unlaundered sheet draped over him. He now remembered where he was. He was lying in the middle of Tony Marino's speakeasy. Joe Murphy lay sprawled unconscious across the sofa against the wall. Malloy took another deep breath and sat himself upright, his neck and spine cracking like a symphony of broken walnuts. His brain shrieked and his stomach went into overdrive, dancing a pirouette around his ass. Satisfied that everything he'd consumed the night before was going to stay put, he steeled himself for his next great effort. Pushing the blanket aside, he slowly got to his feet. He stood still momentarily, glancing around him to confirm his whereabouts. Right. Now that the hard part was over, he was ready to tackle the day. There was just one thing he needed before he got the morning off to a running start: a drink.

Michael Malloy was an alcoholic's alcoholic. By all accounts, he would drink whatever was put in front of him. When it came to gin, whiskey, bourbon—anything distilled or brewed—he was an equal-opportunity consumer. He was not a man of moderation. During those days of Prohibition, he took it where he could get it. It was not uncommon for him to wake up on the floor of Marino's and, as it was testified to in court, help himself to the contents behind the bar before shuffling off to find whatever odd job he could get for himself that day. Murphy would later admit on the stand that he joined Malloy at the bar on those mornings for a little hair of the dog. With these two leeches clinging to his establishment, relieving it of its inventory with such uncouth regularity, perhaps it's no surprise that Marino complained that his business was sinking faster than an olive in a dry martini.

Prohibition was a bummer. It was a fact startlingly evident in the flagrant contempt and disregard of the law exercised by countless enthusiasts for the devil's milk. At midnight on January 16, 1920, the National Prohibition Act was ratified as the Eighteenth Amendment to the U.S. Constitution, making it illegal to "manufacture, sell, barter, transport, import, export, deliver, furnish or possess any intoxicating liquor." Thus, the ill-conceived effort to legislate American morality got under way. Whiskey, gin, brandy, rum, beer, wine, ale, porter, all spirituous, vinous, malt and fermented liquors—the staples of Michael Malloy's diet—sold containing half of 1 percent or more of alcohol by volume and fit for getting drunk on were outlawed.

Beer taps ran dry, wine bottles were smashed and barrels of whiskey went to the ax. Its doors padlocked and its windows boarded up, the New York saloon was quickly banished to the realm of fond memories. This social experiment, said President Herbert Hoover, was "noble in motive and far-reaching in consequence." That consequence, though probably not one envisioned by Hoover, was a quasi-underground revolution. According to a 1929 *New*

York Times article, it was a struggle waged in "office buildings, restaurants, downstairs and upstairs, around the corner, everywhere." When New York was wrung dry, the speakeasy was born.

Within a decade, noted the *Times,* such establishments were "familiar institutions of metropolitan life. And it ranges from the waterside back room or the cellar gathering place, to the deluxe speakeasy where smart New York meets." Unlike Marino's, the establishments frequented by the roving *Times* reporter boasted "handsomely appointed dining rooms, soft lights, well-trained waiters, a French menu and the clink of ice in wine buckets." Gaining access meant learning the secret ritual, whether it be a special knock or the drop of a name. For those who knew the secret password, a delicious world of prohibited pink lady cocktails and illicit gin fizzes awaited.

The basic formula for any speakeasy was a room and a couple of bottles, according to New York Police Commissioner Grover Whalen. It was a formula adhered to by many, much to the chagrin of the authorities. In 1929, Whalen estimated there were more than thirty thousand speakeasies in the city. To tackle these dens of inebriation, the Prohibition Bureau assigned to New York a meager force of two hundred agents—not all of whom were untouchable. In terms of the police, the city's population of 6 million was watched over by eighteen thousand policemen—less than four thousand of whom were available for patrol during any twenty-four-hour period, according to the *Times.*

"These men must patrol 5,000 miles of city streets and 175 square miles of the port," the paper reported, more than implying that the odds were stacked in favor of the speakeasy owner. And why not? Proprietors of such businesses had an impressive arsenal at their disposal, for the siren song of a cold cocktail garnished, maybe, with an olive or fruit decoration, and drank to the sounds of live horn and piano, was a powerful and corrupting tool. For those moments, however, when an officer of incorruptible moral fiber and his posse busted down the door, there were measures a proprietor could take. The pulling of a lever or applied pressure to a certain floorboard could send an establishment's inventory crashing through a trapdoor, or conceal the bar behind a bookcase or secret wall.

The speakeasy was another world, one that offered a respite—if only briefly—from the realities of the Depression. Down that hidden stairwell or beyond that nonchalant storefront, accompanying the percussion of ice cubes in martini shakers was, perhaps, the tinny sounds of a piano in a smoke-filled corner. In the more upper-class establishments, it would not be uncommon to drink to the live sounds of smoky jazz. The bartender—in his white shirt and loosened black tie—would vigorously rattle the contents of his shaker: a glass of gin, lemon juice, a teaspoon of sugar, a hint of grenadine and half a glass of fresh cream over cracked ice to produce a New Orleans Gin Fizz. Working his way down the bar, he catered to the illicit thirsts of his patrons. An empty cocktail glass stood waiting on the polished mahogany. Into it went a measure of rock candy syrup, rye whiskey, and juice from a freshly squeezed lemon. Where moments before there had been nothing, there was now a Rock and Rye. Those who came to forget their troubles, or just feel the slow burn of hard liquor, were men in suits and blue-collar immigrant workers. Joining the ranks were women, originally barred from the saloons in the days of legalized drink. Elbow-to-elbow, the sexes jostled at bars and squeezed into booths, hoisting glasses, tilting bottles and giving life to an element of what Stanley Walker, city editor of *The New York Herald Tribune*, called "the madhouse that was New York."

Stanching the flow of illegal liquor into the city was law enforcement's secret to battling the speakeasy scourge.

"Stop the flow of liquor and the speakeasy cannot operate," Police Commissioner Whalen said. "The number of drinking places proves that the distilling and smuggling of forbidden drinks is common practice. Let the enforcement officials stop the flow at its point of origin and they need not worry about speakeasies." But it was easier said than done. A 1929 study by law enforcement of liquor seized in 273 raids "showed the average quantity to be about four gallons—or perhaps a day's supply," reported the *Times*. "If there is anything like 30,000 speakeasies and each one requires four gallons a day, the total becomes impressive. Practically the whole of this liquor is delivered by hand or motor car." And herein was the problem, for officers hesitated to stop every man they saw "carrying a package or hauling something in his car. It invokes the delicate question of search and seizure . . . And how shall the policeman say that the man entering a basement with a package is, in fact, a carrier of contraband?"

The problem, when stripped to its most basic element, however, was that law enforcement simply lacked the necessary manpower to tackle the large-scale distilleries and the back-road rumrunners. So, the liquor continued to flow and the speakeasies continued to flourish. But beyond the mere selling of alcohol, speakeasies posed additional problems. Both Whalen and Maurice Campbell, prohibition administrator for New York, agreed that speakeasies were sinister breeding grounds for evil activity. As if describing Marino's place of business, Campbell said some establishments were downright "disreputable," serving as nothing more than a "common meeting ground of criminals and indirectly contributing to the planning of crime."

Such planning would soon become a major headache for Marino and the lads. On the night Frank Pasqua blatantly suggested whacking Malloy, Marino—imbued with a new sense of hope for the future—staggered home high on drink. Surely, Malloy's innards had nearly corroded in their entirety under the intense onslaught of cheap booze. Like some bizarre oral growth, there seemed to be a bottle or glass permanently affixed to his lips. As for their dastardly plan, Marino and the boys believed it to be brilliant in its simplicity. The only foreseeable challenge—as far as Marino could tell—was insuring Malloy. What reason could they give the man for wanting him covered? Since when had they become so caring? Maybe they wouldn't have to act like they cared at all. Perhaps it was possible to insure someone without that person even knowing it. Yeah, that was something to consider.

The next step, once Malloy was insured, would be determining the best method to rid themselves of him. Preferably, it would be something clean. There would be no severed limbs or arterial spraying. It would have to appear as though it were an accident. The last thing anyone wanted—especially the proprietor of a speakeasy—was to have the cops sniffing around. From his shady past, of course, Marino had experience to draw on. He had dispatched the unfortunate Mabelle Carlson without drawing attention to himself. Surely, a feeble drunk would pose no greater challenge. The money to be doled out after Malloy's death would be divided equally among the plotters—therefore, the fewer people involved the better. It was imperative, for that reason alone, not to let Anthony "Tough Tony" Bastone in on the plan.

"Until Bastone muscled in, life at [3775] Third Avenue was all harmony," *The New York Herald Tribune* later reported. Tough Tony was an enigmatic individual. By all accounts, he was a brute who took great pleasure in dispensing savage beatings. The papers of the day identified him as a "gangster." Later, in court, it would be hinted at that Tough Tony played a vital role in supplying Marino's speakeasy with liquor. If this was the case, then it's not going too far to suggest that Bastone had a sinister, yet important, connection.

The age of Prohibition spawned a new breed of criminal. In cities like New York and Chicago, they drew lines of battle and waged war for control of the metropolitans' illegal liquor trades. New York City's five boroughs fell under the violent jurisdiction of men with names like Dutch and Little Frenchy. The Bronx—as well as Harlem—was the eminent domain of Arthur Simon Flegenheimer, better known as Dutch Schultz. Through killing and intimidation, Schultz—a man of notoriously ill disposition—ascended the underworld's ranks, achieving for himself the status of "Beer Baron of the Bronx." It was in the Bronx where Schultz was born and raised. One can argue he had ties to the alcohol trade from the very beginning: His father, who abandoned the family when Schultz was fourteen, was the owner of a New York saloon.

Recently released from a one-year stint in prison for burglary, Schultz was eighteen years old when America went "dry." It was not long before he saw in Prohibition an opportunity to make a quick buck. He began working the ranks of various bootlegging operations. He broke legs, busted chops and inflicted harm of a more permanent sort for some of the heavier characters in the liquor-smuggling business, including Jack "Legs" Diamond and Arnold Rothstein. It was not until 1928, however, that Schultz took his first major step toward becoming "Beer Baron." It was that year that Joey Noe, a friend of Schultz and the son of a beer pipe cleaner, opened his own speakeasy—the Hub Social Club—in a Bronx tenement at 543 Brook Avenue and took Schultz on as his junior partner.

A lot of people were thirsty. Consequently, business was swell. From their Brook Avenue address and the profits garnered therein, Noe and Schultz sowed the seeds of a burgeoning empire. It was not long before they were scouting new locales and opening other speakeasies throughout the Bronx. Courtesy of their connection with a New Jersey brewer named Frank Dunn and a couple of beat-up trucks, Noe and Schultz branched out further, taking it upon themselves to supply beer to their competitors. For the speakeasy owner who maintained he was happy with the supplier he had, ample reason to switch was soon provided. It came wearing a flashy suit with, perhaps, a gun holstered under an arm and knuckles that had dislodged many a tooth. Sometimes it brandished a baseball bat.

Smashing up a joint may have been a last resort, but there were times when even that failed to force a proprietor to see the error of his ways. When that occurred—as a Bronx speakeasy owner named Joe Rock discovered—more drastic measures were employed. Rock was a partner with his brother, John. One night, Noe and Schultz dispatched a couple of goons to pay a visit to the Rock establishment and sample some of the home brew. It was not, they determined, a satisfactory concoction. Voicing as much, the goons implied that it would be wise for the Brothers Rock to secure their beer from a supplier of higher quality. John quickly got the message. Joe, made of tougher stuff, told them to piss off. This they did, only to return a while later in a collectively violent mood. They ransacked the Rock establishment, busting barrels, smashing glasses and breaking bottles. When they were done, they dragged a bloodied and beaten Joe from the premises. He was taken to a remote location and hung by this thumbs from a meat hook. According to legend, he was blindfolded with a handkerchief smeared with muck collected from a gonorrheal discharge. The unfortunate episode left Joe blind and sent a clear message to other speakeasy owners.

Though lucrative, the Noe-Schultz partnership was not long-lasting. It ended in a frenzy of gunfire on the morning of October 16, 1928, outside the Chateau Madrid on West 54th Street, near Sixth Avenue. The target was Joe Noe. The gunmen, rivals of the Noe-Schultz collaborative, blazed away from the confines of a blue Caddy. Noe hit the pavement with slugs in his spine, chest and left hand, but not before squeezing off a few rounds of his own. He died five days later at the Bellevue Hospital prison, leaving Schultz in sole command of a liquor empire that had now spread from the Bronx to Manhattan's lower west side. It was an empire Schultz ruled with an iron fist.

Being in the business he was, Marino must have known of the brutality that befell the defiant Joe Rock. Marino's own establishment was less than two miles from the Hub Social Club. The fact that Marino was operating a speakeasy in the Bronx made it likely he was securing liquor from Schultz; otherwise he would not have been in business. Seeing as it was implied that Bastone was providing drink to Marino's operation, it's not hard to imagine that Bastone had dealings with Schultz's people. If not, he was either very brave or very stupid. Whatever he was, he was intimidating. "Everybody was afraid of him," Marino said. Pasqua would take it one step further, saying Bastone was "a very bad character, a gun man."

Marino's speakeasy was five miles from his house on Pilgrim Avenue. He had a lot to think about as he walked home that evening after agreeing to Pasqua's plan. How would they secure the money to pay for the insurance policy? How much would they be able to insure Malloy for? And, most important of all, how much would he see once Malloy was taken care of?

As was often the case, he had left the speakeasy that evening in the care of Joseph Murphy who, along with Malloy, had promptly set about getting sloshed.

Francis Pasqua considered himself a respectable member of the Bronx business community. He had attended school at P.S. 85 before moving on to Mount Carmel Catholic School on 115th Street—between First and Pleasant Avenue—and then dropping out and going to work in the family trade. After ten years helping his father with the grim duties inherent in running Pasqua's Burial Service, he now boasted the title undertaker and co-ran the operation. But despite his entrepreneurial pursuits, Pasqua was not always the smartest of individuals. Later, when asked in court how long he had worked for his father, he answered, "Thirty-four years."

"You have not been alive that long, have you?" Pasqua's inquisitor countered.

"No," the undertaker replied.

Married to Elvira, with a four-year-old son, Pasqua had a marriage that, unlike Marino's, seemed a harmonious one, free of nasty venereal issues. According to his wife, Pasqua was home every evening "by six or seven" and would not leave once he was there. But like Marino, Pasqua was a shady operator working on the fringes of the law. It was he who had brought the crosshairs to bear on Michael Malloy with nothing more than a simple suggestion. The Irishman had stumbled into Pasqua's life uninvited, emerging from a shabby existence in some dingy room or maybe a back alley. The fact is no one really knew much about Malloy, and no one really cared to. If he had family, he never mentioned them. The only friends he thought he had were now plotting to kill him. Yes, life was tough.

Pasqua believed offing Malloy would be an easy thing. It would also help his business. Once the guy was dead, Pasqua would handle the funeral arrangements and then overcharge whatever company insured Malloy to cover the costs. It was a grand scheme. The death certificate would not be a problem. He knew someone who could cater one for any special occasion. His job put him in contact with those who could help him skirt the system when circumstances called for such measures. The immediate challenge was securing some sort of policy. As far as Pasqua knew, insurance companies weren't in the business of covering incorrigible drunks who sometimes slept in doorways. Certain aspects of Malloy's life would have to be refined to make him a more desirable insurance prospect. Pasqua would have to come up with a job for Malloy, other than full-time inebriate.

Although Pasqua had suggested Marino be the one to insure Malloy, it was Pasqua who actively sought coverage. He wasted no time and set about this self-appointed task with vigor. If all went well, Malloy would be buried by month's end and Pasqua would be a few hundred dollars richer. On the morning of July 29, 1932, Pasqua kissed his wife goodbye and left his house at 1959 Hobart Avenue, dressed in his best undertaker's black. He was a dapper-looking young man who carried himself with an air of hardy righteousness. His black hair was perfectly coifed, slicked back against his scalp. He had a full, oval face and pursed lips that leant something of a snobbish demeanor to his appearance. He drove to the speakeasy and found Malloy behind the bar chatting amicably with Marino and Murphy.

"Hey, Mike," Pasqua said. "What do you say we go get you some insurance?"

Not being of obstinate mind, Malloy readily agreed to the plan. "Sure," he said, "whatever you fellows say."

Pasqua hoped everything progressed with such ease, for simplicity was the key word by which the gang would operate. The plan certainly seemed devoid of complexity when it was broken down into its three key steps:

1. Insure Malloy.
2. Kill him.
3. Collect said insurance.

The fourth part of the plan entailed nothing more than celebrating the successful completion of parts two and three. Pasqua had arranged a meeting this morning with an agent from the Prudential Life Insurance Company. From the speakeasy, Pasqua drove Malloy to the funeral parlor. Pasqua's father, Ralph, was already there. Not long after Pasqua arrived with Malloy, the agent appeared in the doorway. His name was Joseph Frumento and he was relatively new to the company, having sold insurance for less than a year. But he was no stranger to the Pasquas, for he was often observed visiting nearby shops and homes in his attempts to generate business. There were the customary pleasantries of introductions before the men tackled the matter the matter at hand.

"Are you the man to be insured?" Frumento asked Malloy.

Malloy, in a rare moment of sobriety, answered in the affirmative.

"What type of policy do you desire?" Fremento asked, opening his briefcase to retrieve a bundle of papers.

"Well," said Malloy, "I'll leave that up to Mr. Pasqua."

"What kind of policy, Mr. Pasqua, do you want to give him?"

"Let me know the different rates on the policies," Pasqua replied.

Frumento recalled: "I took out my rate book and I quoted him a figure on the ordinary policy where you pay every three months for $2,000, but that seemed too steep."

"That's above my means," Pasqua said.

Frumento tried a different approach. "What about a policy payable by the month?"

"And what does that cost?"

"That costs $8.08 per month."

That was more like it. "He asked me the different provisions under the policy, and I told him all about it," Frumento said. "It contains disability and double indemnity, and he seemed pretty well satisfied." Having settled on figures Pasqua could work with, Frumento took out an insurance application and began to fill it in. "I asked Mr. Malloy his name. He said it was Michael Malloy."

When asked for his address, Malloy—although he only used it sporadically as such—gave Marino's speakeasy as his place of residence. He told Frumento he was born in Ireland on June 5, 1885, thus making him forty-seven years old instead of sixty. He said he worked as a porter at Pasqua's funeral establishment where he "cleans and takes care of the store." Malloy had been versed in what to say, probably on the drive over from the speakeasy. Asked about his family, Malloy told Frumento he hadn't "any friend or relative except Frank Pasqua."

"Then who do you want to name as beneficiary?" Frumento asked.

"Well, the only friend I have here who has been doing good to me is Frank Pasqua," Malloy said. "He gave me a job and feeds me."

Thus, the insurance was to be payable at death to Frank Pasqua. His relationship to the person insured was recorded as "Friend." Pasqua would also pay the premiums. Frumento wrote on the application: "I collected $8.08 in advance on this whole life." The agent then had Malloy sign his name, and Malloy scribbled it in the appropriate blanks.

It was just a day or two later when the application for policy number 64827 hit the desk of Charles Minervini, assistant superintendent for the 13th district of the Prudential Life Insurance Company. As assistant superintendent, it was part of Minervini's "official duties" to authenticate applications and rule out any insidious intent on the part of the applicant. After reviewing Pasqua's application as submitted by agent Joseph Frumento, Minervini took it upon himself to pay a visit to Pasqua's Burial Service where he hoped to interview Michael Malloy. What struck Minervini as odd was the fact that the beneficiary was the person who had taken the policy out on Malloy—a person who, obviously, was of no relation. Minervini attempted several times to make contact with Malloy at the mortuary, only to be told each time by Pasqua that Malloy was unavailable to chat. "After making two or three calls, I could not find [Malloy], and an arrangement was made that the agent was to bring Michael Malloy to the office," Minervini said.

It was between 11:30 A.M. and noon on the first Saturday of August when Michael Malloy showed up at Minervini's East 125th Street office. He was accompanied by Francis Pasqua, again dressed to the nines. Also present at the meeting was Joseph Frumento. The assistant superintendent and the undertaker cordially summed each other up in prelude to their passively hostile encounter. Minervini sat at his desk with the application in front of him. There were hand-scribbled notes on it.

"Mr. Malloy," Minervini asked, diving right in, "who do you intend to make beneficiary?"

"Frank Pasqua," Malloy said.

"I see. And who is to pay for the policy?"

"Frank Pasqua."

Minervini nodded, scribbling additional notes on the back of the application. Pasqua looked on nonchalantly. "So," Minervini said, "you intend to pay the premium, Mr. Pasqua?"

Pasqua nodded.

Minervini scribbled some more.

"You see," Pasqua said, "Mike works for me at the undertaking parlor as a sort of caretaker. He sleeps there and hasn't got no relatives or friends. I want the policy for protection. In case he dies, there won't be a cost of a funeral or any such thing."

Again, Minervini put pen to paper. It was beginning to make Pasqua nervous. "Just so I know I have this correct," said Minervini, "Mr. Malloy is in your employ, and you're seeking coverage for him to defray the cost of burial should he pass away while under your supervision."

"That is correct," Pasqua said.

Minervini stared at the two men. He would later describe Malloy as having a "red nose" and being "somewhat corpulent." Malloy's face, Minervini said, "was heavy and round with thick lips." He turned his attention back to the application. "Aside from your own protection, Mr. Pasqua, you really don't have any insurable interest in the life of Mr. Malloy."

Pasqua wasn't sure if what Minervini was saying was a question or a statement.

Minervini stood up, his hand outstretched. The meeting was apparently over. "Thank you for your time, Mr. Pasqua, Mr. Malloy. We'll be in touch."

The meeting had lasted no more than ten minutes. Pasqua left the office with an empty feeling inside, for Minervini had done little to veil his skepticism. On the street, Malloy suggested a drink might make things better. In Minervini's office, the scheme was already beginning to unravel. The seasoned insurance man sensed in motion the workings of something sinister. What was it about Pasqua that leant a dubious quality to the whole thing? It wasn't that Minervini considered undertaking to be a shadowy profession. He simply didn't buy into Pasqua's sincerity. He had been in this business long enough to recognize the workings of a bullshit artist. And, right now, his nose was picking up something unpleasant. His cynicism was evident in one of the remarks he penned on the back of the application during the meeting: "The applicant is to be employed by the beneficiary, an undertaker who is to pay premiums. This beneficiary desires this policy, he claims, for protection."

There was also the fact that Pasqua said Malloy lived at the undertaking parlor. The parlor's address was 246 East 116th Street. On the application, it stated that Malloy rented a room at 3775 Third Avenue. It was a discrepancy unaccounted for. What really bothered Minervini, however, was that there were no blood ties between Pasqua and Malloy. In essence, Malloy was being insured by a stranger—one who had set himself up to benefit from the insured's death. As far as Minervini was concerned, "there was no motive for the insurance of [Malloy]." He typed his notes up in report form, saying as much, and had the report dispatched to the Prudential home office. Under normal circumstances, he would have ordered a Prudential physician—in this case, Dr. Melsiner, located "somewheres around Brook Avenue and 141st Street"—to perform a comprehensive physical on the insured-to-be. But he decided that on this occasion an examination was not warranted, as Pasqua's application failed to stand on its own merit.

On August 24, the application for Prudential policy number 64827 was turned down. The word "REJECTED" was stamped across its face. Frumento returned to Pasqua's place of business and refunded him the $8.08 advance. Word of the rejection was a major setback. In the speakeasy's back room—where the plot had been hatched—Pasqua and Marino sat in dark contemplation over shots of cheap booze and pondered their next move. As far as Malloy was concerned, it was all inconsequential.

For the time being, it seemed that fate had sided with the hapless Irishman.

Perhaps it happened over an illicit glass of liquid fire at the local speakeasy. Maybe it was passed on during a casual business conversation between two associates working the same trade. Whatever the circumstances, Joseph Frumento shared word of Pasqua's rejection with Joseph Porreca, an agent and collector with the Metropolitan Life Insurance Company. A four-year Metropolitan employee, it was Porreca's job to "solicit insurance and collect premiums." Maybe, Frumento told him, it would be worth Porreca's time to approach Mr. Francis Pasqua and see if Metropolitan could better meet his insurance needs. Porreca, agreeing it was a noble idea, called Pasqua's Burial Service and made an appointment to meet with Mr. Pasqua.

Porreca made the trek from the Metropolitan office at 125th Street in Harlem to Pasqua's parlor one fall morning less than two weeks after Prudential had turned Pasqua away. Sitting down to discuss business, Porreca told Pasqua he had been sent by "the Prudential man."

"I understand your case was rejected," Porreca told him. "If there's something I can do for you, I'd be willing to do some business with you." It was at that point, Porreca recalled, that Pasqua "spoke to me about a man who was working for him." Whereas Pasqua had told Prudential he employed Malloy as a "caretaker," he told Porreca that Malloy worked the parlor's security detail as "the night watchman."

"May I meet him?" Porreca asked.

"You can't see him now." Pasqua said. "He'll be in late tonight, around nine or nine-thirty."

It's hard to believe Malloy was scheduled that evening to stand guard over coffins and formaldehyde. By nine o'clock on most nights, he was either out cold or desperately clinging to Marino's bar as the last vestiges of consciousness slipped away from him. But if Pasqua was delaying for time, it worked.

"Well," said Porreca, "when can I see the man?"

"I will arrange for an appointment," Pasqua said.

The appointment was set for the afternoon of September 12 at what Porreca described "as some speakeasy on Third Avenue." He met Pasqua at the burial parlor and together they drove in the undertaker's car to Marino's establishment. Business—as it was most days—was slow. Malloy was hunched at the bar with a glass in front of him when Pasqua introduced him to the insurance man. Another gentleman, whom Pasqua failed to acknowledge, loitered quietly in a corner keeping company with a bottle.

After the friendly introductions, Porreca—anxious for a new client—opened his briefcase and pulled out some paperwork. Pasqua had already told Porreca he wanted to spend no more than $8 per month to insure his employee. "Of course," Porreca said, "I selected the most protection for the cheapest rate." The lowest rate Metropolitan offered was $8.10 a month, for which Pasqua could insure Malloy's scrappy existence for $3,000. The policy Porreca offered was an "Endowment at 85," which sounded good to Pasqua. But, really, what did Pasqua care? By the time his eighty-fifth birthday rolled around, Malloy would be a decomposed pile in a cheap pine box.

Shortly thereafter, the application for Metropolitan Life Insurance policy 804677D was submitted to the company's home office. As it had with the Prudential plan, circumstance again intervened on the side of Malloy. Metropolitan rejected the policy for the same reasons cited by Prudential. The first month's premium was immediately returned to the disheartened Pasqua. In Porreca, however, the undertaker had a determined—yet completely unsuspecting—ally, one who did not easily succumb to the burden of defeat. In Pasqua, Porreca saw a business opportunity ripe for the taking. He was determined to sell this man a policy that would stick. So able was Porreca at his profession that he convinced Pasqua to take a policy out on himself. But if Metropolitan was anything, it was consistent. This application also was rejected.

It was dawning on Pasqua that the inner workings of the insurance industry were a vastly complex and paranoid affair. Surely, he thought, his name—and that of Michael

Malloy—was now familiar among that elite group of New York insurance workers who wielded their red "REJECTED" stamps with what seemed to be Napoleonic fervor. Enormously frustrated, but galvanized by his plan's potential, Pasqua realized that he would have to change tactics. It was time to get wily.

Pasqua convened a meeting with Marino and Kriesberg sometime in October to discuss the unforeseen challenges they had thus far been dealt. Up until now, the involvement of Marino and Kriesberg had been limited only to their agreement that Malloy be whacked. Again, they gathered at the table in the speakeasy's back room. Again, they stared out through the beaded partition and took in the desolate vista of empty chairs. Malloy, of course, was there. Joseph Murphy was also present, but ignorant of the conspiracy. That was about to change. Pasqua's new plan involved pulling Murphy into the fray.

He explained to Marino and Kriesberg the problems inherent with trying to insure Malloy. He told them of his dealings with Prudential and Metropolitan. He said he could not approach them again and submit another application bearing the names Pasqua and Malloy. A red flag would certainly go up in some executive's office. Instead, he proposed insuring Malloy under a nom de plume, with Murphy—because he was of Irish descent—posing as Malloy's next of kin and beneficiary. All of this would be done without Malloy's knowledge. Pasqua conceded that the scheme would require one or two preparatory measures, but it was nothing he could not handle on his own. Having heard the plan out, Marino and Kriesberg thought it to be a fine idea—even if it did mean sharing the final spoils with one more person.

Joseph Porreca was a man enthused with insurance and the art of selling it. Even after Metropolitan had rejected

Pasqua twice, Porreca maintained contact with his prospective client. He called on him regularly and discussed possible avenues open for exploration. "I thought he was a good prospect," Porreca said of Pasqua. The lure of a commission—which, for a Metropolitan agent back then, was five and a half times the rated premium—undoubtedly fueled the agent's dogged determination. But determination had failed to overcome the company's screening process. In truth, Porreca had run out of options. Then, one day in early November, he received a phone call in his eighth-floor office. It was from, of all people, Francis Pasqua.

According to Porreca, Pasqua told him he had a friend who "wanted some insurance on him as soon as possible." This friend had even given Pasqua the money to purchase a life insurance policy. Porreca considered Pasqua a humble man of kindhearted humility. Here he was, trying to help yet another person fortify himself against life's uncertainties with reliable coverage from a trusted firm. And, in another example of Pasqua's magnanimity toward those who were less well off than himself, he had allowed this "friend" to move into his Hobart Avenue residence. So, as Porreca believed it to be, it was Pasqua, his wife, child and "friend" all living blissfully under one roof.

"All right," Porreca said. "I will come and see him."

"Well, that's not possible," Pasqua replied. "He comes home late and it is very hard to see him."

It was a pretty limp excuse, but Porreca accepted it as fact. Not once did the insurance agent question its veracity or seek an appointment to chat with the "friend" elsewhere. "I was anxious to get the business," he later said. Thus, on a blustery day in the second week of November, Porreca dropped a blank life insurance application off at the mortuary. This was a blatant violation of Metropolitan company rules, which asserted that insurance agents "be present to witness the signature of the applicant."

"I had so much faith in him," Porreca naively said of Pasqua. Perhaps it was a faith instilled more by his desperation to sell a policy than a legitimate assessment of character. Whatever the reasons behind Porreca's naïveté, he had fallen into Pasqua's little trap. Unwittingly, Joseph Porreca—quiet insurance salesman—was playing a minor, but significant, role in a crazy little episode that would soon be tabloid fodder.

CHAPTER 3

Double Indemnity

Anthony "Tough Tony" Bastone made things his business, according to Marino. He kept his ear to the floor, and when the reception got muddy he found the source of the disturbance and bloodied his knuckles on it. Through intimidation and the threat of physical pummeling, Tough Tony generally got things done his way. Rare was the man who possessed the moxie to face him in confrontation. He had a habit of drawing back his coat to reveal the two revolvers he kept tucked in the waistband of his trousers.

Through various criminal undertakings, Tough Tony was an individual well familiar with the art of scheming. He had crafted more than his fair share of insidious plots and knew when something was afoot. For some time now, he had suspected Marino and Pasqua of conspiratorial planning. It seemed that greengrocer fellow—the one who came in for a regular drink—also was involved to some extent. Tough Tony simply referred to him as "the Jew."

In Tough Tony's cryptic line of work, preservation meant paying attention to one's surroundings—not only keeping an ear out for things, but maintaining a sharp visual surveillance of nearby happenings. Over his bottle of whiskey, Tough Tony had observed the snide glances the men shared and the conspicuous whispering—and there were those meetings in the proprietor's room. It was Tough Tony's opinion that such secrecy could only mean that a plan for financial gain was in the works. It was a plan, he couldn't help but notice, from which he had been rudely excluded.

A one-time bartender, the forty-three-year-old Bastone—a husband and father of five who resided at 2152 Third Avenue, just blocks from the speakeasy—was, according to one newspaper article of the day, "unemployed." That is not to say, however, he did not find work in more illegitimate enterprises. Joseph Murphy said that he sometimes overheard Tough Tony and Joseph Maglione discussing a counterfeiting operation. The printing of funny money was a boom industry during the Depression years. "Spurious Money More Prevalent Than Ever," declared a *New York Times* headline one week before Tough Tony was gunned down. "Idleness and hunger lead to desperation, and desperation has turned more than one honest man into a counterfeiter, according to [United States Secret Service] Chief W. H. Moran," the article said. "Much of it is prepared by the photo-engraving process and is easily detected. Money made from engraved plates usually gets by until it reaches banks. In a few cases counterfeits have been accepted by banking experts."

In the evening, Bastone and Maglione would arrive at the speakeasy and order their drinks. They were a contentious duo, constantly at odds over the profits garnered from their shady activities. According to Murphy, they would sometimes discuss "stick-up jobs."

"After they come in from a job," Murphy said, "they

would argue who is going to get the money . . . They come in and argued." In terms of their counterfeiting endeavor, they would frequently tell Murphy they had been busy going about "changing" their bogus twenty-dollar bills. There was a furniture shop they frequented on Tenet Avenue, where they cashed in their fake notes for "proper money."

Despite their sniping, Maglione and Tough Tony had more in common than they may have cared to admit. They both enjoyed the company of the bottle. "At least three or four nights a week found them leaning over the bar at Marino's," Murphy said. The men could relate to each other, as they both had to provide for large families. Maglione had four children waiting for him at home. Tough Tony had five. There was little money to spend on familial necessities, and what money the two men did have more often than not wound up in the register of various gin joints. Undoubtedly, this occurred beyond the knowledge of the Home Relief Bureau, which provided financial aid to both men because of "their inability to find a job."

The (Bronx) *Home News,* in reporting Tough Tony's death, stated, "While Bastone had been a familiar figure in Harlem for several years, he gained public prominence for the first time on Dec. 30, 1930." On that night, he was tending bar in a speakeasy on Eighth Avenue at 120th Street. A small crowd was gathered at the bar, toasting the imminent end of a depressing year. Outside, while Bastone's clientele lamented the loss of a golden age, four armed bandits readied themselves for a daring heist. As reported by the Bronx paper, the culprits "entered [the speakeasy] and lined Bastone and several customers against a wall. They were methodically searching their victims for cash when Policeman George Rouse, 35, 1812 Harrison Ave., near W. Tremont Ave., chanced to look through one of the front windows."

Witnessing the crime in progress, Rouse ran to the speakeasy's entrance in a side alley off the main road and rang the door's buzzer. His plan was to storm the premises, taking the bandits by surprise once the door was open. What he failed to realize was that he'd already been spotted. One gang member, standing sentry by the window, saw the cop approach. When Rouse sounded the buzzer, the gang was ready for him. In the alleyway, Rouse heard the sound of a lock turning on the other side of the door. The door swung inward to reveal a darkened hallway beyond. When the officer drew his sidearm and tentatively stepped across the threshold, one of the bandits lunged from the hallway's shadows and swiped Rouse across the head with a blackjack. Rouse staggered backward, his hand coming up to the bloody wound on his head. He fell through the doorway and collapsed in the alley.

The bandits—having relieved the speakeasy's customers of their wallets, cash and watches—charged out the door, stepping over the fallen officer as they fled. Rouse, although stunned and his aim unsteady, fired several rounds as he pulled himself to his feet. One bandit returned fire. A fusillade of hot lead tore into the doorjamb near Rouse's head and chipped the pavement at his feet. Two bullets hit the policeman in the right leg and sent him back to the ground with a bruising thud—only now Tough Tony had joined the action. Kneeling at the policeman's side, he grabbed Rouse's revolver and blazed away until the hammer harmlessly clicked home. Again, the volley was returned. "As the men fled, a final shot struck Bastone in the abdomen and he too collapsed. Both he and the policeman recovered," the Bronx paper reported.

Tough Tony's forays to the side of good, however, were few and far between. His "second fling with prominence" occurred on April 28 the following year. Again, the setting was a speakeasy—this one being at Manhattan Avenue and 120th Street. And while the ambiance of the establishment is unknown, the quality of its liquor is not. Simply put, it sucked. On the night in question, the quality of hooch was the focus of much pontification among the clientele. Opinions were exchanged freely in heated review, and glasses were slammed on the bar to emphasize displeasure. There was little consideration for the hardships inherent in distilling one's own poison or brewing beer, of which crafting five gallons took roughly three weeks. So ill-tempered did people become that night over the taste of what was being served that a melee erupted. It was a bar brawl in the classic sense of the word, replete with flying furniture and broken bottles being wielded as weapons. In the midst of it was Tough Tony, fists flailing and obscenities flying. He proved a hard man to put down. "Tables were overturned, mirrors shattered and shots fired," *The Home News* reported. "When police reached the scene they found that Tough Tony was suffering from wounds to the abdomen and left arm, as well as a cut on the head where he had been hit with a bottle."

As he had done the previous December, Tough Tony made a complete recovery.

Tough Tony's behavior was only mildly reflected on his rap sheet. At the time of his death, his police record showed four arrests, but only one conviction. On July 9, 1929, he was sentenced to thirty days in county jail for a violation of the Sullivan law, or carrying a concealed weapon. He was arrested for felony assault on April 29, 1931, but the charges were quickly dismissed. On August 16, 1932, he was arrested for again violating the Sullivan law, but as with his run-in the year before, the charges were dropped.

Maglione's criminal history was also surprisingly bland. He was "sent to the Reformatory [in 1920] for petty larceny." It was his sole conviction. Bastone and Maglione were driven to scheme by their perpetual desperation for a buck. Wherever money was concerned, Tough Tony, Marino said, always "chiseled his way in." Within the seedy environs of Marino's, Tough Tony—like some crazed mystic—knew all, saw all and heard all. Perhaps it was his fearsome reputation that prompted those around him to simply spill their guts. Whatever it was, it did not take long for Tough Tony to learn of Marino and Pasqua's plan. Once he did, he made it clear in no uncertain terms that he was to be involved—at least that is what Marino claimed.

It was an evening in early November when Bastone allegedly shared his intentions with Marino. Displaying an admiration for the democratic process, he supposedly told Marino that a vote should be held to determine the hierarchy of power within the speakeasy. Marino, despite the mental aggravation of combating syphilis and chronic blue balls, was sharp enough to read between the lines. When Tough Tony implied something, it was more an order than a suggestion—lest one wanted to taste one's own blood. It's not clear how many people were present in the speakeasy that night, or if such an event even took place. Pasqua was not there to challenge Tough Tony, nor was he likely to have done so had he been. Bastone's actions came as no surprise to Marino. Ever since opening his speakeasy three years prior, he'd been hopelessly fighting a losing battle to keep Tough Tony out of his affairs. It was like contending with another disease.

"Let's vote," Tough Tony allegedly said. "We're gonna vote for the leadership down here."

Marino, behind the bar with Murphy, quietly acquiesced. The whole thing, needless to say, made a complete mockery of the electoral process. The outcome was little in doubt. A vote against Tough Tony meant a future rife with intensive dental work, or legs that no longer served any purpose. Hence, no one raised his hand in favor of Marino or Pasqua. The undertaker's absence was noted by Tough Tony, who wasted no time in asserting his newfound authority. "If Pasqua don't like it," he told Marino, "you should go and knock him off." The lure of insurance money was a powerful draw, as was any chance to inflict grievous bodily harm on someone. It was just the sort of work at which Tough Tony, by all accounts, excelled.

Later that evening, according to Marino, Pasqua made an appearance at the speakeasy. He was leaning against the bar with a glass in hand when Tough Tony ambled over for a brief chat. The conversation was unpleasant for Pasqua, as the gun-carrying Bastone laid down the new law. Civility not being one of Bastone's finer points, he threatened Pasqua by telling him he'd be "a dead Guinea" if he made a fuss about the way things now stood. Malloy, meanwhile, was absent from the proceedings. When such an anomaly occurred, it can easily be assumed he was drunk or passed out elsewhere.

Malloy was not yet even insured, but already the plot was veering ever-so-slightly into the realm of chaos. Evolving from a simple suggestion discussed among three guys over drinks, the plan was now outgrowing them. The intent had been to keep the number of those involved to an absolute minimum, thus ensuring maximum payoff once Malloy was in the ground. With Bastone forcing his way into things, the number of participants now stood at five, for whatever venture Tough Tony was involved in, so too was Joe Maglione. By the time Tough Tony made his power play, however, Pasqua had already concluded that outside people—namely Joseph Murphy—would be necessary for the scheme's success. Of course, there was a big difference between Joseph "Red" Murphy and Anthony "Tough Tony" Bastone.

In events envisaged by Pasqua, Murphy would play a simple role, posing as Malloy's grieving next of kin. All he had to do was act distraught in front of the insurance man and collect the check. It was nothing too extreme—he just had to play it subtle. At most, it called for several hours of sobriety on Murphy's part. But subtlety was not a concept with which Tough Tony was familiar. He brought an element of volatility to the scheme that did not bode well for the overall outcome of things. Vital to the plan's success was making Malloy's death appear innocuous. There would be no convincing of officials that Malloy's demise was accidental if his body was pumped full of lead.

Marino's speakeasy did not have a phone. If someone wanted to reach Marino or one of his customers, they had to call the candy and cigar store on 167th Street. Acting as a secretary of sorts, the store clerk would take the message and deliver it to the intended party. Pasqua called the candy store the November morning Joseph Porreca dropped off the blank insurance application. He left a message for Marino, saying "there was an application at my office." In essence, Porreca had delivered Michael Malloy's death warrant into Pasqua's hands. All Pasqua had to do was scribble a phony signature then provide Porreca with the information necessary to fill in the blanks.

According to Pasqua, after his message had been delivered to the speakeasy, "[Tough] Tony and what's-his-name came down, Joe Maglione, to pick up the application and they brought it to the Bronx, and they came back with that signature on it." The signature was that of a gentleman named Nicholas Mellory. This was the name of Pasqua's supposed friend who was seeking coverage. In reality, it was the alias under which the gang was seeking to insure Malloy. This brief version of events as later recalled by Pasqua was a lie, a pallid attempt to divert some of the wrongdoing from himself.

Nicholas Mellory was Pasqua's own creation, and he went to some lengths to ensure that this figment of his imagination would withstand close scrutiny from Metropolitan should the company investigate the matter. It was

Pasqua's intent to make Mellory a more desirable insurance prospect than the haggard Michael Malloy. To do this, he put a business contact to good use. As an undertaker, Pasqua frequently organized floral arrangements for burial services through Michael Del Gaudio, a Manhattan florist. Del Gaudio's place of business was at 2255 Second Avenue near 116th Street. Around this time, Pasqua paid a visit to Del Gaudio's flower shop to seek meaningful employment for the nonexistent Mellory.

The conversation between the two men was brief.

"It was no conversation, exactly. He just come in," Del Gaudio said. "He said if anyone would inquire about Malloy—Mellory, rather, that you say he worked for you." Pasqua did share with Del Gaudio the reason for his odd request: "He was telling me that this man could not get insurance unless he showed he was working someplace." Del Gaudio complied with Pasqua's wishes. The undertaker, after all, was a good customer and he wished to continue doing business with him. Mellory, a man who lived only on paper, was now an expert floral arranger. His other duties included buying and selling floral specimens, as well as making deliveries.

So, that was that. Satisfied with the somewhat paltry tale he had weaved, Pasqua turned his attention to a few minor details. He shaved a few years off the Irishman's age and changed the man's nationality. Mellory would be an American born to Irish parents. Convinced he had all his bases covered, Pasqua called Porreca on the morning of November 16 and told him the application was ready to be picked up. Porreca, undoubtedly excited by this news, agreed to swing by the funeral parlor that afternoon and fill in the mandatory details. When Porreca eventually arrived, he and Pasqua sat down and went over the application. In a blatant violation of Metropolitan policy, Porreca simply filled in the blanks with the information Pasqua fed him. As Porreca jotted down the many untruths without a hint of skepticism, the undertaker was overwhelmed with sinister glee.

Each poisoned word that dripped from Pasqua's tongue and each stroke of Porreca's pen breathed more life into the elusive Nicholas Mellory. According to application #121—dated November 16, 1932—of the Metropolitan Life Insurance Company, Nicholas Mellory was born in Illinois on December 27, 1888, making him nearly forty years old, according to the application—though the math was clearly wrong. He was single and resided with Pasqua at 1959 Hobart Avenue, the Bronx. A "florist" by trade, his "exact duties of occupation" were "taking care of and selling" flowers. He was a man of average height, standing five feet, six inches and weighing a trim 147 pounds. He had a history of good health and had never suffered from such nasty maladies as "Consumption, Diabetes, Disease of Brain, Disease of Heart, Disease of Kidneys," or any ailment inflicting the liver. He was also free of "Syphilis, Ulcer or Open Sores and Varicose Veins."

He had never been turned down for insurance by Metropolitan in the past, nor had he ever filed "any other application on said life pending with this company." Mellory himself had signed his name to the paper in neat, fluid cursive. His brother, Joseph, was listed as beneficiary. It all looked and sounded good to Porreca, who willingly scribbled his name on the dotted line requiring the agent's signature. How was he to know he was signing away Michael Malloy's life? Here was another example of how Porreca's enthusiasm for the job—and his blind faith in Pasqua—may have clouded his better judgment. In retrospect it is easy to criticize, but one wonders if Porreca ever noticed the similarities between the names Nicholas Mellory and Michael Malloy.

Names aside, the two men boasted similar physical builds. Malloy was six feet tall. Mellory, standing five-foot-six, was not much shorter. The fact that Mellory was so elusive also failed to arouse Porreca's suspicions. The edge one would expect him to have after four years of selling such policies was noticeably blunt. Even when the information required for the application was provided by someone other than the applicant, he did not query the matter. Defending his actions in court, Porreca would simply say, "I filled in whatever [Pasqua] told me." Once that was done, Porreca signed his name to the application for Metropolitan policy number 1536363M, right under the typed print that read: "I certify that each question in Part A was asked of the Applicant and answered . . . and that I believe the answers are correct."

It was an $800 policy with a monthly premium of $5.02. As Porreca capped his pen, Pasqua produced the first month's payment. The two men shook hands and Porreca departed—the application tucked away safely in his briefcase—for his office. The form was filed with Metropolitan on November 18, 1932. Two weeks later, on December 1, some anonymous cog in the vast Metropolitan machinery stamped his seal of approval on the paperwork. The application was accepted, thus providing Nicholas Mellory, aka Michael Malloy, dependable coverage in the event of some heinous accident.

Pasqua and company rejoiced.

Their celebration was one of snide joviality. Pasqua shared the news in quiet conversation with each of them. In the proprietor's room at Marino's, they toasted their first successful step on the path to financial well-being. But the celebration was short-lived. Not long after the glasses had been raised and the liquor consumed, simple mathematics came into play. Marino began thinking. Metropolitan was to pay out $1,600—under the double-indemnity clause—upon "Mellory's" accidental death. Split between the five conspirators, that worked out to barely $300 each. It was pretty lousy considering all that was at risk.

Marino shared his concerns with Pasqua. Marino was a desperate man in a desperate situation, perhaps more so than the others involved. At times of great stress or excitement, he was prone to thumping headaches in the back of his skull. He also frequently suffered from dizzy spells. These episodes made him "nervous and excitable" to the point where "I don't know what I'm doing at times." The more "nervous and excitable" he got, the more seismic his headaches became. Combating blue balls and syphilis did little to ease his temperament. He had spent much time recently lost in the swirling, thumping misery of his head. He was not sleeping well. He spent many nights wandering around the downstairs of his house, pondering the survival of his business and how much he would need to stay in operation. Tough Tony's supposed ascension to power only exacerbated matters. It also meant less cash in Marino's pocket once the deed was done.

It was sometime during the first two weeks of December that Pasqua placed another call to Porreca. He said he had concerns with the policy and wished to discuss them. Porreca was always one for good customer service and made the trek to Pasqua's Burial Service, where the undertaker told him he "wanted more policies issued." Pasqua said he was looking out for Mellory's interests. Should Mellory ever marry and start a family, the current policy would do little to ease the financial and emotional burden of his widow and children should something tragic (God forbid) happen. It was a dangerous world full of dangerous people. Who knew what could happen?

"I want to know," Pasqua said, "if I can have more insurance, more policies issued?"

Porreca told Pasqua that it was indeed possible to take additional policies out on Mellory, but "if he wanted to have more insurance on the same party it required a physical examination."

Well, that certainly posed a problem. But, by now, Pasqua was pretty quick on his feet. He also had Porreca eating out of his hand. Pasqua said arranging a physical examination might not be possible. He reminded Porreca that Mellory worked late and slept during the day. Porreca suggested an alternative approach. "I told him," Porreca said, "that I had somebody in mind, a friend of mine that he could approach and ask to insure the man, the same man, for some insurance." The "friend" was a fellow insurance agent named Frederick Freyeisen, who worked for Prudential. Pasqua thought this was a wonderful idea, and asked Porreca to call the agent and arrange a meeting.

Prudential Agent Frederick Freyeisen covered a specific territory "located at Tremont and Third Avenue and covering Monterey Avenue up to 178th Street, and also 180th Street, a few houses." Pasqua's home fell within this area. After Porreca had managed to iron out the details, Pasqua met with Freyeisen on Saturday, December 10, in Freyeisen's office in the Kaplan Building. The fact that Mellory was already insured for $800 through Metropolitan did not concern Freyeisen. During his initial conversation with Porreca, Freyeisen had asked for the applicant's name and place of work. "He's a florist," Porreca told him, and gave him Michael Del Gaudio's contact information. Freyeisen promptly called Del Gaudio, who confirmed that, yes, Nick Mellory did work for him. Satisfied, Freyeisen arranged a face-to-face with Pasqua.

The meeting on December 19 was a well-attended affair. Pasqua was accompanied by Porreca and one Nicholas Mellory. "Mr. Pasqua brought a man whom he called Mr. Nick Mellory and told me he was a friend and would like to get insured," Freyeisen said. "I wrote him up for weekly insurance, two policies." Pasqua must be given credit, for this was an exceedingly cunning move. Who was this mysterious man playing the role of "Mr. Nick Mellory"? It could not have been Michael Malloy, as Porreca had met Malloy at the speakeasy when Pasqua was trying to insure him under his real name. One can only speculate as to who this individual was. Perhaps the pocket of an inebriate from Marino's had been lined with a few dollars. Maybe he was a minor player in the overall scheme of things. Regardless of who it was, Pasqua had moxie.

This was not the first time Pasqua and Freyeisen had met. The two men had briefly made each other's acquaintance at a funeral some time before. Pasqua had handled the burial arrangements for a client of Freyeisen's who passed away—one hopes from natural causes. Seeing as the two men had previously done business with each other, Pasqua went into the meeting with a slight advantage. Also lending further weight to his credibility was the fact that he had secured insurance through Porreca at Metropolitan. After hearing Pasqua explain the needs of his friend, Freyeisen produced the applications for the two policies and proceeded to fill them out—with information provided by "Mellory" and Pasqua—there in the office.

"These policies, do they contain the same clauses as the other policy, such as double indemnity and disability?" Pasqua asked.

"All our weekly policies contain the double-indemnity clause," the agent replied.

Pasqua nodded in silent approval.

The personal details given were pretty much the same as those filed with Metropolitan. But casual examination of the Metropolitan and Prudential applications reveals two inconsistencies, the first being a change in Mellory's birthday. On the Prudential application, Mellory's date of birth is recorded as December 27, 1892, making him four years younger than he is on the Metropolitan application. Despite this aberration, both applications state, in the box asking for "Age NEXT Birthday," that Mellory would be forty years old. The apparent miscalculation of age on the Metropolitan paperwork is unaccounted for. It seems no attention was ever brought to it. Nor was it mentioned by prosecutors or defense attorneys during the subsequent trial.

The second abnormality is found in Nicholas Mellory's signature. It's hard to believe both applications were signed by the same man. On the Metropolitan policy, Mellory's signature is penned in neat fluid cursive. The letters are short and round, shaped by graceful curves in thick, black ink. Elegant tails extend from the capital "N" and "M." The signature on the Prudential application is scratched across the dotted line in a spidery scrawl. The letters are not rounded off in elegant curves, but instead are sharp and pointed. The words are stretched and elongated, as compared to the short, compact appearance of the Metropolitan signature. Also, the handsome tails are missing from the "N" and the "M." The strange alteration in signature is also left unaccounted for.

The Prudential policies were for $494 each, both with a weekly premium of 65 cents. "I asked the party I insured for the premium on the application," Freyeisen said.

Going through his pockets, Pasqua—acting on "Mellory's" behalf—realized he did not have $1.30 on him.

"Mr. Pasqua said he would pay the money for it but he did not have any change, but he would give me the money through Mr. Porreca," Freyeisen said. And that was what he did. The following day, Freyeisen received from Pasqua, via Porreca, 65 cents for Prudential policy number 93439381 and another 65 cents for Prudential police number 93510104. Both applications were reviewed and accepted within the week.

Upon Prudential's acceptance of the policies, Freyeisen

delivered them to Porreca at the offices of Metropolitan. His reasoning for this was understandable. "Because I could not get in touch with the party that was insured . . . I gave it to [Porreca] to deliver, as he knew all about it," he said. In hindsight, the reason for Mellory's elusiveness eventually began to dawn on Freyeisen. After comparing the details on paper to the actual physicality of the man who presented himself as Mellory, Freyeisen would later say, "I admit that the man was somewhat taller than [five-foot-six] after thinking over the whole matter." And instead of weighing 160 pounds, "he was probably about 170." Of course, by the time he was struck by such realizations, it was far too late.

The vile mechanizations of the plot were now fully greased and ready to be put into motion. The members of the Murder Trust—Marino, Pasqua, Kriesberg, Murphy, Bastone and Maglione—could slap one another on the back and rejoice in the imminent success of their crafty undertaking. True, up until this point, Pasqua had shouldered the majority of the burden. But in the weeks ahead, everyone involved would find himself playing a pivotal role. The line of battle was drawn. On one side stood the gang, confident in its skills and sure in the outcome of its undertaking. On the other side was the object of its conquest, oblivious to everything. All was in place. Beyond the grime and cheap booze of Marino's, Pasqua and company envisioned a bright future, one where maybe chilled champagne flowed into long-necked glasses. On the two Prudential policies, Malloy's death would garner $988 each for a total of $1,976. From the Metropolitan policy, they stood to make $1,600. Thanks to double indemnity, there was $3,576 to be made from eradicating one hapless drunk from existence.

And what of Malloy? His body ached from the want of

a soft mattress on which to sleep at night. Rare was the occasion he could walk in a straight line or speak without slurring his words. His was a floundering existence. Feeble and weak, he remained ignorant to all that could not be found in a bottle. Liquor was as much a crutch to him as the bars on which he leaned when begging for a free drink. It was in this sorry state he stood on the precipice of his greatest struggle, unaware that his finest hour was at hand. The stage was set and the participants were ready.

The killing of Michael Malloy could now begin.

CHAPTER 4

On the House

Born of necessity, the cocktail was the child of Prohibition. Garnished with a slice of lemon peel or an olive, perhaps topped with a cherry, these Technicolor concoctions blunted the bitter taste of bathtub gin. Gin and whiskey crafted by amateur hands often went down like liquid fire. It watered the eyes, cleared the sinuses and put hair on the chests of men and women. The cocktail lent an air of refined civility to the wicked stuff.

Practitioners of the distilling arts were limited by the primitive props at their disposal. Many improvised their methods and the tools they used, but the procedure was pretty much the same for those thirsty enough to take measures into their own hands. For a libation on the cheap, one could simply pour sugar water into a tub, throw in a vast quantity of bread yeast and let it sit for a while. If one desired a more potent concoction, the process took on a new complexity. It required the production of ethyl alcohol, the intoxicating agent found in alcoholic beverages. This was accomplished by ridding denatured alcohol—alcohol unfit for consumption, but ideal for removing paint—of its toxic contents. There was never anything all that pure, however, about gin brewed in a bathtub where Grandma and the kids scrubbed themselves on a semi-regular basis, even if the tub was clean.

It was with this stuff that the gang planned to do Malloy in. They thought it was a brilliant idea. Instead of using deadly force and risking some kind of direct confrontation with their prey, they would actively encourage Malloy to bring about his own demise. His ravenous thirst would be his undoing. Since Marino cut him off, Malloy had been having a hard go at it. The energy expended on begging for drinks and endearing oneself to others was almost as exhausting as working full-time. And while Malloy often worked behind Marino's bar for his booze, the time he spent catering to the needs of others severely cut into his own drinking time. His luck was now about to change.

Under the auspices of the murder ring's plan, Marino was ready to free Malloy from his purgatory and reinstate a line of credit. The idea sat well with the other conspirators—except Tough Tony. He was less than enthused, according to some. He supposedly shunned creativity and preferred a more straightforward approach. Why mess around when you could simply pull a trigger or drag a sharp blade across an exposed throat? As Pasqua had allegedly feared, Tough Tony failed to realize the importance of being subtle.

Malloy's reputation as a raging alcoholic was well established. It was explained to Tough Tony that it would behoove everyone if Malloy's death came across as a result of his own liquid excesses. Should Malloy's corpse bear signs of physical violence, police and insurance investigators would be all over them. Tough Tony's reputation for packing heat would only arouse suspicions and induce closer scrutiny. Supposedly, Tough Tony pondered this point and acquiesced to Marino's more stealthy approach—but he was not happy with it. Caressing the handles of his pistols, Tough Tony warned the others that he would be watching them carefully to make sure no one shortchanged him. And as everyone knew, Tough Tony's paybacks had the potential to be eternal downers.

Marino was confident in his plan and saw no reason why it should fail. As was later attested to, Malloy already "appeared to be broken in health from too much drinking." The whites of his eyes looked like a page from a road atlas with thin red lines crisscrossing here and there. The tip of his nose was a massive red blotch and his cheeks were patches of red and purple. His jowls sagged and his posture was slightly bent from endless days leaning over the bar. And that was just on the outside. God only knew what disturbing processes were taking place beneath his skin.

The history of drunkenness is a long, sordid affair rife with tales of debauchery. It was a colonial physician who, in the wake of the American Revolution, first catalogued the deterioration of the body brought on by excessive drinking. In 1785, Dr. Benjamin Rush published his book *An Inquiry into the Effect of Spirituous Liquors on the Human Body and Mind.* Those who suckled too long from the bottle were likely to experience—among other things—a "decay of appetite," feeling sick to their stomach and being hampered by the "puking of bile and discharging of frothy viscous phlegm." When not discharging disgusting substances, a drunk, Dr. Rush wrote, might very well engage in acts of extravagance, such as "singing, hallooing, roaring, imitating the noises of brute animals, jumping, tearing off clothes, dancing naked, breaking glasses and china." Bad breath, epilepsy, consumption, expanded gut and "frequent and disgusting belchings" were other symptoms of what Dr. Rush dubbed an "odious disease."

While Marino and Pasqua were sure Malloy would easily succumb to the vast amounts of alcohol that would soon be thrust upon him, they decided to set the foundation for a backup plan just in case. Pasqua asked Marino if he knew anyone they might be able to bring in on the scheme at minimal cost. Boasting an affinity for the criminal was one thing, possessing the lack of emotion and the steel mentality to blatantly take a life was another. But after careful consideration, Marino was pretty sure he knew two men who might be up to the challenge—and do it for cheap, of course.

Edward Smith and John McNally were regulars at Marino's, swinging by each evening to toss a few shots down the hatch after a day of ominous business dealings. At thirty-six, Smith boasted an impressive list of criminal undertakings and convictions dating back to when he was seventeen. In 1914, he was arrested and convicted in New Jersey of breaking, entering and receiving stolen property. He spent a year in Rahway Reformatory and was released on May 1, 1915. He was busted again the following year, this time for burglary in the third degree and assault. He was convicted on the burglary charge and whisked away to the Elmira Reformatory for a year. Released in 1916, he kept himself out of trouble—or at least succeeded in not getting caught—until 1918. On October 17 of that year, he was nabbed for grand larceny. Again, he was sent packing to a reformatory, only to be released a short time later. On May 4, 1921, he was apprehended by an Officer McCadden of the New York City Auto Squad for stealing a car. A judge promptly sent him back to Rahway.

Following his release some months later, he left the New York area and ventured south. His travels brought him to Knoxville, Tennessee, where he was busted on May 28, 1922, for grand larceny. Considering his prior record, the judge burdened Smith—who conducted his many nefarious schemes using the alias William Jones—with three to ten years in prison. He served three years and was released in 1925. In 1930, he branched out from burglary and larceny, and got sent up the river for "impairing the morals of a minor." For this debauched episode he was sent to prison. Somewhere in the midst of his very busy criminal career, he was hauled off for possessing a revolver in New York City. Most recently, he had ascended the criminal ladder and was taking part in more audacious operations. He had several schemes simmering on the back burner. One was a plot to steal two tons of bricks from the construction sight where he sometimes worked, at 141st Street between Fifth and Lenox Avenues. There had also been some discussion, allegedly with Marino, about burning down a speakeasy on Westchester Avenue—for a fee, of course. Then, there was Thomas McMahon's butcher shop at 141 Willis Avenue, which seemed like a pretty good place to hold up at gunpoint. Indeed, there was no shortage of work for Mr. Edward Smith, aka William Jones.

But as colorful as Edward Smith's criminal adventures were, his true claim to fame was a prosthetic appendage of his own design, which earned him the nickname "Tin Ear." In 1926, during a brief stint of honest employment, Smith lost his right ear in a mine explosion. Following his initial recovery, he took it upon himself to craft an artificial replacement. He experimented with various materials and worked hard on mastering the art of sculpting an acceptable-looking substitute. He finally settled on using wax, as it was easy to mold and shape. Invoking what one paper called "the art of a sculptor," Smith "perfected the artificial ear." While it took him three years to master this strange art, he eventually honed his skills to the point where he could manufacture an artificial ear in a mere fifteen minutes. But, as *The Home News* reported, "His 'tin ear' has no part in the case . . ." It was, as far as the media of the day was concerned, just an interesting aside.

By 1933, Smith's pal, John McNally, had been convicted only three times. In 1924, he was busted for unlawful entry. Seeing as prior to this point his life had been supposedly crime free, he received a suspended sentence. Five years later, in 1929, he was convicted of grand larceny. This time around, there was little leniency from the judge. McNally was shipped off to the New York State Reformatory. In 1931, the charge was disorderly conduct. The sentence was "30 days on the island." Like Smith, McNally also had several schemes in mind, most notably the plot with Smith to torch the Westchester Avenue speakeasy.

It was a frosty evening in early December when Marino approached Smith and McNally and enticed them with the words "I may have a job for you." Marino was behind the bar with Murphy. Smith and McNally had come in to blunt the senses with a little juice. Both Smith and McNally had known Marino for about a year and a half. In between drinks, they would discuss jobs they were working on and schemes worth keeping in mind for the future. Hence, there was a certain level of trust between the three men.

In those dark days of the Depression, "job" was a magic word. When Marino uttered it from the corner of his mouth, it instantly seized Smith and McNally's attention. What sort of job was it? Marino told them the speakeasy was not the place to discuss in detail matters of such a delicate nature. Despite Marino's secrecy, Smith and McNally voiced their enthusiasm between shots. Pleased, Marino looked toward the end of the bar, where Tough Tony and Maglione were conversing over a bottle of hooch. He called the two men over and introduced them to Smith and McNally. Marino would only say a plan was in the works to take care of a problem he shared with some other gentlemen. And that was all he was willing to part with on this particular evening. Marino was simply baiting the two men to get a sense of where they stood. That said, Smith and

McNally knew what was being implied. Marino was talking about having someone "bumped off."

The subject was not broached again until sometime in mid-December. As far as Smith could recall, it was "between about the tenth and the fifteenth." As usual, Smith and McNally had stopped by on their way home to partake of the sauce. The weather was growing increasingly frigid and the winter ahead promised to be a hard one. As such, the two men were eager to learn more about Marino's scheme, and whether or not there was a place in it for them. They were greeted by Marino as they entered the speakeasy. Maglione wandered over and joined them for a drink as they sidled up to the bar. With their similar backgrounds, they had plenty to talk about.

It was not long before Marino joined in the tête-à-tête, and soon the topic of conversation turned to food. Caring little for how his wife felt about it, Marino asked Smith, McNally and Maglione over to his place for dinner. It sounded like a fine idea, and all four men went outside and crowded into Smith's car. Marino sat in the front with Smith, while McNally and Maglione sat in the back. "I was going to drive him home for supper and McNally in the car, says, 'Marino, how about that job you promised us?' " Smith said. "When we got to Marino's house, Marino gave me a case of beer. I put it on [Maglione's] lap in the back of the car. He said, 'I will take you around there now.' So I told him to guide the way, I would drive the car."

Dinner could wait.

"He told me to go round this corner and that corner." Smith said. "I didn't take notice of the streets, but it was only a few blocks from his house. When we got there, there was supposed to be a little gray roadster stopping in front of the fellow's house that would indicate he was home. When we got there, [Marino] said, 'That is the car there.' I pulled up in back of it. Marino got out, McNally got out and I got out. Maglione sat in the car. We went in, the three of us."

The "fellow" of which Smith spoke was Francis Pasqua, who greeted the men at the front door and invited them in. The house was small and cramped for space. The smell of food drifted through the place. Pasqua's wife could be heard in the kitchen, pots and pans clanging as she made the evening meal. A young child was making a ruckus in a nearby room. Marino introduced Smith and McNally to Pasqua. Although the two men frequented Marino's establishment, they had never formally met. Turning to Pasqua, Marino said, "These are the fellows I was telling you about."

Pasqua nodded his approval. "Step into the bedroom there," he said, pointing down the short hallway to a door. "I will be there in a minute." The three men crowded into the small bedroom while Pasqua went into the kitchen and told his wife to keep dinner warm. These men were business associates and he needed a few minutes to discuss some work-related issues. Pasqua joined the others "two or three minutes later" in the bedroom. They all huddled together between the bed and a chest of drawers.

Pasqua eyed Smith and McNally before getting to the point. "Now, you fellows don't look to be chumps," he said. "I don't think you will take me for one. So we have got a fellow here insured. I want to know will you do the job."

So far, the terms and purpose of "the job" had been veiled behind a lot of cryptic speech, first by Marino, and now by this undertaker chump. Sure, Smith and McNally knew what it was they were being asked to do, but they wanted to hear the actual words for themselves. The two men exchanged glances before Smith asked of Pasqua: "Come on, tell me about it. What is it all about?"

"We got a derelict, a bum," Pasqua said. "He is always drunk. You got a car. I want to know will you run over him. If you men throw him, I will give you two hundred dollars."

Here was the crux of the matter presented in simple language, but Smith didn't like what he was being told. It was not that he had suddenly decided to embark upon a life of Godly servitude. Rather, he did not take kindly to being insulted by such a paltry sum of cash. He shook his head in disgust, motioned to McNally and pushed his way through Marino and Pasqua toward the bedroom door.

"Now, wait, wait, don't be in such a rush," Pasqua said. "Come back here."

There followed a brief but animated conversation between Pasqua and Marino in Italian. When they finished, Pasqua turned to Smith and offered him $400. Smith put his hat on his head and bade a good evening to his hosts. As he and McNally stepped out into the hallway, Pasqua called them back into the bedroom. "Don't leave," he said.

Pasqua opened a drawer and began fumbling through some clothes. Amid his underwear and socks he had hidden the insurance policy from Metropolitan. "Then he had a policy in his hand, and I pulled the policy out of his hand and looked at it," Smith said. "Eight hundred dollars? Suppose this man dies of an accident, then what do you get?"

Pasqua and Marino exchanged glances. "We get double indemnity," Marino answered.

Smith shook his head in disgust. "Don't you think you have a hell of a nerve offering me two hundred dollars to kill a man when you get sixteen hundred dollars?" Obviously, Smith was not wholly aware of all the facts. Marino and Pasqua may have been cheap, but they were—at least on this occasion—smooth operators, withholding from Smith and McNally the true amount they had insured Malloy for.

Marino snatched the policy away from Smith. "Well," he said, "we ain't sure we're gonna get it."

"Right, that will do with that then," Smith said. For the third time that evening, he and McNally made to leave, and, for the third time that evening, Pasqua called them back. Smith did not want to waste any more time. He was thinking of Maglione in the back of his car with that case of beer all to himself. It was time to bust out with the hard negotiations. "How about half of that policy?"

Pasqua began mumbling something under his breath that neither Smith nor McNally understood. "Well, it will take six weeks anyhow to change it over, to give it time to die down and have a beneficiary sign to it," Pasqua said. "When we need you, Marino will let you know."

That was more like it. "All right," said Smith, visibly satisfied. "I will think about it anyhow."

Negotiations were over. McNally followed Smith down the hallway and out the front door. Marino scurried not far behind. As perturbed as Marino and Pasqua were, they could take solace in the fact that Smith and McNally's services would be called upon only as a last resort. They were certain the booze would kill Malloy. Pasqua saw his visitors out and stood on the front step, watching them pile into Smith's car. He waited until the vehicle's taillights had disappeared into the night then went inside to eat his dinner.

There was silence in the car, which only underscored the contrast of moods between the front and back seats. Marino, in the back next to Maglione, sat and smoldered. He had miscalculated Smith's penchant for deviousness. The man had outmaneuvered Pasqua at every turn, while Marino had offered no support for his besieged comrade. From the front—where Smith and McNally sat—there radiated a sense of mocking joviality. "You fellows don't look like chumps," Pasqua had said. Goddamn right—though Pasqua had been taken for a ride!

It was Marino who finally broke the silence and asked to be dropped off at home. Smith pulled up in front of Marino's house and let him out. The evening, however, was just getting started for the other three. There was still that case of beer to contend with. Maglione had exercised extreme self-control while waiting in the car outside

Pasqua's. Smith drove them all to McNally's place at 3058 Third Avenue, where they proceeded to get thoroughly sloshed.

Behind the bar at Marino's, the gang had stockpiled its arsenal. It was an impressive array of whiskey and gin bottles—each one a potential elixir of doom. After decades of abuse, Malloy's innards were battered and sclerotic—or so the gang believed. In normal human beings, excessive consumption of alcohol does more than send the room into a ferocious spin. It sets in motion biological processes that make grown men shudder. It can wreak havoc with the testicles and decimate the libido. In extreme cases, it can actually decrease penile size.

Such risks were of little concern to Michael Malloy, a man who cared not for carnal matters. There was only one lady in his life. She had a long, slender neck and curves in all the right places. She was, of course, the bottle. Like women of the flesh-and-blood variety, she could be both bitter and sweet. She could keep a man warm at night but leave him regretting his actions the morning after. She could be refined and sophisticated, or cheap and in bad taste. Sometimes she was hard to handle. On other occasions, she went down easy. There were nights when she left you wanting more and others when there was none to be had. Sometimes she was smooth, sometimes she was bubbly. At times, she blew her top. She could be flat or robust. She could knock a guy off his feet and leave him speechless. Sometimes she was complex and accessorized; other times she was simply neat. And, if you dared to push her too far, she could cost you everything. It made for a complex relationship, but it was one in which Malloy was willing to invest his time and energy.

Murphy and Malloy—when the latter was permitted to

drink at Marino's—would each "obliterate 15 shots of whiskey" in the early part of the day, according to *The New York Herald Tribune*. It was an impressive example of Malloy's iron fortitude, prompting the gang to wonder just how much alcohol it would take to kill him. It was an evening in late December when they decided to find out. Malloy entered the speakeasy to commence his nightly ritual of begging. Arranging bottles behind the bar, Marino called to Malloy. By now, Malloy had grown accustomed to Marino's inhospitality and his refusal to serve him. Marino harangued Malloy almost nightly for his begging. Business was scarce enough as it was, Marino would tell him. Having a beggar on the premises did nothing to improve prospects. Thus, when Marino summoned him that night, Malloy expected nothing more than another verbal lashing. But much to his surprise, he was greeted with open arms.

Marino explained that competition from other speakeasies was forcing him to ease house rules. Thus, in recognition of his steadfast loyalty, Malloy was being granted an open-ended tab. In essence, his drinks were on the house. It was too good to be true, and suddenly Malloy's world was one of limitless abandon. No longer would he suffer the scourge of an empty bottle. His glass would always be full. It was a brief, but dazzling, moment that reinvigorated Malloy's existence with purpose. Life suddenly had meaning. Whether Marino noticed a flash of clarity in Malloy's bleary, red-rimmed eyes as the Irishman absorbed the immensity of his good fortune, no one can say for sure.

And so it was that Malloy started drinking. He wasted no time in lavishing himself with the liquid riches so generously placed at his disposal. The other members of the gang watched from the periphery, their own bottles in hand, as Malloy unwittingly took the first steps on the path that would lead to his end. But in the dirty yellow light of the speakeasy—as the conspirators sat waiting in the shadows—they failed to realize that they had inspired in their prey a new vigor for life. One gin after the other, Malloy chugged like a champion. No sooner had his empty glass touched the bar, than it was filled again to the brim by Marino. Between shots, Malloy expressed to the barkeep his sincere gratitude. He was, the papers later reported, "thankful for munificent comrades." Like a man who stumbles across an oasis after days of parched torment in the desert, Malloy could not get enough. He simply had to drink. Sobriety presented too many challenges—there was too much thinking involved. For a "drink cadger" like Malloy, life was more pleasant surrendering to the whims of intoxication. It blunted the sharp edges of reality and instilled a certain sense of liberation. Things were more manageable when drunk. Life was not as cruel.

As Malloy rambled on between gulps, Marino stood at the ready with a bottle in hand. He listened for the first minor slurring of words and looked for signs that Malloy might be losing his equilibrium. It was a standoff between Marino's patience and Malloy's iron constitution. But it was a showdown Marino was destined to lose. Police later said, "Malloy had been a hard drinker all his life, and he drank on and on." And then he drank some more. The hour was growing late, and Marino and the others were growing weary. The place gradually began to empty, like the bottle from which Marino poured the gin. How long this would last was anyone's guess. Malloy eventually had his fill. He dragged the back of a scruffy sleeve across his mouth and thanked Marino for the outstanding service. Then, with legs that were surprisingly steady, he shuffled out into the merciless embrace of the wintry night.

But robust and thirsty, he returned the following day, ready to reexert his dominance at the bar. "Best place I ever drank in," Malloy supposedly said. "Another 'mornin's morning,' if ya don't mind."

He was greeted warmly by Marino, who placed a glass in front of him and filled it from a loaded bottle. Together the two men—quiet combatants facing off over the no-man's-land of the bar between them—reenacted the previous night's episode. Malloy guzzled all that was put before him, while Marino stood at the ready with the refill. As Malloy drank, he cast his watery eyes over the lunch tray at the end of the bar. He wondered aloud if the house courtesies extended to the offerings on the tray. Marino assured him they did. Thankful once again for his friend's charitable nature, Malloy made himself a sardine sandwich and merrily munched on it as he drank. The fetid scent of booze and sardines was now heavy on his breath. He left at closing time, smelling like a cross between a distillery and a cannery.

An air of anticipation had now settled over Marino and the lads as they waited for the alcohol to induce some sort of sclerotic meltdown. The only thing was, it didn't. On the third day, Malloy was back. Chagrined, Marino greeted him with a forced civility and charm that had to be mustered from deep within. Sardine sandwich in hand, Malloy again went to task on Marino's stock. He was drinking whiskey now, as well as gin, and helping himself to all the sardines. The mere sight of it was hard to stomach. Malloy's refusal to keel over simply perpetuated Marino's disgust. So it was, that at the end of the third night, the gang again watched Malloy leave. They remained lightened by a faint sense of hope that perhaps Malloy would pass out on the street and die from exposure. Maybe he would choke on his own vomit while he slept or something—just as long as he died!

What little hope they had began to fade on the fourth day when Malloy strutted in and took his place at the bar. "Great stuff," Malloy reportedly said as he made himself comfortable. "Best stuff I ever drunk."

A burgeoning sense of failure and the first slight pangs

of desperation were now settling in. Malloy remained oblivious to any signs of unease his "friends" may have displayed, being focused as he was on his haute cuisine. It carried on for three more days, as the gang's expectations of a quick victory were slowly routed. Their dream of easy money was succumbing to the light of a harsh reality: Malloy had no plans of going anywhere. Instead, he was blasting his way through Marino's inventory with unencumbered vitality. How much he drank exactly in that one-week period is known only to those who witnessed his Olympic feat of endurance.

Had Malloy been burdened with the normal biological limits of the human body, he surely would have died. But for reasons unexplained by medical science, he wasn't, so he didn't. Bent over the bar, he indulged his addiction with binge sessions of staggering magnitude. Such drinking generally produces a toxic level of alcohol within the body, which corrupts the bloodstream and wreaks havoc with the central nervous system. When alcohol poisoning occurs, the body is overwhelmed by the onslaught of toxins and basically begins to malfunction.

Certainly, Malloy was getting drunk, but he never breached a level of intoxication indicative of the vast amount of liquor he consumed. He had drunk himself unconscious in the past on multiple occasions—and those were on nights when the number of drinks was limited by the number of bills in his pocket. But now, with liquor flowing unabated, Malloy seemed impervious to its more dire side effects. The gang was baffled. Had normal biological processes associated with alcohol poisoning occurred, the symptoms would have manifested themselves in a number of ways. His breathing would have become slow and labored. His flesh would have grown clammy. He would have felt dizzy. As his breathing continued to slow under the incessant intake of alcohol, his skin might have turned a suffocated blue. Vomiting, and possibly uncon-sciousness, would have followed.

Had this happened, the gang might have gathered around Malloy's prostrate form to witness his final mo-ments. Out cold, Malloy would have presented death with two options: asphyxiation or simple surrender. Vomiting when drunk is a defense mechanism enabled by the central nervous system to expunge excess alcohol not yet absorbed by the body. This may occur regardless of a person's state of consciousness, hence the unpleasant end for those who asphyxiate on their own vomit while lost in the depths of a drunken oblivion. The second option was thus: A depres-sant, alcohol decelerates the brain's control centers and the functions they regulate. When the amount of alcohol con-sumed overwhelms the body and its defenses of last resort, the body will simply cease to function. This is a result of the brain slowing to a point where it's no longer communi-cating with the body's vital organs. Everything eventually slows to a complete stop, inducing death.

It was a scenario such as this—minus the technical de-tails, of course—that the gang had envisioned. But Marino wondered if he and the others were guilty of a miscalcula-tion. It seemed that years of rampant alcoholism had ren-dered Malloy's innards pickled and well preserved, thus fortifying them against further ravages from the bottle. Marino convened a meeting in the speakeasy's back room to discuss the lackluster results of their plan thus far. Ac-cording to Marino, Tough Tony argued that the gang was trying to be too clever. He strongly suggested, not for the first time, that they use a more straightforward approach. His plan was to have someone lie in wait and shoot Malloy as the drunk staggered home one night. In light of recent events, the plan was not so quickly dismissed by the others. But af-ter some consideration, it was put on the back burner.

For the moment, subtlety was still the way to go.

* * *

Murphy had so far sat idly on the sidelines. He watched the ineptitude of his boss's plan slowly reveal itself with each glass Malloy polished off. Part of him thought it best to remain as detached from the proceedings as possible, for the situation was growing increasingly tense. Although Malloy was not yet dead, the individual members of the murder ring were already taking steps to protect their self-interests. "Everybody, Marino—they all had guns. If one wasn't carrying one, the other was," Murphy said. Despite his alleged unease, Murphy decided, while listening to the others, that it was time he contributed something to the scheme. He saw a chance to play upon his fascination with chemistry. Speaking up, Murphy suggested that they switch Malloy's whiskey and gin with shots of wood alcohol. Surely, Murphy said, Malloy would not prove resistant to its toxic qualities.

The consequences of drinking such lethal stuff were already well known to the public. Over the New Year's weekend of 1927, a report issued from Bellevue Hospital asserted that blindness could result from downing three drinks comprised of 4 percent wood alcohol. The report's findings were underscored by Dr. Nicholas Murray Butler, president of Columbia University, who publicly voiced his opinion that the use of denatured alcohol in beverages was akin to "legalized murder." By 1929, about fifty thousand people nationwide had succumbed to impure alcohol. Of course, what Murphy was suggesting wasn't merely to give Malloy shots laced with wood alcohol. Rather, they would serve Malloy wood alcohol straight. The plan was enthusiastically approved by the others, who encouraged Murphy to set about it posthaste.

The whole thing excited Marino. According to Pasqua, Marino declared he was going to "give [Malloy] all of the drink he wants, all that 'smoke,' what you call wood alcohol, and let him drink himself to death." Kriesberg was equally enthused. "Yeah, feed 'im wood alcohol cocktails," he said, "and see what happens." Although he maintained a low profile, Kriesberg was no less excited by this sinister endeavor. Hawking vegetables had grown as stale as the heads of cabbage on his failing grocery stand. There was little money to be spent in those days, even less on produce. That being the case, Kriesberg was partners in another criminal undertaking, alongside Marino's cousin. Her name was Marie Baker, and she would later achieve notoriety of her own right in the press when it came to light that she was the so-called "Pants Bandit."

With a penchant for the Bonnie-and-Clyde lifestyle, Baker was the mastermind behind a number of armed robberies throughout the Bronx, according to *The Home News*. It was her modus operandi, however, that garnered considerable attention. In the commission of her crimes, she forced her victims to remove their trousers at gunpoint after relieving them of their wallets, jewelry and any other valuables with which she could abscond. Without pants, her victims were unable—or, more accurately, unwilling—to give chase in public as she made her getaway. When she was out on the job, she brought with her a male accomplice whose only task was to act as a lookout. This was Kriesberg's job, for which he received a small share of the spoils.

But Kriesberg was not really cut out for a life of crime. He lacked Pasqua's guile and Marino's blatant cold savagery. He was not hard like Murphy, who had grown emotionally numb following a vagabond childhood and a life on the streets. At his core, Kriesberg was a family man who spent most of his time worrying about his kids. It was for them, he claimed, that he partook in the Malloy scheme. The lure of that insurance money was too powerful a draw to resist. It would certainly exceed the proceeds he earned as "aide to the Pants Bandit."

That evening, after Murphy's plan had been approved, Kriesberg returned to his home on Cauldwell Avenue and, like the others, hoped Malloy's end was finally at hand.

CHAPTER 5
"He Didn't Die"

Murphy purchased the wood alcohol at a nearby paint shop for 10 cents a can. With the wood alcohol in a brown paper bag, he returned to the speakeasy confident success was at hand. Some minor planning was required. A certain panache would be necessary, for he couldn't simply put a glass of poison in front of Malloy and expect the man to drink it. Though who was to say Malloy wouldn't? No, Murphy decided to wean Malloy on to it gradually. Again, the plan called for Malloy to down "as many drinks as he wished for the asking."

It began with a shot of "cheap, impure whiskey." Hunched over the bar, Malloy smacked his lips and asked for another. Murphy was happy to oblige and filled Malloy's glass as Marino casually looked on. Without adverse reaction, Malloy downed the stuff and promptly followed it with another shot. The wood alcohol was behind the bar, ready to be wielded when the time was right. The idea was to loosen Malloy up a little and blunt his wits. Murphy hoped the onslaught of cheap booze would overwhelm Malloy's senses, thus rendering them useless for when he poured Malloy a glass of the awful poisoned swill.

Once convinced that Malloy was "feeling good," Murphy began tainting the shots with "smoke." Malloy downed them with unabated enthusiasm. His expression remained neutral. The others saw nothing in his body language that betrayed any sense that something was wrong. In fact, Malloy asked for more. He downed several poisoned shots that evening, expressing his pleasure with each—much to the startled amazement of the others. He continued to drink, eventually reaching quite an advanced state of intoxication. This, however, did nothing to impede his consumption. According to *The Daily News,* he "merely slept it off and appeared at the speakeasy the next day none the worse for this exposure."

Upon Malloy's return the following afternoon, Murphy set about in the same manner he had the night before. First there were shots of whiskey. Once Malloy began to teeter, there followed shots spiked with wood alcohol. "They fed him rot gut whiskey so flavored with arsenic that there was more poison than hooch," reported *The Daily Mirror.* "He flowered like a rose to water." This time, however, there was only a temporary pulling of the punches. The tainted shots soon gave way to belts of pure smoke. Malloy remained blissfully clueless, as always, and continued to believe in the charitable nature of his "friends." Their warm welcomes and continued proffering of drinks made him, according to one account of the day, "an almost permanent 24-hour customer." But this was just another grizzly exercise in what *The New York Post* described as "a gamut of exhaustive laboratory experiments" by an unseemly group boasting a "knowledge of murder that bettered the best efforts of the Borgais (sic)."

The wood alcohol's terrible taste and odoriferous properties were lost to Malloy in his intoxicated haze. Perhaps the drink's foul qualities struck him as being no different than bathtub gin. Whatever the case might have been, he never voiced an opinion on the matter. "Malloy drank the stuff and liked it," Marino said. *The New York Evening Post* reported: "[Malloy] could drink all he wanted and he wasn't asked to pay a cent. He didn't know that what he was drinking was wood alcohol, and what he didn't know apparently didn't hurt him. He drank all the wood alcohol he was given and came back for more."

The gang was becoming increasingly "dismayed by his immunity." In a vain attempt to speed things along, Kriesberg bellied up to the bar one particular evening and invited Malloy to partake in a duel. "Let's see how much liquor we can drink," he said, presenting Malloy with a challenge no serious drinker could turn his back on. Malloy eagerly accepted. The rules were thus: Murphy would pour Malloy drinks from one bottle and pour Kriesberg's drinks from another. "I drank whiskey," Kriesberg said, "[Malloy] drank wood alcohol. But he didn't die." Again, Malloy was defying the dictums of medical science and the bounds of human endurance.

On some nights, Kriseberg—a gaunt-looking individual described as "a sallow, thin, dark-haired man" with a long face and sloping forehead—would arrive at the speakeasy and find the place stinking of wood alcohol. Wafting out from behind the bar and carried on Malloy's breath, the odor permeated every corner of the establishment. But not once did Malloy portray any physical symptoms—other than those of typical inebriation—that might indicate something was taking an ill hold on him. Not merely was he drinking wood alcohol, "he thrived on it." Kriesberg said that on one evening he watched Malloy consume a "quart and a half" of the deadly stuff.

This was how it carried on, night, after agonizing night,

until something finally happened. It began with a scene by now common to the whole gang, but the members endured the predictability of it in the hope that their efforts would pay off. Murphy was pouring shots of smoke just as quickly as Malloy could drink them. He was leaning against the bar and downing them in rapid-fire succession. No one knows for sure how much Malloy drank that late-December evening, but it seemed that he had finally consumed more than his battered body could handle. He swayed on his feet; his speech became a jumbled slur of incomprehensible nonsense. Struggling, yet determined, he brought another glass up to his lips and slurped the contents down. It's always the final drink that pushes one over the edge.

He hit the floor in a crumpled heap. He lay there motionless before a small, but startled audience. They got up from their chairs and surrounded him in an air of anticipation. Murphy felt an overwhelming sense of accomplishment at being the man to lay Malloy flat. This was the moment they had all envisioned, for as it was later reported: "The scheme had begun to cost them money." Insurance premiums were being paid and money had been fronted. Buying the liquor and poison in the amounts necessary to unravel Malloy had not been cheap. Alas, it now seemed it had not been for naught.

Assuming his duties as undertaker, Pasqua knelt beside the body and performed a brief examination. He checked for a pulse and heartbeat, and placed his ear to Malloy's mouth to see if the man was still breathing. Signs of life were weak and the breathing was slow and labored. Pasqua assured the others that it was only a matter of time before Malloy snuffed it. The gang left Malloy on the floor and waited for the inevitable. The perpetrators receded to the shadows and watched Malloy's chest rise in jerky intervals beneath his crumpled shirt. The minutes ticked by and propelled them deeper into the still of that tense night. Then something happened: Malloy's breathing lost its arrhythmic quality, and a sound not unfamiliar escaped the unconscious man. Michael Malloy was snoring.

The guy was merely sleeping it off. He spent the night on Marino's floor like so many times in the past. In the cruel light of the morning after, he staggered out to no one knows where, only to return later that afternoon. For Marino and the lads, the whole episode was one of false hope. The plotters had foolishly believed they had succesfully breached the wall of Malloy's iron constitution. But it was a fleeting moment, harshly brushed aside by Malloy's refusal to die. His bizarre physiological makeup proved resistant to the onslaught of toxic brew and the murder ring's most dastardly scheming.

If not dead, Malloy should have at least been blind. The key ingredient in wood alcohol is methanol, a clear, volatile toxin produced from the distillation of wood. It's the primary compound in paint thinner and is often found in antifreeze, as well as many industrial products. Ten milliliters is enough to cause blindness. Two to eight ounces of the stuff is enough to kill an adult. As a prologue to death, there are a number of physical symptoms and ailments that mark a slow, but steady progression toward an unpleasant end.

Death by methanol poisoning is a grueling and painful process. Consuming the poison in minute amounts, Malloy may have felt nothing more than a mere throbbing between his temples. There may also have been shortness of breath. Had his body reacted normally, it would have metabolized the poison and produced formaldehyde, a toxic by-product. This would have caused severe nerve damage and spiked the acidity in his body's tissues and fluids. The acid would eventually sizzle its way through his veins and arteries. His liver and kidneys would also begin to dissolve. But Malloy drank nothing in moderation. Consumed in greater quantities—such as those found in the prolonged company of a shot glass—the methanol should have proved catastrophic. If the plan had worked as Murphy, Marino and the others had hoped, a scenario such as this might have played out:

Poised comfortably against the bar, Malloy downed another shot of smoke and let rip a thunderous belch. The stuff was rough on the gut, even more so than the swill he usually consumed—but it seemed to do the job. It blazed a molten trail on the way down and smoldered in the pit of his stomach. Like most spirits of the day, the taste left a lot to be desired and the smell was not kind on the nose, but it was free. Besides, taste and quality mattered little. He just wanted to get drunk. He ordered another shot, his words stumbling slightly over his tongue. Murphy obligingly refilled the glass. Malloy nodded his thanks, raised the glass and downed its contents in one not-so-fluid motion. Swallowing the stuff left him short of breath, and the fumes made his head swoon.

That last one packed a real punch. For one uncomfortable moment, he felt sure he was going to serve it up all over the bar. Once confident everything was staying put, he motioned for another. It was then he noticed there were two Murphys behind the bar. One, slightly translucent, was superimposed over the other, though not perfectly aligned. There was nothing strange about that, but there was something else, too, a feeling of malaise. This somehow differed from the general sensation of airiness that came with a buzz. It felt as though his strength was slowly being sapped from his body like beer from a tapped keg. His legs were losing their sense of solidity. He felt drunk, but in an unfamiliar way. Perhaps it was time to call it a night. He tried to tell Murphy as much, but the words didn't merely stumble over his tongue, they fell in a jumbled heap.

His heart thumped heavily in his chest and flooded his

system with poisoned blood as he staggered to the door. The others bade him well and watched him leave, knowing it was a dead man who stumbled out into the cold night. Beyond the walls of the speakeasy, Malloy's life was a mystery. Where he went on the nights he didn't crash on Marino's floor or sleep in the back room of Pasqua's mortuary was one of those great unknowns. Later, not even the authorities would be able to paint a precise picture of the man's routines. Bronx District Attorney Samuel J. Foley would admit that much in court. Presumably, however, he sought shelter in the squalor of a nearby tenement. Returning to whatever wretched domain it was he'd emerged from each morning, Malloy sought the mercy of unconsciousness.

The onset of severe symptoms of methanol poisoning is sometimes delayed by eight to thirty-six hours after ingestion. Thus, in the bitter light of the morning after, Malloy may have thought he was suffering from an extraordinarily bad hangover. His stomach was a hot, bubbling cauldron. But there was more to it than that. It was pain that pulled him from the shallows of an uneasy sleep. Lying amid dirty sheets, he curled his body against the sharp abdominal cramping and violent waves of nausea. His clothes clung to clammy skin, which had turned slightly blue in color. In angry protest, his stomach propelled its acidic contents upward. Malloy puked all over himself.

In many such poisoning cases, these ailments are often coupled with confusion. As the hours tick by, the brain—soaked in toxins—transmits unintelligible messages. Along with muddled thoughts and clouded memory, Malloy's surroundings descended into haze. Things appeared wavy and ill defined, as if veiled behind a heavy mist. The mist gradually became a blizzard, and a flurry of snow swept across his vision. Internally, things deteriorated even further. His body continued to metabolize the wood alcohol and produce more formaldehyde, which continued to spike the levels of acid in his body. His thoughts grew more convoluted and breathing became increasingly difficult.

Every organ and system in his body was now contaminated. As the day progressed, Malloy's condition worsened, pushing him closer to that grim conclusion so desperately sought by his "friends." In the stark abandon of his miserable little flat, he finally lapsed into unconsciousness. The sun sought cover behind the horizon as if unable to bear witness to Malloy's convulsing body. And then came blessed relief. The trauma of it all induced a massive coronary and killed Michael Malloy where he lay. Not until the repugnant smell of musty vegetables seeped into the hallway and neighboring apartments was the body discovered.

Of course, none of that actually happened.

"The 'syndicate' grew desperate," stated *The Mirror*. "It was spending money for poisons that seemingly were so much stimulant to Mike. They ran the gamut. Cyanide to carbolic."

"This stuff would not work on him, and they said they would fix him another way," Murphy said. After each methanol binge, Malloy just slept it off. "The plotters," the police told the *Times*, "tried to kill the man with good liquor and bad, but there was something about Michael Malloy that even denatured liquor could not affect." *The New York Evening Post* would later dub the Irishman "Michael 'Iron Man' Malloy," while another reporter would describe "the durable bar fly" as a "hard nut to crack." The gang was painfully aware of Malloy's stellar immunity long before these somber salutes made their way into print. Time was running out for the Murder Trust. Like a hungry cat that only prolongs the mouse's agony by swatting it here and there, the gang had messed about with Malloy for too long. It was time to take far more drastic action.

"The plotters thought out a scheme which they believed meant certain death and which might be diagnosed as a natural death . . . They were out of patience and nervous," the *Times* reported. Marino believed Malloy's ongoing survival would eventually prove catastrophic to his establishment. A man of such insatiable thirsts could very well put the shabby speakeasy out of business, drink through its entire stock and leave nothing but shelves of empty bottles and the broken dreams of a few desperate men in his wake. Varied plans were discussed and courses of action were debated. Tough Tony—who bragged incessantly about how he had "given it to a lot of wops in Harlem"—advocated sheer brute force. But Pasqua and Marino still favored a stealthy approach.

It was Pasqua who devised the new scheme, which he pitched to an increasingly anxious Marino. Having taken note of Malloy's love of sardines and oysters, Pasqua said it was time to let loose with a full-frontal gastrointestinal assault. There would be no more messing around. This was the real deal. Pasqua's plan called for dropping oysters in a jar of denatured alcohol and, after letting them soak for a while, serving them to Malloy. Pasqua was certain that would do the trick, because "Alcohol taken during a meal of oysters . . . will almost invariably cause acute indigestion, for the oysters tend to remain preserved." Pasqua knew from professional experience that such a culinary concoction could prove fatal. Marino and the others agreed to the plan—but the question on everyone's mind was: Will it work?

There are, unfortunately, no exact dates on which one can place these events. What is known through media accounts and court testimony is that the gang's futile attempts to kill Malloy via gin, whiskey and wood alcohol

consumed all of December 1932. Hence, the oyster
scheme probably commenced sometime in early January.

Malloy sauntered in one evening and took his place at
the bar. He got comfortable on his bar stool and greeted
Murphy in his usual fashion by asking for a drink. Murphy
opened a bottle of smoke and poured Malloy a shot. Malloy remained oblivious to the repugnant vapors emanating
from his glass. He downed the poison and expressed his
satisfaction. Murphy smiled his approval and shot a quick
glance to the smattering of oysters that was festering in a
jar of methanol behind the bar. The gang had left them sitting "for a few days" and was anxious to conclude this
frustrating endeavor.

Marino took up position behind the bar. He was ready
to yield the oyster platter with deadly consequence. Once
Malloy had slipped comfortably into his early evening
buzz, Marino placed the oysters in front of him. Malloy
was again taken aback by this display of seemingly bound-
less generosity. He plucked the oysters from the plate one
by one and thoroughly masticated each mouthful. A meal
such as this was not one to be rushed. Indeed, each
morsel—its taste and texture—was worthy of his fullest attention. As Malloy ate, Marino and Pasqua watched from
the sidelines with morbid anticipation. Pasqua was sure the
alcohol would act on the oysters like formaldehyde on a
corpse. It would preserve them and render them impreg-
nable to the ravages of Malloy's stomach acids as they
passed through his digestive tract. They would nestle like a
lead weight in his gut and cause all sorts of grotesque problems. Malloy would soon find himself crippled with the
worst case of indigestion he'd ever had, or so Pasqua believed. It would begin with an uncomfortable twinge above
the belt line, a slight cramp accompanied by mild bloating.
But the soft edge of these discomforts would soon harden,
perhaps resulting in the loosening of his belt. There would
follow a fusillade of nasty expulsions that brought the taste

of oysters back to Malloy's mouth and left the state of his undergarments in question.

His stomach would continue its revolt against the imperishable intrusion and become an angry sea of acid. There would be chills and sweats and violent bouts of diarrhea and vomiting, undoubtedly rendering the cramped lavatory in the back off limits for quite some time—that was, of course, if Malloy could even muster the strength to stand. Pasqua theorized that the stomach pains would be unbearable. Of course, he and the others would feign concern. They would approach Malloy's quivering, bent-over form and ask—their voices conveying the utmost sincerity—if he was feeling all right. "What's that? The oysters? Oh dear, could be a touch of food poisoning. You sure ain't looking too good. Maybe another drink will do the trick. No? Perhaps you should go and sleep it off."

Pasqua had once buried a man who'd suffered a similar fate. In that particular case, the man had washed down a meal of raw oysters with several glasses of impure whiskey. The whiskey preserved the oysters and caused a massive gastrointestinal infection that sent the man into shock, then ultimately killed him. Without proper medical attention, Malloy would be dead within two days. The undertaker was sure the plan was a winner.

And so the gang watched and waited. They attended to their own drinks and sought reprieves from the anticipation in games of pinochle—a particular favorite of Tough Tony's. With smacking gums, Malloy finally pushed the fully cleared plate away from himself. Pasqua took the Irishman in with a watchful eye and noticed—much to his dismay—that "he seemed pleased rather than ill." It was later claimed in court that this "astounded the gang." Malloy betrayed no signs of gastric distress. There was no rush to the lavatory to forfeit the meal. Nor were there any disruptive noises to indicate that any violent gastrointestinal processes were taking place. All the gang could do was reel in silent amazement—stunned by their own glaring incompetence—when Malloy suddenly "called for a drink."

"By this time, according to police," *The Home News* reported, "the plotters decided [Malloy] was an iron man, that he bore a charmed life and couldn't be killed, but they had paid the premiums on his insurance and wouldn't give up without trying everything." It was also becoming apparent to the few patrons of Marino's who were not directly involved in the gang's ploy that something was afoot. The smell of poison liquor had become commonplace, as had the clustered meetings between Marino, Pasqua and the others. It seemed they were meeting on an ever more frequent basis. With increasing desperation came the slow erosion of secrecy, though they tried to keep things under wraps. "As far back as I can remember," Murphy said, "only the fellows that are implicated in the thing [talked about it]. They didn't do much talking if anybody was around that couldn't be trusted."

Having finished his meal of poisoned oysters, Malloy saw the evening through in his usual fashion: He got drunk. When he staggered from the speakeasy later that night, he left behind him a raging torrent of confusion and frustration. When he returned the following day in high spirits and unblemished health, the group descended into quiet turmoil. "Never felt better in all my life," Malloy said, when asked by a curious Marino how he was feeling. How was any of this possible? Surely, Malloy was not blessed with the powers of immortality! The gang decided it was time to meet again and conferred later that evening. In their frantic discussion the members breached new lows of depravity, for they were not burdened by any guiding moral conscience. It had reached the point where nothing was beyond consideration. Desperation had evolved into obsession. Killing Malloy had become a matter of principle, though profit still remained the underlying motivator.

* * *

There was much debate over what new course of action to take. One proposal called for simply beating Malloy on the head until he was dead. They could do it as he sat at the bar, or jump him in the street and dress it up as a random mugging. It was Murphy—described by one newspaper scribe as "shifty-eyed and nervous"—who proposed the winning plan: "Try poisonous sardines with tin garnishings." Apparently, the barman was convinced that tainted seafood was still the way to go. But raw shellfish soaked in denatured alcohol was one thing, digesting jagged shards of shrapnel was something else entirely. The gang agreed and decided to move forward with Murphy's recommendation.

Rare was the occasion that Murphy could contribute to matters of such importance, but twice now the gang had gone along with a plan of his devising. Outside the speakeasy, he was an individual of little consequence. He walked with a severe curve to his spine, shoulders slumped forward under the heavy burden of failure. Amid the happenings of 3775 Third Avenue, however, he was part of a semi-clandestine operation, and he liked the feeling of self-importance that came with making a contribution.

Along with slabs of sandwich meat, the sardines were a regular feature on Marino's free lunch tray. It was his meager way of adding a sense of culinary sophistication to the otherwise drab surroundings. He knew there were fancier places about town wowing patrons with gourmet offerings. In one place, west of Sixth, behind the fake cigar shop facade, beefsteaks—complemented with liquor and cigars—were the featured item on the menu. The Little Maison Doree on West 52nd Street served dishes rich in garlic, while another speakeasy on 46th Street was known for its veal scallopini. But such scrumptious treats cost money. And seeing as Marino found money in short supply, sardines and cold cuts it was. Marino's clientele did not seem to mind, least of all Michael Malloy. On most nights, before he drank enough alcohol to kill his appetite or render his legs useless for the task, Malloy helped himself to the lunch tray's contents, cramming between slices of bread a rather large heaping of sardines.

It was a ritual duly noted by Murphy, who purchased a can of sardines to make a special dish just for Malloy. The can was opened and placed on a shelf out of sight, allowing the sardines to sour. Murphy let them rot for several days, deciding they were fit for serving only after he found himself repulsed by the smell. Before Malloy came in one evening, Murphy smeared the contaminated fish on a piece of bread. To the slimy spread he added not salt and pepper or a dash of mustard, but numerous metal slivers. Via the services of "a local machine shop," Murphy had reduced the can to nothing more than tin shavings. Bits of broken glass were then carefully placed amid the mush, along with some carpet tacks. Another slice of bread was lovingly placed on top.

When Malloy showed up on the evening in question, Murphy—as was now the custom—poured him a shot of his regular poison. He then offered him the sandwich. Malloy accepted and ravenously sunk his teeth into the fishy treat. Murphy watched and waited. Any minute now it would happen. The first sharp shards would tear through Malloy's internal workings, piercing and shredding pipes and tissue as they made the torturous descent to his gut. But Malloy chomped, chewed and swallowed that first mouthful without so much as a grimace. Satisfied, he did it again and continued to do so until the sandwich was gone. Murphy was not a man prone to deep thought or inquisitive spirit, but even he was taken back by Malloy's durability. Was it possible to chew a mouthful of broken glass, carpet tacks and razorlike splinters of tin and not feel anything?

Was Malloy immune to pain? Was his body resistant to such injuries? None of them should have been surprised, for Malloy had thus far proven himself to be a biological powerhouse.

The sandwich had been a particularly vile creation. Its potential to cause grave bodily harm was far greater than the methods previously employed. It was the ring's most brazen attempt yet on Malloy's life. Later, keeping tally of the gang's efforts, the *Herald Tribune* reported that Malloy had withstood "wood alcohol . . . survived a dose of poisoned oysters and sardines mixed with tin." But as far as Malloy was concerned, the sardine sandwich was a well-crafted meal. Those gathered that evening did not want to believe what they were witnessing. But much to Murphy's begrudged amazement—and that of the other plotters— "Malloy ate it and liked it." As with the oysters, he washed it down with a shot of wood alcohol, "grateful for the food and drink with which they plied him," reported the *Times*. The evening was still young, and the plotters were firm in their belief that the sandwich's less-than-appetizing properties would soon inflict fatal damage. There had been plenty of talk from Pasqua about food poisoning and internal hemorrhages. Perhaps Malloy would wake up in the night, spewing blood from several orifices and die a slow death—or perhaps not. "The durable Malloy," it was later reported, "never weakened on this diet."

Malloy was thirsty the following evening, and hungry. Sitting at the bar, he asked for another sandwich. The gang was far from amused. It was time to up the violence. The oyster and sardine ploys had been born of desperation, but all they did was exacerbate the Murder Trust's anxiety. If he was as vital a player as they said he was, Marino and Pasqua should have paid more attention to Tough Tony. As he kept claiming, he had enough experience giving it to "wops in Harlem" to know you didn't go about this sort of work being overly inventive. You simply pulled the trigger and got the job done. Alas, his advice was being ignored—much to his increasing chagrin. But the man so feared by others because he "packed a gat" was exercising amazing restraint. Perhaps it was the enticement of insurance money that kept Bastone's temperament in check.

Although Marino claimed Bastone had ascended to the head of the gang via his non-hostile takeover some weeks earlier, it is evident that Marino and Pasqua were still exercising control over the scheme. But their ways had met with nothing but failure—something the others must surely have been aware of. It was a situation that not only cast Marino and Pasqua in a bad light, but also made Tough Tony look weak, for he had done nothing to force his will upon them. That Tough Tony was feared is a fact not under dispute, but one has to wonder how much say he really had in the grand scheme of things. He certainly had some, but there is little doubt that Marino and Pasqua still firmly clasped the reigns of power.

Bastone's influence on Murder-Trust policy temporarily came into play following the failed poisoning attempts, when it was decided to try a more straightforward approach. They would get a machine gun and whack Malloy Chicago-style, cutting him down in a fiery blaze of lead. Malloy's stomach may have been ironclad, but the gang was willing to bet it wasn't bulletproof. The press, relishing the murder ring's comic failures and Malloy's penchant for survival, would later write "the gang had arranged to shoot [Malloy] with a machine gun, but Malloy eluded the trap." This was not necessarily true. The plan, in fact, fell apart because Marino was unwilling to dole out the cash necessary to get his hands on a quality product. And for the 1930s hit man, quality meant the Thompson submachine gun.

Developed under the ominous codename "Annihilator," the tommy gun pumped out one hundred rounds in less than a minute and could rip a human target in half. It was the firearm of choice among Chicago's heavy hitters, thus resulting in one of its many nicknames: the Chicago Typewriter. Marino apparently thought he knew where he could get his hands on one, but when that fell through, he went to another source. Neither court records nor media accounts name Marino's contact. Marino, however, eloquently summed up the episode himself: "I was supposed to make connections about a machine gun, but the parties that I wanted to get were not there. Later I come back, and who is this says 'Did you get it?' and I says 'The nigger wants $50.' The nigger come in the place and says, 'You got $50?" and I says, 'No.' "

And that was that—short and sweet. Once again, Michael Malloy—still oblivious—had evaded the snapping claws of death.

The year 1932 slipped into history, and New Yorkers celebrated "with noisy revelry." Reported *The New York Times* on the first of the New Year: "It was not particularly rejoicing that a new page of history had been flipped by time, for 1933, though it was welcome, was greeted with a prudence born of the past."

Past lessons were something the Murder Trust would have been wise to take into consideration.

CHAPTER 6

The Drunk Who Came In from the Cold

Marino closed shop at eleven that evening. He was tired and, like his comrades in conspiracy, felt the shame of defeat gnawing away at his pride. The gang's mood was grim. The planning, the preparation, the investment of time and resources had thus far yielded a zero-percent return. Malloy's broken appearance was deceiving. His blood was impervious to contamination. Objects not meant for consumption were no match for the cast-iron machinery of his stomach. Blatantly defying death, he was playing them all for a pack of fools. So what now? What new dark avenues were there left to explore? Death is infinite in its designs, but Malloy's penchant for survival seemingly knew no bounds.

Outside, the street was quiet. The dim glow of yellow light colored some of the windows of the neighboring tenements. Marino turned his collar up against the raw January night and the light snow that had started to fall. His breath came and went in clouds of white vapor as he slowly trudged home. The sting of winter made his nose run and his ears burn, but there were more important things on which to focus his attention. His conspiratorial mind pondered all that had transpired up to this point. How quickly the best-laid plans go to hell. Every contingency had been considered except for the one that plagued them now: their inability to kill a worthless drunk. They were certainly working hard for their money. Was it worth it? It was quickly reaching the point where the effort extolled was not worth the reward.

Marino's woes were many.

For starters, the killing of Michael Malloy had become a crowded affair. There were so many conspirators now jostling to do the Irishman in, that the murder's proceeds would amount to nothing once evenly split among all the participants. Tough Tony was further complicating matters with his desire to whack John McNally, friend of Edward Smith and a Marino regular. Tough Tony's reasoning was simple: "I don't like the Irish cocksucker," he reportedly told Marino. Well, that was fair enough—but it was one hell of a time to act on a personal grudge. The gang could hardly cope with one plot to kill, let alone two. But on the issue, Tough Tony would not be placated. "We got to knock him off," he allegedly said. Where this deep-rooted animosity suddenly sprung from is not entirely clear. Unlike Malloy, McNally was not a valuable commodity. Whereas the appearance of Malloy's passing had to be carefully planned so as to ensure maximum financial benefit, there were no restrictions to hinder whatever random acts of violence might befall McNally. The restraint Tough Tony was supposedly forced to exercise in the Malloy affair was proving too much. Stripped to its basic essence, Tough Tony's violent inclination toward McNally was nothing more than desperate bloodlust.

"Count me out of the fucking thing," Marino said after Tough Tony shared his intentions.

Things had already breached an unforeseen level of complexity. There was no need to add to the chaos, nor did Marino want to implicate himself in another murder. Tough Tony, however, remained adamant. He asked Marino to show him where McNally lived. "He had a couple of guns and I had to go with him," Marino said. On the evening in question, Marino, Bastone and Joseph Maglione staked out McNally's house at 3058 Third Avenue, near East 157th Street. They loitered in the shadows and waited for their intended victim to return from whatever it was he was out doing. The hour grew increasingly late and the weather grew increasingly cold. Marino's patience grew increasingly short. "Two o'clock, I went home," Marino said.

"Listen," Tough Tony said as Marino turned to leave, "if you don't keep your fucking mouth shout, I'll give it to you, too."

"I ain't going to say a word," Marino shot back.

They had failed in yet another task. Tough Tony found the situation increasingly intolerable. Blood had to be spilled, and he cared not whose it was. He found someone the following day to bear the brunt of his violent impulses. Tough Tony arrived at the speakeasy that afternoon and told Murphy he was going to beat the hell out of a shoe shiner he saw working on 118th Street. He ordered a drink, threw it back in one shot and asked Murphy to join him on his endeavor.

Marino, who was present at the time, said, "They had the guns down in the cellar in one of the gas stoves in the place." Murphy and Bastone scurried down the basement steps to retrieve their arsenal. Once packing heat, they scrambled up the stairs and out of the speakeasy, ready to inflict pain. Yes, the shoe shiner would pay for Malloy's refusal to die. The shoe shiner would bear the brunt of Bastone's frustration. Marino waited for them to return from their conquest. If anything, this was merely a morale booster. It was an exercise in self-reaffirmation—a chance for Tough Tony to prove to himself his aim remained true.

When Murphy and Bastone walked through the speakeasy door an hour later, their faces were etched with the agony of defeat. "When they come back, they says, 'No good,'" Marino said. The two went downstairs and put the guns back in their hiding place. At the bar, they set about drowning their frustrations in a bottle. The shoe shiner had proved elusive. If it weren't so depressing, it would have almost been comical—but the gang's failure was becoming habitual. Were they all really this incompetent? At this point, robbing a bank would have been quicker and more to the point.

Marino and Pasqua had never liked the thought of sharing. Already, there had been discreet mumblings between the two about how to handle the money. It was of Pasqua's opinion—and Marino was apt to agree with him—that once Malloy was dead and the money secured, it should be split among the plan's original architects. Pasqua had quietly shared his intentions with Marino one night while sitting at the bar. "Outside of Danny and Murphy, no one is entitled to it," Pasqua whispered. "They are the only ones that done the work."

This, however, was not entirely true. Pasqua had thus far done the lion's share of the work. Without his efforts, Malloy would not have been insured. Murphy also had made vital contributions via his suggestions. It seemed the plot had roused in him a vigor that had not been there previously, but this was not to say he had surrendered his old ways to a life of sobriety. He was still drunk most of the time. In fact, he still did plenty of drinking with Malloy.

While Malloy downed massive quantities of smoke, Murphy continued to poison himself with excessive amounts of whiskey. And while Murphy's plans had proved as big a failure as the others, he had put into his work a noble effort. Kriesberg was owed a cut primarily because he was present when Pasqua and Marino hatched the plan. He had kept his mouth shut and had been a loyal compatriot. In terms of contributions, he had offered little. But he was one of Marino's few repeat customers and a partner-in-crime with Marino's cousin, which worked in his favor.

But Marino was the glue that held everything together, for he provided the locale where they could ponder and execute their dastardly deed. When it came time to count the money, no one could say he wasn't worth his generous cut.

The others had done nothing for the betterment of the scheme. Granted, they were all accomplices by association. If word got out of what they were conspiring behind the empty storefront on Third Avenue, they would all be sent upriver.

There was something else to consider: Money made men—especially this lot—do violent things. How would the others react when they discovered they were being cheated? Marino and Pasqua would undoubtedly find themselves on the receiving end of something brutal. This was one aspect of Pasqua's plan worthy of further contemplation. It would have to be discussed, for they were not dealing with reasonable individuals. Indeed, there was no short supply of things to worry about. But was it worth dwelling on the future when so much of the present remained uncertain?

Like the cold, all these things gnawed away at Marino as he walked home.

The weather chilled him to the bone and steered his thoughts back to the unfortunate Mabelle Carlson. How easy it had been to rid himself of her. His only weapons had been his cunning, guile and the chill of an unseasonably cool spring night. As he pondered the particulars of this earlier success, Marino was suddenly staggered by a flash-bang of inspiration. He stopped short in his tracks and shook his head at the wonderment of it all. Why hadn't the idea struck him sooner? He had already committed the perfect crime once, who was to say the same modus operandi wouldn't work twice?

Marino quickened his pace in his excitement. He now knew what to do, and tomorrow was a new day.

Malloy sat at the bar and exuded immortality. His mere presence had become a slap in the face of each man plotting his demise. It was like salt in the wound every time he walked through the door and ordered a drink. Those in the loop would stir uncomfortably and exchange knowing glances. Like soldiers hunkering under fire in a frontline trench, they were bound by a unique experience known only to them. By now, no one was sure what to make of Malloy. Was he a marvel of human engineering, or simply a freak? It seemed that the harder they tried to kill him, the more enthused with life he became. The free meals and the drinks on the house had blessed him with unwavering vitality.

While the city's newspapers ran stories of people keeling over from alcohol poisoning at alarming rates, Malloy continued to drink his smoke with unbridled abandon. The reeking stench of it was at times intolerable. The fumes were enough to cause headaches, nausea and other unpleasant sensations, but the gang was probably suffering more from the smoke than its intended target. Their indirect approach had failed. There were low murmurings that it was time to get violent.

Then, one day in January, something unusual occurred: Malloy did not show up. His absence at the bar was glaring—and remained so over the next several days.

Where was he? Had the wood alcohol finally done its thing? Had he suffered a delayed reaction to the tainted sardines and poisoned oysters? Was it possible that after all their efforts, their conniving and scheming, all the setbacks and frustrations, the gang had finally killed "Iron Man" Malloy?

Of course not.

He was back in the speakeasy less than a week later, his return promptly bringing an end to the jovial speculation. As he pulled up a stool at the bar, he told Marino where he had been. "He went away to the Fordham Hospital," Marino said. "He went up there for his leg. He had a running leg." Malloy had taken leave of his drinking duties to seek treatment for an oozing sore. Disgusting as this was, it was proof of Malloy's physical fallibility. Despite everything, there was still some hope. Malloy was not invincible after all.

It was an evening in mid-January when Marino acquainted Pasqua with his plan to subject Malloy to the Mabelle Carlson Treatment. They had every reason to be confident. The basic elements of the plan remained the same. As they had done with Mabelle, they would feed Malloy drinks until he was hopelessly drunk and leave him to sleep it off in the cold embrace of a wintry evening. High temperatures that month rarely breached the upper forties. At night, the mercury plunged to the low twenties.

They acted on "one of the coldest nights of the winter." Malloy came in that afternoon, blowing into his cupped palms to warm his frozen hands. Marino told him he knew what would do the trick and poured Malloy a shot of smoke. Malloy graciously accepted, and so began the boringly commonplace routine. There was casual conversation about the weather and other mundane topics as Malloy drank. All the while, Marino played the gracious host and made sure Malloy's glass remained full. Mere drunkenness would not suffice. For the plan to succeed, Malloy had to transcend all levels of basic inebriation and drink himself into a raging stupor. But this was not hard to accomplish, for the simple act of pouring a drink was an invitation for Malloy to drink it. And after countless refills, Malloy drank himself unconscious.

Marino knew he could not take Malloy back to his place. What would be the odds of having another person die in his residence from excessive alcohol consumption and exposure? Malloy would instead be dumped in Crotona Park, as it was only a few blocks away. Marino and Pasqua took Malloy by the arms and legs and carried him out to Pasqua's "little gray roadster." They tossed him gracelessly into the backseat and drove to the park in silence. There, they dragged Malloy from the car and carried him into the darkened grounds with their gentle hills of grass and rock now white under a blanket of snow.

The weather was frightfully cold. One paper described it as "an arctic day." Marino and Pasqua carried Malloy along a path, looking for the ideal place to dump him. They finally settled for a park bench. With heaving breath, they stretched Malloy out on the bench lengthwise. The task of transporting him from the car to this solitary spot had been most challenging. Neither Marino nor Pasqua was an ideal physical specimen. The challenge of hauling Malloy's deadweight was made all the more cumbersome by the bucket of water they had brought along. After all that had transpired, they were leaving nothing to chance. "Malloy's clothing was stripped from his chest and water poured over him," *The Home News* reported. The fact that Malloy did not stir is a testament to his severe state of intoxication. Satisfied that their work was done, Marino and Pasqua stole away. They returned to the car and drove back to the relative warmth of the speakeasy.

Malloy's body had withstood the shock of poison, broken glass and tin—but would it yield before the chilling savagery of Mother Nature? Whether Malloy froze to death on that bench or suffered a slow, choking demise from pneumonia over the days that followed, Marino didn't really care. The end result would be the same. That was the beauty of the plan: There was no discernible escape from its grim outcome. But Marino thought it unlikely Malloy would make it out of the park alive. Certainly, he would freeze to death. It was an unpleasant demise far removed from the pleasures of drinking oneself into an eternal oblivion.

Lying on the bench, Malloy's breath came and went in rapid bursts. It materialized above him in frosty clouds that quickly dissipated in the wintry gusts that blew about him. How long he remained sprawled in the cold of that January night no one can say. Indeed, the events that transpired on that park bench are forever lost to time, but one thing is certain: Michael Malloy woke up. How frantic and confusing those first moments of consciousness must have been. Where was he? This wasn't his bar stool, and this certainly wasn't the speakeasy! Once confusion gave way to startling clarity, circumstances may have played out like this:

Malloy sat up, but not with the deliberate care of one who has had too much to drink, but with the urgency of one propelled by the direness of his situation. The cold blade of the wind against his exposed flesh sucked the air from his lungs. Already, his body had begun to yield to the merciless weather. A painful numbness blanketed his entire being and seeped deep beneath his skin. If characterized as a killer, cold, it can be said, is an unpredictable slayer. The physiology of freezing is a complex matter. One person might survive a subzero ordeal, while another perishes in temperatures as mild as forty-five degrees. In cold enough conditions, the body's temperature drops three degrees about every half hour. Depending on how long Malloy remained unconscious on that bench, he may have come to with a body temperature of ninety-five degrees—three degrees below the body's normal core temperature of 98.6. This would constitute a case of mild hypothermia.

When he moved, the bitter cold clung to him like sodden leaves. His extremities ached and his hands had lost much of their flexibility. Beneath his skin, his body's entire network of capillaries had contracted against the cold, flooding his torso with blood. At the expense of less vital anatomy, the body was attempting to keep its central cavity warm. He could feel muscles in his back and legs bunching up. Once his body temperature dipped again, they would begin to contract uncontrollably in a meager effort to generate body heat, causing violent shivering. Malloy struggled to his feet. Still drunk and unsure of his whereabouts, he floundered in the snow trying to gain some familiarity with his surroundings. Why was his shirt open? Had he done that? He wasn't too sure of anything at the moment.

His body began to shake. His teeth banged together. He was unable to gain a firm hold on his thoughts. In these conditions, and with his body temperature continuing to drop, his mental processes were growing sluggish and the clarity of his thoughts—already dimmed by alcohol—were dulled even more by an encroaching mental fog. He stumbled left, then right, not sure which way to go. The ache that accentuated every move he made had, somewhere along the line, become a biting pain. The cold was now like countless icy needles piercing his skin. Had he been on the bench long enough for his body temperature to drop to ninety-three degrees, his situation would have been further complicated by the gradual onset of dementia.

Considering the severity of nocturnal temperatures that January and the fact that Malloy had no choice but to escape his predicament on foot, no one can say how degenerative his condition became. In the worst-case scenario—the one Marino and the others were hoping for—Malloy's sense of urgency would have been dulled by a mental fugue. Unsure what he was doing or where he was going, he simply began to walk, almost oblivious to the elements swirling around him. But the going was not easy. No longer was he shivering. His muscles had ceased their frenzied activity. They now seized up like rusty hinges. Trying to move his legs—to bend them at the knee and put one foot in front of the other—was an excruciating exercise. His body was breaking down. Physical movement had become nearly impossible, but it was something his mind was only partially aware of.

His mind was wandering off in wild directions, exploring alternative realties and doing little now to register the goings-on in the real world. Having reached this stage, his body may have surrendered what little strength it had left and collapsed, leaving itself to the mercy of whatever came next. It would not be death, not yet. When the body's temperature hits the low nineties, everything is lost to the senses. A further decline in body temperature would have pushed Malloy far beyond the danger zone. His rate of breathing would have decreased dramatically and his blood would have started to coagulate, growing thick and soupy as it pushed ever more sluggishly through his veins. From this point on, it would have all been a rapid degeneration.

Hallucinations would abound. Perhaps the swirling static of the snowy night would give way to the familiar stretch of bar in Marino's. All the stools are taken except for one, which is reserved for Malloy. He takes a seat and Marino serves him a glass of his regular. If Malloy reached this stage, the harsh realties of the outer world would continue inflicting their toll even while he reveled in the warmth of his mental make-believe. Once the body's core temperature hits the mid-eighties, the heart begins to malfunction. The cold fries its circuitry and causes it to beat irregularly. The level of blood moving slowly through the veins drops like a river in summer.

Malloy's final moments would have been spent curled up in a fetal position amid the snow and slush on the ground as the wind and cold tore the life from him.

What did Malloy actually go through that night in the park? Whatever it was, it wasn't pretty. When Marino arrived at his speakeasy the following day to open it up, there was a surprise waiting for him. Lying on the floor in the middle of the basement was Malloy's ragged and unconscious form. In his battered and weather-beaten condition, he had somehow traipsed half a mile through the ugliest of winter nights to the speakeasy's front door. Perhaps Murphy, in a drunken state after helping himself to his nightly cache of drink, let Malloy in to sleep it off. Half-frozen, Malloy probably made his way down to the basement to thaw himself out near the gas stove. Unlike the previous ordeals the murder ring had put Malloy through, this one seems to have caused the hardy soul some real discomfort. His mere appearance must have told some tale of physical anguish, for Pasqua briefly referenced it later when being grilled by authorities: "Red had given [Malloy] some smoke, some wood alcohol, and the fellow was in agony in this park, Crotona Park, and, well, the following morning, they happened to find the fellow got from Crotona Park down in the basement. I suppose the fellow got up at night and walked over to the speakeasy, and I suppose [Marino] figured that didn't work, they would try something stronger."

When it was later reported in the media, the true barbarity of the act was overshadowed by the man's comedic penchant for survival. After reviewing the episode's morbid facts and describing how Malloy had been prepped for the ordeal, *The Home News* simply told its readers: "This didn't bother him a bit." *The Daily News* took it one step further: "He didn't even get the sniffles and was back the next day for his alky ration."

The episode presented yet another peculiarity in the strange case of Michael Malloy. The laws of common sense dictate that one would surely question what sequence of events had led one into such a predicament, but Malloy did no such thing. He slept his condition off on the speakeasy's basement floor and, after coming to, failed to pursue the matter with his supposed friends. Perhaps he thought he only had himself to blame. After all, he had drunk himself into a raging stupor. It wasn't the first time. But waking up to headaches and vomiting was one thing; stripped to the waist on a park bench in the middle of winter was something else entirely. Regardless, it failed to rouse in him any questions. This spectacular lack of curiosity would not serve him well in the near future.

Marino and Pasqua were not quite ready to surrender all hope. The prolonged exposure to the cold would surely induce an illness. Malloy's body was weak; it would be susceptible to nasty things, some sort of bug—perhaps a phlegm-producing monster accompanied by a molten fever. They pictured Malloy bedridden, hacking and short of breath as he shivered beneath dirty sheets. Maybe he would cough himself to death. Better yet, perhaps he'd drown in his own pink, frothy sputum. Naturally, this was not to be. And it was not long before everything was back to normal—or as normal as things could be at 3775 Third Avenue. Malloy was again showing up for his free fill of drinks, while the murder ring found itself hurtling hard and fast toward the breaking point.

After one particular evening of watching Malloy chug his way through a jug of methanol, Murphy felt compelled to comment. "This stuff ain't killing him," he said, referring not only to the poison, but to the gang's gauntlet of evil schemes. "We gotta try something else."

This "something else" would prove to be the most violent undertaking yet. Subtlety would be cast aside in favor of brute force. It was a declaration of all-out war. Their patience had been tried and their resolve only strengthened by Malloy's penchant for life. It was time to resort to the backup plan. But what the gang could not have known was that the plot was about to enter its most outrageous and convoluted stage.

CHAPTER 7

Ticket to Ride

His name was Harry Green—"Hershey" to his friends—and he drove a cab. It was a nondescript job calling for nondescript skills, just a good sense of direction and steady reflexes. A gift for gab might be deemed a prerequisite for such a profession by some, but Green was not a conversationalist. He would not ask fares how their day was when they entered his cab, nor would he wish them well when they exited. He cared not for the opinion of others and was more than happy to admit he cared only for himself. For Green, if anything, was startlingly blunt. He didn't like people as a general rule. An amendment to that rule was that human life was of little value to him. Simply put, Harry "Hershey" Green was a deeply disturbed young man.

He had made it to twenty-four without acquiring a criminal record, but this was hardly a reflection of his character. True, he had never killed anyone—but there was certainly something provocative in the idea of rubbing someone out.

In maintaining his reputation for straightforwardness, he would later admit that he was eager to take a life—and his job provided ample opportunities for someone looking to practice the art of murder. On the occasional days and nights when he worked, he drove around the Bronx and Harlem picking up potential victims, though he never acted on his impulses. Simply killing someone for the sake of killing didn't hold Green's interest. What he really wanted to do was kill for cash. He needed the money.

Green lived at 2530 Lurting Avenue in the Bronx and drove his cab out of a garage at 619 Wales Avenue, an establishment owned by a gentleman named Alex Polk. Green had worked for Polk on and off for about six months, but no more than two or three days a month. It behooved Polk's drivers to drive as much as they could, as he paid his employees a commission based on the fares they brought in. Consequently, Green was broke most of the time. "On a night when he booked five dollars, he turned in two and kept three," Polk said.

One could hardly eat and get drunk on that. No, what Green sought was a new opportunity—a chance to break into something different. That chance was about to come along.

Marino sat in the musty corner shadows of his speakeasy. Failure tormented him like the syphilitic burning in his crotch. January would soon pass into February, and another month's premium would be due. It should have all been over by now. Desperation had drained the gang's creativity. There would be no more tainted seafood or broken glass sandwiches. Marino was sitting at a table with Joseph Maglione and John McNally.

Edward "Tin Ear" Smith was skeptical of Marino and Pasqua's plan to run Malloy over. He wasn't sure it was worth the risk, but McNally remained hot on the idea. The problem was McNally—who remained ignorant of Tough Tony's attempt on his life—didn't have a car. Christ, if it wasn't one thing it was something else!

Since he and Smith had rejected Pasqua's blundered business proposal, McNally had returned to the speakeasy two or three times just to see how things were progressing. Marino said he was still interested in having Malloy flattened in the street. On this particular evening, however, Marino followed up the reiteration with a new proposition. "On one of these occasions the conversation was about Smith, I remember," McNally said. "He had made advances to Maglione's sweetheart, and I remember Marino saying to Maglione, 'How about Hershey?'"

From that point on, the two men conversed in Italian, leaving McNally out of the loop. Marino and Pasqua had already discussed breathing new life into the death-by-car idea. They decided that now was not the time to be cheap. During his conversation with Maglione, Marino laid most of his cards on the table—though he opted not to mention the two Prudential policies. According to Maglione, Marino told him "he had a [Metropolitan] policy for $800 and that if we would run Malloy over we could take the other half of the double indemnity, so me and McNally spoke it over. So McNally says to me, 'See if we can get somebody to drive a car.' So I said, 'I have a friend of mine, Harry Green, he is a cab driver, we will speak to him.'"

McNally went to the bar and had himself a drink. "When I was ready to leave, Maglione asked me to wait for him, that he would walk down with me," he said. "When we got to Westchester Avenue, he told me to walk over to Westchester and Jackson Avenue with him, and he would walk me down to Harlem."

Half the double indemnity for McNally and Maglione meant $400 a piece. As they walked, they discussed how much they should offer Green for his services. They settled on $150, with each contributing $75. They walked to a small eatery in Harlem where Maglione knew Green would be dining that evening. Joining him at his table, they ate spaghetti and dispensed with the small talk before finally "putting the proposition to Green."

Green happily accepted.

The individual members of the Murder Trust were not gentle men, and those who were pulled into their dark orbit were quickly corrupted by the gang's lack of moral decency. One man, however, was immune to their corrupt ways. He was godfather to Marino's son, and his name was Jimmy Salone. Unlike those he associated with, Salone was—by comparison—an upstanding citizen. When District Attorney Foley later called Salone into his office for questioning, he praised the young man, saying, "I know you are a clean, good kid." Such compliments were not forthcoming about the others. Whether Salone was really an all-around decent bloke or a crook who excelled enough at his craft to not get caught, no one can say. What is known is that Salone, who lived at 473 East 136th Street, occasionally worked as a driver for Krasne Grocery Store.

During his off time, he enjoyed visiting Marino's once or twice a week. There he could sit and enjoy a drink. "I am not a drinker, see," he said. "I drink to be sociable." Being "sociable" meant learning to play pinochle. His tutor was Tony Bastone, who enjoyed a good game of cards. Salone was a quick learner. "He learned me an Italian game how to play," Salone said. "I was wise to the game playing before that with the others. All he had to do was give me a touch of it, and I caught on to it."

But there was more than drinking and games of cards taking place at 3775 Third Avenue. There were sly murmurings and sideways glances and hushed conversations in the shadows. Simply put, Salone knew there was something not quite on the level going on—or at least being planned. Such scheming was to be expected in a speakeasy. But there was something overtly sinister about what he saw and heard, for Salone was witness to an emergency meeting of the Murder Trust. When the plan was still in its infancy, its concept simple, the number of plotters at a minimum and its outcome foreseen with little hindrance, the meetings had been a covert affair. Then, the Murder Trust had been an enterprise built on confidence and hope. Now, it was broken in spirit, desperate and really pissed off. The loss of patience meant caution had been thrown to the wind.

The meetings had moved beyond the privacy of the speakeasy's back room and were now taking place wherever: at the bar, in a corner, around a table. While it became obvious to the few not directly involved that something was afoot, Michael Malloy remained lost in his own little world of drunken ignorance. It is hard to imagine how he could have been so oblivious to such goings-on, as the place was not very large. From the point where one entered through the fake facade of the storefront to the back wall of the speakeasy, the distance was only thirty-five feet. The width of the room was a mere twelve feet, the same length as the bar. This left little room for maneuvering and covert planning.

One evening in late January, Salone swung by Marino's for his social drink and "to fool around with the fellows." The gang was present and accounted for, nursing their bruised and battered egos with the sauce. It had been merely a matter of days since the failed attempt to freeze Malloy to death. Tough Tony—if his involvement was as great as Marino claimed it to be—had been right all along. There was no room for sly creativity when it came to whacking someone. The only way to do it was to simply do it. Harry Green was a firm believer in this line of thought, and when Salone entered the speakeasy that evening, he found the cabbie in conference with some of the others.

Salone, presently unaware of what was in the works, had a drink at the bar and chatted briefly with Kriesberg "about old times." He then took a seat at a table on the right side of the room. A few members of the gang were conferring nearby, standing next to the partition that hid the speakeasy's interior from passersby on the street. What Salone heard came as something of a surprise. "The first time I heard any conversation, I walked in the place and heard Harry Green talking about running over some man," Salone said. This was not your typical cocktail chatter, but, by now, there was nothing typical about the situation. "There was Bastone, Marino and Pasqua who took part in the conversation," Salone said. Noting the way they were huddled close and trying to keep their voices low, Salone knew "there was some secret talking going on." Indeed, there was. Kriesberg sat at the bar and watched the proceedings over the rim of his glass. His major contribution was yet to come.

This was Green's first encounter with the other conspirators, though he had known Maglione for about five years. As far as he remembered, the meeting took place "in the latter part of January." He immediately fit in well with the others. They shared a common lack of values and sought only to better their own circumstances at the violent expense of someone else.

Green was eager to play his part and demanded to know what was required of him. His eagerness was almost enough to infuse Marino and the others with a renewed sense of optimism. But unlike Green, they knew what it was they were up against: an indestructible force of nature. That night in the park, not even God had been able to do Malloy in. There is no record of the gang telling Green of Malloy's impressive track record. Perhaps they didn't want to frazzle his nerves—if such a thing was even possible. What they told him was to make sure Malloy got it with all four wheels. If there was any doubt, Green was to back over the bastard and make sure the job got done right. By God, there would be no chance as to Malloy's fate this time around.

Green had a drink with his new friends. Of primary concern to him was the $150, though he thought the price was "pretty cheap." But if the truth be told, he would have killed for less, as his financial circumstance was quite dire. Also, he wasn't being asked to do much. His task would be easy and he foresaw no problems. Minimal planning was required. The underlying factor critical to this endeavor's success was speed. He would need a nice stretch of road where he could really put his foot down. He didn't want Malloy to become jammed under the car and end up smeared across the asphalt. Nor did he want the guy to come over the hood and bust the windshield. For that matter, he didn't want the front grill dented, the hood ornament bent or the headlights smashed. Any such damage would lead to bothersome questions from his boss. Under the circumstances, he would rather not draw attention to himself.

The gang picked the night of January 30, 1933, to run Malloy over. They would wait until the hour was late, drive him to some deserted road and clobber him with eight cylinders. Once again, the plan called for Malloy to be properly sloshed. They wanted him "limp with drink," according to Murphy.

Just like the clinking of glass and the sound of liquor over ice, the smell of wood alcohol had become a sweet siren song for Malloy that beckoned him to the bar with its promise of intoxication. Malloy's ordeal by blizzard had left him undeterred. His resolve to get plastered on a nightly basis remained intact. He had no fear that he might again wake up half-naked on a park bench. That strange episode was behind him. Besides, everyone on the juice has a story to tell at some point. Malloy now had his: "Well, lad, you think you had a rough morning after, let me tell you about one I had not too long ago . . ."

When Malloy came in that afternoon, he was greeted with the warmth and graciousness he had come to expect. He took his seat at the bar and started drinking. Murphy drank with him, taking slugs from his own bottle. The other gang members settled down with their own glasses and waited for the rumbling approach of Green's taxi.

CHAPTER 8
The Mean Streets

Green arrived at the speakeasy sometime before 10 P.M. He parked the cab in front and sauntered in, ready to perform his duties. On this night, unlike his new partners in crime, Green was a man of indomitable spirit. He did not realize his fellow conspirators were desperately trying to claw their way free of a swirling, sucking eddy of failure and incompetence. Unbeknownst to him, he was—in a way—their last hope. When Green entered the speakeasy that night, Malloy was already drunk at the bar. He seemed anything but a formidable target. His legs had failed him, rendered useless by the stinking swill he was gulping down.

As the hour was not yet late enough, Green had a drink himself and discussed the evening ahead with the others. It was going to be a crowded affair. Present were Maglione, Marino, Murphy, McNally and Bastone—and all of them wanted to play a part. They wanted to see Michael Malloy's end for themselves and be free from this waking nightmare. The task, of course, required no more than two people: one to drive the car, the other to drag Malloy into the middle of the street. But Green wasn't going to complain, although he would soon have reason to.

If Green was unaware of the ineptitude with which the others conducted their affairs, he would soon find out. The first problem presented itself before they even left the speakeasy. How were they going to cram seven people into the taxi? It was going to be a tight fit, requiring several beer guts to be sucked in. According to Maglione, it was sometime between 11:30 P.M. and midnight when they decided to head out. The short car ride did not promise to be a comfortable one. The prospect became even grimmer when Bastone announced that he was bringing along a friend, a man known to the others only as "Johnnie." This brought the total to eight.

There was no point arguing about it. Besides, there were more important things to worry about. They finished their drinks and got up to leave. Malloy and Murphy were still at the bar and fumbling with their respective jugs of drink. Bastone walked over and helped Malloy off his stool. What excuse they gave Malloy for denying him further liquid refreshment is not known, though it probably didn't matter. Malloy was so drunk he had no coherent concept of what was happening. Murphy stumbled out from behind the bar and followed the others into the street. The night was clear and crisp. As they struggled to work out the physical logistics of getting themselves into the car, "it just started to snow," McNally said.

Johnnie got in the car first.

"Bastone and Murphy came out with Malloy," McNally said. "Then Marino and Maglione and myself. Green had jumped in the driver's seat. I think Marino asked Murphy for the key to close the place up."

They shoved themselves in for a very awkward fit. Bastone's friend sat on the left rear seat, while Maglione sat in the center rear seat. As McNally remembered it, "Marino sat on Maglione's lap, Bastone sat on the portable seat, Murphy sat on Bastone's lap and Malloy was thrown on the floor. He was all bundled up, he was pressed against my legs and Marino had his feet on top of him."

After making sure everyone was in, Green fired up the engine and pulled away from the curb. "We went up Third Avenue as far as Fordham Road," Green said, "then turned left and went as far as Gun Hill Road, and across from Gun Hill Road until about a quarter of a mile before Baychester Avenue."

It was here Green stopped the cab. The street was deserted. The snow was still falling. The ground was lightly frosted. This was the spot to do it. From the backseat, Maglione had lost track of where they were: "We went up some road, I don't know exactly the name of that road that they took. He was going down the road, and Bastone and Murphy takes Malloy out of the car and they walked ahead with him, giving Green orders to run him over as they got a little ways from him." It would be over in a matter of minutes. The scourge of the Murder Trust's existence—the very thing that had brought it into being—would be a lifeless lump in the gutter. Then there would be rejoicing, for there would be much to celebrate. How funny it would seem when it was over. The tales they would share! The revving of the taxi's engine signaled Malloy's imminent end. Bastone, Murphy and Malloy were small, hard-to-see figures in the windshield. Green gunned the motor some more and released the break.

The reverberation of the engine shook the taxi as the wheels spun momentarily, searching for something to grip. The car jumped forward with a powerful lurch. With his foot heavy on the accelerator, Green catapulted the car down the center of the roadway. In the street, Murphy and Bastone held Malloy by his outstretched arms. Their legs were bent and their bodies wound tight as they prepared to jump clear at the last possible moment. The car's headlights grew larger and the engine louder, like the roar of some charging beast. In the car, the men braced themselves for the awful impact—and then Maglione noticed something that made him yell at Green to stop the cab.

"Just then a woman happened to light a light in a window, and they changed their minds," Maglione said.

The car screeched to a violent halt. As McNally remembered it: "Green drove up to Murphy and Bastone and Malloy, and told them to put Malloy back in the cab, which they did, and proceeded straight ahead, and Green turned left off on to another, a more lonely road. Murphy and Bastone dragged Malloy out of the cab, held him in the middle of the road, Green reversed the cab again, and on the first attempt missed Malloy and nearly hit Murphy and Bastone instead. Green swung around, got the same distance between them, about a block or block and a half, and on the second attempt, Murphy and Bastone they threw Malloy and jumped out of the way themselves, and the cab hit him. Green went straight ahead for about three blocks before he turned around. On the way back we saw that another car had already stopped by Malloy and a man was bending over Mike Malloy's prostrate form, so we passed the body up, passed Mike up, and we picked up Murphy and Bastone."

McNally's account may give Green too much credit. Maglione would later recall it took the cabbie *three* tries to successfully plow Malloy down. After being scared away by the woman in the window, Green turned the cab around and drove to Baychester Avenue. Here, once again, Malloy was manhandled by Bastone and Murphy and dragged from the car. They stood on either side of him—his arms slung around their shoulders—and walked him into the middle of the street.

"They got some distance away and Green drove fast," Maglione said, "as he got near him, Bastone and Murphy jumped away from him, but Malloy jumped out of the way himself. That was done again the second time, the same as the first."

For a man "limp with drink," Malloy was proving to be surprisingly quick on his feet. Although nothing about Malloy should have come as a surprise by now, the men in the car were shocked by his apparent nimbleness. Murphy and Bastone took hold of Malloy in the street again, repositioning him in the center of the road so that his back was to the oncoming cab. This, too, failed to work. "He heard the car coming on top of him," Maglione said. "He saw Murphy and Bastone jump out of the way, and he jumped out of the way . . . but on the third try they hit him and they were going over him again when another car came down."

Even Green admitted his aim was off: "Bastone and Murphy took Malloy out of the car again and walked down the road to Baychester Avenue. I turned around and drove as far back as Gun Hill Road again and then started down Baychester Avenue in another attempt to kill Malloy. As I drove alongside of them, they tried to throw Malloy in front [of the cab], but somehow or other he was missed. I then went up Baychester Avenue about another two hundred yards and came down on the side of the street in an attempt to kill Malloy again, and the same thing happened. He was missed again."

As Maglione remembered it, "The man jumped out of the way too quick for him."

It certainly wasn't meant to be this hard. Green slammed on the breaks and brought the cab to a jarring halt. He stuck his head out the window and looked back down the street. He could see Murphy picking up Malloy's "staggering" form. Bastone was running toward the cab. Green put the car in reverse and backed up to meet him. Breathing heavy, Bastone leaned into the window. He said it wasn't working. If they stuck around much longer, someone was bound to notice something. In full agreement, Green quickly devised a plan.

"I made up a signal with Bastone that I ring the horn twice when I came down the road for him to know it was me, and that we wouldn't miss [Malloy] this time. He agreed, and I drove down to Baychester Avenue and Gun Hill Road again and came up this time and hit Malloy, and I went up Baychester Avenue another two hundred yards, turned around and came down on the other side. As I was coming back I seen a car stopped at the side of Malloy's body, but I didn't stop there. I continued down and picked up Murphy and Bastone."

Murphy said the evening was a blur. "I was feeling pretty good," he said. "I can't say I was drunk, but I can't say I was sober." Murphy fell asleep not long after Green pulled the cab away from the speakeasy. Despite the recollection of others who said Murphy helped Bastone hold Malloy in the middle of the street, Murphy insisted he did no such thing. Instead, he said he brought a bottle of booze with him in the car and, after helping himself to a couple of belts, dozed off.

Murphy said it was the "thud" of the cab slamming into Malloy that disturbed his slumber. "What attracted my attention was when [Malloy] was hit and I woke up. [The car] gave a jerk. That is the time it hit Malloy; that is all I can remember." He then did his best to play innocent. "I asked them what they were hitting him for, and they told me to shut up. Tough Tony said, 'If you don't shut up, you will get yours.' So I had to shut up." Although Murphy's story was a blatant lie, he at least admitted to tagging along that night. It was more than Marino would cop to. Referring to the others who went on the violent joyride, all Marino would later say was "The car came up and they went in the automobile. Where they went, I don't know."

Green hit Malloy with "tremendous force." As Malloy

grew larger in the taxi's windshield, Maglione could not bring himself to watch. He diverted his eyes to the blurred scenery out the side window and looked down at his hands. The others in the car urged Green onward, while Maglione supposedly steeled his guts for the sickening lurch. "As soon as he come on top of Malloy, I buried my head," Maglione said. "I could not bear to see it." It was a strange admission from the man who approached Green and made the $150 offer, not to mention helped Tough Tony and Murphy drag Malloy from the car. "I helped push him toward Bastone," he said. "I just gave him a shove towards Bastone."

There was a loud thump as Malloy bore the brunt of all eight cylinders, and the sound of rolling thunder as his trashed body rolled up onto the hood and rocketed up the windshield. Then he was airborne. He hit the asphalt and rolled into the gutter. There was a lot of excited yelling in the car, for what a spectacle it had been! Green stomped on the brakes. Maglione slowly raised his head from the crook of his arm. All he saw in the windshield now was light snowfall swirling in the beams of the taxi's headlamps. Murphy and Tough Tony were standing on either side of the roadway, breathing heavily and rejoicing in their bravado. Malloy was nothing more than a mangled, unmoving heap. Although the gang was certain Malloy was dead, the arrival of the mystery motorist denied them their chance to confirm it. Whoever it was could report the accident for the gang. The following day's paper would surely carry news of a body being found on Baychester Avenue. This would play perfectly into their plan. Murphy, posing as "Mellory's" distraught brother, would call the authorities and claim possession of the body. Pasqua could then secure the death certificate and the insurance money could be collected.

God, they were good!

They drove into the night and left Malloy's body for

someone else to worry about. They returned to the speakeasy in high spirits. They spilled out of Green's cab and congregated on the sidewalk, glad to be free of the car's cramped confines. The hour was late and the night's adrenaline was wearing off, but they could easily imagine Malloy's broken body being loaded into a meat wagon for its trip to the morgue . . .

They decided to part ways for the evening. The hard part was done, but tomorrow there was still much work to do.

McNally showed up at the speakeasy "sometime the next afternoon." Business was slow as usual. In eradicating Malloy, Marino had rid himself of his most loyal customer—although, granted, he was a customer who never paid for anything. When McNally arrived, there were only three people in the place. Marino and Bastone were sitting at the bar with a newspaper spread out in front of them. Murphy was behind the bar, tending to some bottles. McNally pulled up a stool and ordered a drink. Marino and Bastone were lost in *The Home News,* their attention rapt. They were running their fingers down each page, scanning headlines and articles for some mention of a fatal hit-and-run accident the night before.

"Marino and Bastone, each of them were looking at the newspapers," McNally said. "I asked Marino if there was any news about Mike Malloy."

Marino flipped disparagingly through the paper and shrugged his shoulders. "I don't understand it," he told McNally. "I don't see nothing."

Marino slid the paper down the bar and asked McNally to have a look. The lead headline on page one read "Bronx Grand Jury Opens Inquiry Into Charges of Balloting Frauds." There was no mention anywhere on the page of a fatal hit-and-run. McNally turned to the inside pages. "Church Group Rehearses Minstrel Show" declared one headline. "Mrs. Schryver Is Given Party by Mizpah Group" read another. The account was riveting: "Songs and piano selections were offered and Josephine Haight gave an impersonation of Gracie Allen. Refreshments were served." But be Mrs. Schryver's party what it may, there was no mention of Malloy's encounter with an automobile. Why would the Bronx's hometown paper not report such an incident? The body had been discovered, so someone had to have called someone else. It was all very strange. Perhaps the "accident" had occurred after the paper was sent to press. As McNally puzzled over the possible explanations, Maglione strolled in.

Maglione said that when he walked in that afternoon he found everyone "looking at the papers. When they didn't see his name in the papers, none of us could wonder what was the matter." If Malloy was not dead, they would have surely been burdened by his presence at the bar. But how could Malloy have survived? When Green's front fender made contact with Malloy's hapless form, the taxi's speedometer had read almost 50 mph. The force of the impact had launched Malloy off his feet. With the exception of Maglione, who covered his eyes, everyone had seen the body take flight and land in the gutter. But the fact remained that Malloy was a man who "seemed able to stand almost any kind of treatment."

Green showed up later that afternoon and found Marino and the others still flipping through the paper. He ordered a drink and asked Marino what he was doing. "Marino said he was looking in *The Home News* for some news of Malloy," Green said. "He didn't see any and [asked me] to get the rest of the papers and look in the rest of them."

Green finished his drink and made the rounds to a number of newstands. He brought back a selection of New York's various dailies and spread them out on the bar. One by one the papers were read and discarded with a growing sense of unease. There was no mention of Malloy or any story concerning a hit-and-run accident—fatal or otherwise— in the Bronx. Something was definitely amiss, though what it was no one could possibly fathom. If Malloy was alive, then where was he? If he was dead, who had possession of the body? There was much discussion and hypothesizing, but nothing was reached in the way of a solid conclusion. Recalled Maglione: "They let it go for a couple of days, then we drove in a cab up to the place—the same place—where Malloy was hit. There was me, Mc-Nally, Marino and Green. We started to look in the bushes there, figuring this party that first saw Malloy was afraid."

The men fanned out along the sides of the street. They crouched down on hands and knees and peered into the underbrush. "They said probably he might still be on Baychester Avenue, that nobody had seen him," Green said. They theorized that after Malloy was struck, he crawled away like some injured animal in search of a lonely place to die. The men quietly called out Malloy's name and listened for some sort of response. There was nothing. They soon reached the conclusion that Malloy was not in the street. Increasingly puzzled, they piled into Green's cab and headed back to their base of operations.

It was decided after some consultation that they would let things sit as they were for a couple of days. If Malloy was alive, he would eventually walk through the speakeasy door and take his usual place at the bar. The individual members tried to go about their daily routines with some sense of normalcy. But like the victims of terminal disease who can't escape thoughts of their impending fate, they couldn't stop thinking of Malloy. The Irishman lurked ominously—and constantly—in the backs of their minds.

And so it came to pass that Marino proposed the most diabolical plan yet. There would be no insurance money without proof Malloy was dead. In short, they needed a body—but not just any body. "Marino told us that we got to go . . . and look for a fellow that looks like Malloy so

they could put a card in his pocket and identify him as
Michael Malloy," Green said. In other words, a substitute
victim would be killed in place of the now elusive Irishman. It was less than a week after Malloy's strange disappearance that Marino presented this vile scheme to
Maglione, Bastone, Murphy and Green—Pasqua was not
present for the meeting. It was not a hard plan to sell. For
all the effort exerted in killing Malloy, the gang had no
physical evidence the job was actually done. The members
agreed to back Marino's proposal.

On the afternoon of February 6, sometime between four
and four-thirty, Green swung by Alex Polk's garage on
Wales Avenue to see if there was an available taxi to take
out. Polk ran a fleet of seven cabs. The drivers who worked
the night shift had not yet returned, so most of the taxis
were still on the street. But there was one available. Polk
gave Green the key to a cab, license number 023783.
Green signed the cab out, drove off the lot and ren-
dezvoused with Marino, Maglione, Bastone and Murphy at
the speakeasy. There, the details of the gang's plan were fi-
nalized. They would hunt for their new prey—someone
who would have to stand five-foot-six and weigh 180
pounds—in the speakeasies of Harlem. There was less of a
chance they might run into someone they knew there.

Harlem in the 1930s was in the midst of a renaissance—an
explosion of creative output by African-American writers,
painters, poets and musicians. It was both an artistic movement and cultural offensive, targeting racism and pro-
pelling Black creativity into the mainstream. But Green
and the boys had little interest in such highfalutin pursuits
as the poetry of Claude McKay. What they were interested
in was speakeasies—and Harlem had no shortage of such
establishments. There was the famous Cotton Club, at 142
Second Street and Lenox Avenue, with its chorus lines and

"They Must Die for Murder!" — So read the headline that ran above this picture in the Thursday, March 19, 1933, edition of *The* (Bronx) *Home News*. Here, the members of the Murder Trust are pictured awaiting the verdict to their trial. They are (clockwise from top) Daniel Kriseberg, Joseph Murphy, Frank Pasqua, and Anthony Marino.

Form 556
Jan. 1932
PRINTED IN U.S.A.

APPLICATION TO THE METROPOLITAN LIFE INSURANCE COMPANY

INDUSTRIAL DEPARTMENT

(INCORPORATED BY THE STATE OF NEW YORK)

NOV 18 1932

This ... be filed at the Home Office and not by the Agent.

NO. 12 1
1932

1536363 M

Note: Entries made in red ink by Company entail loss because of handling one and are not a part of answers by applicant to questions in this application.

DEBIT No. **108** NAME OF AGENT **PORRECA** DISTRICT **HARLEM. N.Y.** (Must be stamped) DETACHED SECTION

PART A

1. FULL NAME of Life proposed for insurance **NICKOLAS MELLORY** 2. RACE White / Colored (Cross out to leave correct Ans.) 3. SEX **male**

4. MARRIED, SINGLE, WIDOW, WIDOWER, DIVORCED OR SEPARATED **single**

5. RESIDENCE OF LIFE PROPOSED STREET, ROAD OR PIKE (PRINT) No. **1959 HOBART AVE.** CITY, TOWN OR VILLAGE (PRINT) **Bronx** STATE **N.Y.**
FLOOR **Gr.** APT. NUMBER FRONT OR REAR RIGHT OR LEFT R.F.D. No.

6. DATE OF BIRTH (If aged 9 or 2) **12/27/1888** 7. PLAN OF INSURANCE **15 Y.E.** 8. AGE NEXT BIRTHDAY **44** Years 9. AMOUNT OF INSURANCE **800** 10. W'kly PREM. (If W.P. Pol.) 11. M'thly PREM. (If M.P. Pol.) **5.02**

12. PLACE OF BIRTH (If U.S.A., give name of State) **Itly** 13. TOT. FAMILY WKLY. PREM. MET. $ OTHER CO'S. $ 14. State D.L.P. on MET. W.P. Pol's $ 15. ADVANCE PREM. PAID (If W.P. Pol.) No. of WEEKS (If M.P. Pol.) No. of MONTHS **one**

16A. OCCUPATION (If more than one, state all) **FLORIST** B. NATURE OF EMPLOYER'S BUSINESS **FLOWERS Seller**

17. EXACT DUTIES OF OCCUPATION **Taking care an selling**

18A. NAME OF PRESENT EMPLOYER **MR. DEL GUIDO** B. BUSINESS ADDRESS **2255 - 2nd Av. NYC.**

19. Is said Life now insured in this Company? If not insured, state "No." If insured, give the following details of all Policies in force. No. of Policy Yr. of Issue Age at Issue Amount of Ins. Prem. Plan

20. Was said Life ever rejected or postponed or offered a substandard policy by this or any other Company or Association? Give particulars. If Metropolitan, give number. **no**

21. Is any other application on said Life pending with this Company? Give particulars. **no**

If all policies in force cannot be entered in this space, attach list.

22. Is said Life now insured in any other Company or Society or Association? If so, give Names and Amounts of all such Insurance (see Part D, No. 6, for children). **no**

I hereby apply for the above-described Policy, and all the statements in Parts A and C of this application are made by me to induce the Metropolitan Life Insurance Company to issue said Policy of insurance.

Signature to be made by Life proposed if age is over 14 years; 6 months; if younger, by the parent, guardian or person liable for child's support. **Nickolas Mellory** Relationship of Applicant to Life proposed

Dated at **N.Y.** this **16** day of **nov.** 1932

PART B

AGENT'S CERTIFICATE

1. Was insurance surrendered because of extreme need in family within six months or is application for such concession pending or to be made? **no**

2. Is the Life proposed in good health, of temperate habits and of good moral character? **yes** 3. Was Life proposed seen when application was written and was it signed in your presence? **yes**

4. Do you know, or have you any reason to suspect that the Life proposed has or has had an illness, disease or injury of any kind within three years?

5. Full name of person who will provide premiums. **Applicant.** Relationship to Life proposed

6. Full name of person providing premiums on any Metropolitan policies in force on Life proposed Relationship to Life proposed

7. If application is on a married woman or a child, state amount of insurance carried by husband or wage-earner, in this and any other company.

8. The only insurance on this Life discontinued within six months, or to be discontinued, are the following numbered Policies. Date of Lapse or File No. in Force Premium

I certify that each question in Part A was asked of the Applicant and answered as recorded, and that I believe the answers are correct. Dated **1/18** 193 Agent

---

Dependable coverage: The Metropolitan Life Insurance application for one Mr. Nicholas Mellory. Note the date of birth and the age of the applicant.

(Continued)

PART C

TO THE METROPOLITAN LIFE INSURANCE COMPANY

To induce the Metropolitan Life Insurance Company to issue Policy and as consideration therefor I agree on behalf of myself and of any other person who shall have or claim interest in any Policy issued under this application, as follows: (Wherever nothing is written in the following paragraphs it is agreed that the declaration is true without exception.)

1. I have never had any of the following complaints or diseases: Apoplexy, Appendicitis, Asthma, Bronchitis, Cancer or other Tumor, Consumption, Diabetes, Disease of Brain, Disease of Heart, Disease of Kidneys, Disease of Liver, Disease of Lungs, Disease of Urinary Organs, Dropsy, Fistula, Fits or Convulsions, General Debility, Goiter, Habitual Cough, Hemorrhage, Insanity, Jaundice, Paralysis, Pleurisy, Pneumonia, Rheumatism, Scrofula, Spinal Disease, Spitting or Raising Blood, Syphilis, Ulcer or Open Sores, Varicose Veins, except — **I have stated all exceptions.**

2. I have never been under treatment in any clinic, dispensary, hospital or asylum, nor been an inmate of any almshouse or other institution, except — **I have stated all exceptions, with times and places of such treatments**

3. I am now in sound health and am not blind, deaf or dumb, nor have I any physical or mental defect or infirmity of any kind, except — **I have stated all exceptions.**

4. I have no Disease of the Eyes or Impairment of Sight, except — **I have stated all exceptions.**

5. I have not been under the care of any physician within three years, except (give names of doctors, dates of attendance and illness). — **I have stated all exceptions and every case when I have consulted or received treatment from a doctor at his office or elsewhere.**

I HEREBY DECLARE that the statements recorded above and on the reverse side hereof are true and complete and I agree that any misrepresentation shall render the Policy void and that the Policy shall not be binding upon the Company unless upon its date I shall be alive and in sound health.

Signature to be made by Life proposed if age is over 14 years, 6 months; if younger, the parent, guardian or person liable for child's support. — Signature of Applicant *Nicholas Mullory*

Dated at _____ this 16 day of Nov. 1932

Report of Field Representative.

(APPLICATIONS REQUIRING A MEDICAL EXAMINATION MUST BE ON FORM 2)

PART D

1. RACE	2. Age given	3. If over fifteen years of age HEIGHT AND WEIGHT IN ORDINARY CLOTHING	4. Is there any evidence that insurance applied for is speculative?	5. Did either parent or any brother or sister die of Consumption or has Life proposed during the past year resided with any person suffering from Consumption?
White ~~Colored~~	40 yrs. Apparent age 40 yrs.	5 Ft. 6 In. 147 Lbs.	no	no ... no

6. Statement of insurance in another Company when Life proposed is under Age 14 years, 6 months. (See Question 22 of Part A.)

Name of Company	Plan of Insurance	Date of Policy	Weekly Premium	Age at Issue	Maximum Death Benefit

7. When was Life proposed last under the care of a physician or otherwise under medical treatment?

Date _____ Illness _____ *never*

This is to certify that I PERSONALLY inspected the Life proposed for insurance, and saw made the signature at the end of Part C, on the date stated, and am of the opinion that said Life is in * _____ health. I find the pecuniary circumstances and hygienic surroundings satisfactory and habits temperate and the insurance applied for in toto with the purpose of being continued. I therefore recommend that this application be _____

Agent's Signature _____

APPROVED FOR ISSUE

I also certify to the above. _____

Signature of Asst. Mgr., if present.

*State whether good, doubtful or bad. †Fill in "accepted," "postponed" or "rejected."
Give below any information that will be helpful in considering application.

FOR HOME OFFICE USE ONLY Returned

CLERK'S CERTIFICATE

I certify that the necessary investigation or verification has been made in the District Office records and that I find no record of a Rejection, Postponement or Cash Surrender except as stated in Part A, also that the application has been reviewed to detect any errors or omissions.

Date _____ 193__ _____ Clerk

REPORT OF HOME OFFICE INSPECTOR

A. Did you see Insured?

B. Did Applicant sign the application?

C. Does Insured appear to be in good health?

D. Has Insured ever been rejected by this or any other Company?

E. What is the apparent age of Insured?

F. Is all insurance in force admitted?

G. Are height and weight approximately correct?

Date _____ 193__

H. Are all questions in the application correctly answered?

Inspector _____

Address, if different from that in Part A. _____

NOV 18 AM

NO 1968710

More dependable coverage: Two applications filed with and approved by the Prudential Insurance Company for Nicholas Mellory. Compare Mellory's signature on these applications to the one on Metropolitan's paperwork. Also, note the different date of birth.

AGENT F FREYEISEN   DEC. 12 1932   93 439 381
(PLEASE PRINT)   (FOR H. O. USE ONLY)

Asst. Supt.   J. NEUER   District   N.Y. 16

APPLICATION FOR INDUSTRIAL INSURANCE IN The Prudential Insurance Co. of America

FOR H. O. USE ONLY   Examined by   Approved by

Incorporated under the laws of the State of New Jersey
HOME OFFICE, NEWARK, NEW JERSEY

Questions to be answered by the person proposed for insurance if age is 15 years NEXT birthday or over; if younger, by parent or guardian. If application was written in a new home, check here ☐

MARK KIND OF POLICY WANTED WITH X		
WHOLE/LIFE	Black	
20-YR. PAY'T LIFE	Brown	
X 20-YEAR END'T	Blue	
CONVERTIBLE END'T 25c ONLY	Blue	
END'T AT AGE 60 25c ONLY	Blue	
WHOLE ($1000 Unt. Amt. Industrial) LIFE	Black	

1. Full name of person to be insured (Please Print)
   NICK MELLORY

No.	Street	ADDRESS	Town or City	State
1919	Hobart Ave	N.Y.	N.Y.

2. Age NEXT Birthday **40**   3. Amount of Insurance **494**   4. Weekly Premium **65** Cents   Floor **3rd**   Front Rear   Right Left

5. PLACE OF BIRTH, State, province or country **U.S.A.**   6. DATE OF BIRTH Month **Dec.** Day **27** Year **1892**   7. RACE **WHITE**   8. SEX **MALE**   (Cross out to leave correct answers)   9. MARRIED SINGLE WIDOWED (Cross out)   10. OCCUPATION (Omit if under age 15) **Florist**

11. Is life now proposed now insured in this Company? If so, state, NUMBERS / KIND / AMOUNTS / PREM.
    No

12. Is life proposed now insured in this Company under Paid-up or Extended Insurance? If so, give policy numbers and amounts.
    No

13. Has life proposed ever been rejected or postponed by this or any other company? If so, by what company?
    No

14. Is life proposed now insured in any other company? If so, for what amount? If infantile, attach form 9061.
    No

15. Is any other application for insurance in this company now pending? If so, give particulars.
    No

16. Height and Weight **Ft. 7 In. 166 lbs.**   17. a. What is the present condition of health? **Good**   b. When last sick? Month **never** Year **seriously**   18. Does any physical or mental defect or infirmity exist? **No**

19. Has life proposed ever suffered from Consumption, Asthma, Spitting of Blood, Habitual Cough, Apoplexy, Paralysis, Heart Disease, Insanity, Fits or Convulsions, Rheumatism, Gall Stones, Disease of Gall Bladder, Liver or Kidneys, Cancer, Ulcers or Accident of any kind?   State what disease. **None**

I HEREBY AGREE for insurance of the amount named herein and I agree that any policy which may be granted by The Prudential Insurance Company of America in pursuance thereof shall be accepted by me, subject to the conditions and agreements contained in said policy. I further agree that there shall be no liability on the part of the Company on account of this application and until it shall issue a policy, except that if a premium be paid when this application is made as shown by the receipt detached therefrom and a policy is issued subsequent thereto, payment of the amount of such policy shall be made in accordance with and subject to the conditions and agreements therein contained, if death occur after the signing of this application and before the issue of said policy, PROVIDED THE INSURED WAS IN SOUND HEALTH ON THE DATE OF THE APPLICATION. Unless the answer to question number 8 above shows that the person to be insured is over the age of fifteen years, I further state that I am liable for such person's support.

Signature of Applicant
To be made by the person whose life is to be insured if 15 years old NEXT birthday, or over, but if younger, by the parent or guardian.
   — Nick Mellory
APPLICANT'S MARK NOT ACCEPTED IF ABLE TO WRITE

State relationship of person who signs, if life proposed is less than 15 years old NEXT birthday.

AGENT'S CERTIFICATE

This certificate must be signed by the Agent or Assistant Superintendent after the above questions are all answered and he has seen the person whose life is proposed for insurance, and is satisfied that the person is a first-class risk. If parent's signature is secured by our representative and child is seen by another, the former will write the word "witness" and the date, above his signature.

I CERTIFY that I have this **10** day of **December** 193 **2** collected **64** cents in advance and have personally seen the applicant herein named, who has been asked all the above questions and has answered as reported above, and I recommend the Company to accept the risk. The signature above was made by the applicant in my presence.

Assistant Superintendent   J. Freyeisen   Agent

❋ If application is for decreased insurance, and the existing policy is to be lapsed, a lapse schedule containing particulars of the policy, as well as the policy itself, must be attached to the application.

IND 1—REV 3-31   3000-4-91   PRINTED IN U.S.A.

N. B. C not acc et thi transcript unless the raised seal
of the Depart. nt of Health is affixed thereon.

New York   FEB 24 1933

A transcript of a record on file with th Department
of Health of the City of New York.

A 22659

STATE OF NEW YORK
Department of Health of The City of New York
BUREAU OF RECORDS
STANDARD CERTIFICATE OF DEATH

1986

PRINT FULL NAME Nicholas Mellory

1 PLACE OF DEATH

BOROUGH OF Bronx

1210 Fulton Ave

Character of premises, whether tenement, private, hotel, hospital or other place, etc. Private House

16 DATE OF DEATH Feb. 23, 1933 (Month) (Day) (Year)

18 I hereby certify that the foregoing particulars (Nos. 1 to 14 inclusive) are correct as near as the same can be ascertained, and I further certify that I attended the deceased from Feb 18 1933 to Feb 23 1933 that I last saw him alive on the 23 day of Feb 1933 ... M., that death occurred on the date stated above at ... M., and that the cause of death was as follow:

2 SEX Male

3 COLOR OR RACE White

4 SINGLE MARRIED WIDOWED OR DIVORCED (Write the word) Single

Lobar Pneumonia

5A. WIFE of HUSBAND

6 DATE OF BIRTH (Month) (Day) (Year)

7 AGE 40 ... IF LESS THAN 1 day ... hrs 1 mo ... min

8 OCCUPATION (a) Trade, profession, or particular kind of work Laborer
(b) General nature of industry, business or establishment in which employed (or employer) Florist

Contributory Ac. Bronchitis Grippe

Operation? ... State kind ...

9 BIRTHPLACE (State or country) U.S.

duration ... yrs ... mos ... da.

10 NAME OF FATHER Sept Mellory

duration ... mos ... da.

11 BIRTHPLACE OF FATHER Ireland

Witness my hand this 23 day Feb 1933

12 MAIDEN NAME OF MOTHER Anna Kenny

Signature Mark & Manzillo M.D.

13 BIRTHPLACE OF MOTHER Ireland

Address 249 E 116 St

(1) How long in U.S., if of foreign birth. How long resident in City of New York 12 y 10

14 Special INFORMA...n required in deaths in hospitals and institutions and in... of non-residents and recent residents.

Usual Residence

17 PLACE OF BURIAL Ferncliff Cemetery

DATE OF BURIAL Feb. 24th 1933

18 UNDERTAKER R. Pasqua Inc.

ADDRESS 346 East 116 St

35 - 2
11/0
10/8

FILED FEB 1933

This is to certify that the foregoing is a true copy (photographic) of a record on file in the Bureau of Records, Department of Health, City of New York.

Assistant Registrar of Records.

The job finally done: Nicholas Mellory's death certificate.

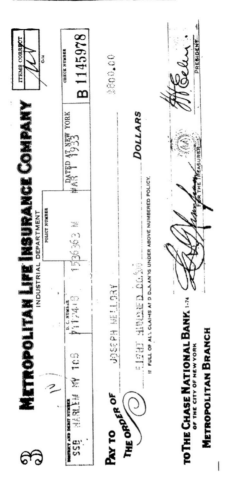

Not-so-easy money: After much sweat and toil, the Murder Trust received this check for $800 from the Metropolitan Life Insurance Company. The money was quickly squandered on payoffs and the purchasing of new suits. It was the only money the gang would make in its crooked endeavor.

A 1933 photo of the store where Anthony Marino's speakeasy was located. *Ossie LeViness, New York Daily News Photographer. Copyright © 2003 Daily News, L.P.*

the vocal styles of Ethel Waters and May Johnson. Or there was Smalls Paradise on Seventh Avenue with its floor shows and Charlie Johnson working the piano. There were countless others. But one would have been hard-pressed to find the sort of bloke the gang was in search of in an upper-class hangout.

"We all walked into a few speakeasies," Green said. "We walked into one speakeasy and looked around on the floor. There were a few bums laying around and they didn't find anybody that looked like Malloy, so we went in a few other places. At 129th Street in a speakeasy there, as we looked around there, we didn't see anything. As we were walking out this here fellow walked in and everybody looked at each other and laughed and said there is almost a double for Malloy, and we took him out."

Initially, McNally did not join them. It was only by co-incidence that he stumbled across his comrades later that evening. It happened at 128th and 129th Streets. On the evening in question, McNally arrived at the locale some-time between six and seven to grab some dinner. He went into a restaurant on the northwest corner of the intersection and took a table. From where he sat, he could stare out the window and watch the world pass him by in the intersec-tion. It did not take long for the world to catch up with him. Shortly into his meal, McNally saw Green's cab pull up at the southeast corner of the intersection. McNally watched the lads spill out of the backseat and onto the sidewalk.

"They went into a speakeasy on the southwest corner," McNally said. "I saw Green get out of the cab, and then Marino and Bastone they crossed to the southwest corner and went into a saloon there. I was in the restaurant on the northwest corner pretty near them. In a few moments they came out, they passed the restaurant and I saw them go into a speakeasy on the block between 128th Street and 129th. In about three or four minutes, they came out with the man Murray, so I walked towards them as they were coming towards me. We spoke, and I crossed over to the cab and rode up to the speakeasy with them."

"The man Murray" was Joseph Patrick Murray, thirty-one, an unemployed plasterer's assistant. He was born in San Francisco but moved to Ireland with his parents as a child. In 1931, he relocated to New York City. It was an unfortunate decision. Like Malloy, he was fond of his drink. Like Malloy, that fondness would put him in a world of serious hurt. Murray had spent the afternoon of February 6 looking for work. While his efforts proved useless, he had managed to work up quite a thirst. "I came home and went up and paid my room rent and came downstairs and went into a certain speakeasy and had a few drinks . . . at 129th Street and 128th and Third Avenue," he said. "I came out again and I was approached on the sidewalk by a man who looked respectable to me."

Murray was in the speakeasy for an unknown length of time. When he left, he stumbled into the annals of bizarre criminal history. The gentleman who approached him on the street—the one whom Murray took as a "respectable" sort—was Anthony "Tough Tony" Bastone. "He asked me if I was working," Murray said. "I said I wasn't working. He says, 'Would you accept a job?' I said, 'Sure I would.' " The job Bastone offered him was that of a "porter." Having accepted Bastone's generous offer of employment without once questioning the motives behind this stranger's intent, Murray agreed to take a proffered ride in Green's cab. Along with Marino, McNally, Green, Bastone and Murphy, Murray crossed the intersection and was bundled into the car.

"[The cab] swung right around and went right over the bridge at Third Avenue; the bridge right opposite Third Avenue—I don't know the name of it," Murray said. "One of them asked me if I drank. I said, 'Yes.' I took a drink out of a bottle and accepted a smoke. Why, I went out.

That is the last thing I remember until I woke up in Lincoln Hospital."

Life is full of small mercies; for Murray, amnesia and unconsciousness were two of them. Green guided the cab back to Marino's speakeasy, where the men gathered at the bar to hoist a few rounds. While the others drank, Green took the cab out to pick up some fares. He didn't want Polk asking why there was no money on the meter. Murray was conscious, but drunk, when Green left. As he had done with Malloy, Marino extended Murray an unlimited line of credit and gave him his drinks on the house. But the offer was not as generous as the one from which Malloy had so merrily benefited. Marino and the others had no intention of waiting for Murray to drink himself to death. They merely wanted him intoxicated and jumbled in thought for the ordeal that lay ahead. They succeeded. Murray eventually lost consciousness. He slipped down the side of the bar and wound up—as Malloy had done so many times before—sprawled on the floor. Marino couldn't get over the resemblance the man bore to Malloy. The similarity had him in fits of laughter.

"Gee, he is almost the double for Malloy," Marino kept saying as he stared at Murray's unconscious form. Their victim was now ready. All they needed was Green to return with the cab. Marino used the extra time to take care of a few important details.

Recalled McNally: "Before I met them on Third Avenue, I remember Marino said to Murphy—Marino was telling Murphy about getting an identification card, so he sent Murphy for this card, this wallet with a card in it, so while Murray was there at ten o'clock that night, Marino asked Murphy where was the card. He put this card in Murray's pocket, along with some silver, some change, I think it was seventeen cents to be exact." The card was an identity card for Nicholas Mellory. Nothing was being left to chance. They eventually heard Green's car pull up outside. "Green went away and said he was going to put money on the clock," McNally said. "He went away and came back about ten o'clock, and Marino says, 'Are you all set?' or 'Are you ready?' Green said, 'Let's go.' "

Murphy and Bastone grabbed Murray by the arms and dragged him outside to the waiting car. As with the excursion they had taken with Malloy, the car ride with Murray proved to be a crowded one. Again, there were eight individuals—including Bastone's mysterious friend, Johnnie—to cram in the cab. It was the same crowd that had gone out before, minus Malloy. "Pretty soon we were all out on the sidewalk again," McNally said, "and Murray was in the car the same as Malloy." In short, they tossed him on the floor and sat with their feet resting on top of him.

Green drove them to Trinity Avenue, but it was still too early. Maglione and McNally were dismayed when they arrived at their destination to see the street bustling with activity. Bastone, however, was not perturbed in the least. As he liked to tell people, he was "tough on Irishmen" just as he was on the "wops in Harlem."

"Murphy and Bastone took Murray out of the cab and threw him in the mud gutter and walked towards 149th Street," McNally said. "Green said he would go around the block before running over Murray. When he turned the first corner, Maglione and I jumped out of the cab and went back to Murray and we pulled him onto the sidewalk. When Green had come around, Marino and Green at the same time yelled what was the matter. Maglione told them they were foolish, it was too early, so Green said: 'All right, put him back in the cab and I will pick up Bastone and Murphy and drive back to the joint.' "

Murray, still out cold, was haphazardly dumped on the speakeasy's floor. They remained at Marino's for the better part of an hour and a half. Nerves were frazzled and tensions were running high, for there was a lot riding on Murray's demise. Marino, eager to be done with the whole sordid episode, was growing increasingly anxious. It was sometime between 11:30 P.M. and midnight when they ventured out again. They had by now mastered the art of getting themselves into the back of the cab. They took their seats and again used Murray as a footrest.

"I know a place over by Southern Boulevard," Green said as he started the engine.

McNally was no angel by any standard, but it seemed to him that the whole Malloy venture had transcended the bounds of mere criminality. The plot had ventured into the realm of lunacy. Vanishing bodies, substitute victims—the whole thing was out of control. And now here he was, riding to some desolate locale to run over some other poor bastard. Such thoughts did not sit well with McNally, who suddenly experienced a crisis of conscience and decided he had had enough. At the intersection of Westchester and Forest Avenues, McNally asked to be let out of the cab. The thought of one member breaking ranks with the gang disturbed the others—especially Bastone, who had never liked the "Irish cocksucker." But there were more important things at present to worry about. Only in time would the gang learn that they should have heeded Tough Tony's advice and whacked McNally.

According to Maglione, Green drove "to the east side of Southern Boulevard." The street was deserted. Green stopped the cab and Bastone got out to have a quick look around. Satisfied, he called for Murphy and the two of them dragged Murray from the car. As they had done with Malloy, they hauled Murray's unconscious form between them and took him into the middle of the street.

"Bastone and Murphy walked down the street with him," Green said. "I went down the street about twenty-five to thirty miles an hour in an attempt to kill him." He would not miss this time. Green made sure his hands were steady on the wheel. "Bastone and Murphy threw him in front of the car and I hit him and rode down to the end of the street, turned around and somebody hollered to run over him again to make sure he is dead. I don't know who hollered it. I went up the street again, turned around and went over him again."

Green ran over Murray's wretched form at 30 mph. The car gave a sickening lurch as Murray took all four wheels. Green looked out the window and eyed the mangled heap. The guy had to be dead. Murphy and Bastone had stood on the sidewalk and watched the grotesque episode play out. Green was about to suggest they check Murray for a pulse when they were suddenly interrupted. "Somebody hollered that there is a car coming and to beat it," Green said. Murphy and Bastone scrambled frantically into the car as Green put a heavy foot on the gas.

Beat it they did, abandoning yet another body in the middle of another street. But there was no reason to worry about the other car. It simply drove by, its occupants either failing to notice Murray's broken body in the roadway or simply choosing to ignore it. It mattered little. Unbeknownst to Marino and the lads, Murray's ordeal had been witnessed by someone else entirely.

Working nights at the Mott Haven Feed Company on Austin Place was not the sort of job that provided one with fun and exciting stories to tell. For Valen Jenkins, his duties were rather remedial. There were bags of feed to stack and orders to process and file. For the most part, the job was mundane and generally not worthy of lengthy discussions at the family dinner table. But on this particular night, Jenkins would go home with a most interesting tale to tell. For at about midnight, he saw something "unusual" unfold in front of his place of business.

Looking out a window onto the street, Jenkins observed several suspicious individuals. What drew his attention to the goings-on outside, and away from his paperwork, was the rumbling of a car engine. "I saw a cab pull up there and three fellows got out," Jenkins said. One of the "fellows," Jenkins could not help but notice, was being pulled about by the other two. Now quite curious, Jenkins watched from his safe place as the disturbing scene played out before him. "So, the cab went on down the street, [with] the three fellows out in the street holding on one fellow," he said. "So the cab went down, turned around and run over the fellow."

As Murray lay in a crumpled heap, the cab came to a stop right in front of the feed company, thus allowing Jenkins to make note of the vehicle's license plate number. An astute and concerned citizen, he jotted it down on a piece of paper. Jenkins's suspicions were further aroused when he witnessed the cab screech away from the scene after the two men who were not hit scrambled back inside the vehicle. Jenkins picked up the phone and called for an ambulance. Help, it turned out, was not far away. The first to respond was Officer John Mortensen, badge number 18647, of the 40th Precinct. He walked the beat from 12:01 A.M. to 8 A.M. It was during the "regular course" of his duties in the early morning hours of February 8 that he investigated the bizarre happenstance at Austin Place and 145th Street. It was brought to his attention by the night duty man at the Mott Haven Feed Company—a gentleman Mortensen knew by the nickname of "Wallet."

Jenkins gave Mortensen the piece of paper on which he had scribbled the cab's license number. Mortensen slipped the paper into his notebook and surveyed the scene. It did not take him long to find what he was looking for. "I found a man lying in the street," he said. "This man was apparently in a very serious condition." Mortensen stayed with the unconscious man and waited for the ambulance. When the ambulance arrived on the scene, Murray was loaded onto a stretcher and put in the back. Mortensen also climbed aboard and rode with him to Lincoln Hospital. Murray remained unconscious for the entire ride.

"At the hospital, the man was put on the stretcher," Mortensen recalled. "He was attended by the hospital doctor. He was examined and searched for property." Mortensen stood over Murray as the orderlies went through his pockets, looking for something that might identify him. In one pocket they found a wallet with a business card inside it. The card was handed to Mortensen. The name on it said Nicholas Mellory. Then Mr. Mellory, as it were, was carted away. He would remain in the hospital—plastered, bandaged and braced, recovering from internal injuries, broken ribs and a major concussion—for fifty-five days.

Returning from the hospital to the 40th Precinct, Mortensen turned his notes over "to the detectives in the department." He recounted the story as told to him by Valen Jenkins and handed over the license plate number to Green's cab.

Elsewhere in town, the gang found itself burdened with yet another dilemma. Although convinced that Murray was dead, they were in the same predicament in which they'd found themselves after killing Malloy: They didn't have a body. They drove back to the speakeasy in contemplative silence. There was the obligatory drink or two to settle the nerves and the disgruntled mumblings of how they had failed in yet another task. Marino eventually decided it was time to go home, so Green drove him to his house. The others also decided to call it a night. One by one, Green drove them to their homes, until Maglione was the only one who remained. The two men drove back to the garage to drop off the taxi. It was nearly two in the morning. Green had had the cab out for roughly ten hours. The car's meter showed he had taken $1.40 in fares.

Green pulled the car into the garage and parked it. He took the key from the ignition and walked with Maglione to the office to turn it in. Polk had gone home but had left a message for Green on the counter. Green hung up the key and picked up the note. While he was out, supposedly picking up fares, someone had called for him. That someone was a Detective Lloyd from the 40th Precinct. The message said he wanted Green to swing by the station house that night to discuss a certain matter. This did not bode well. Green handed the note to Maglione. It occurred to both men that the gang now had a problem on its hands much larger than the mere lack of a body. The note did not offer an explanation for the summons. But could there be any question as to what Lloyd was investigating? Perhaps the occupant of the car Maglione had seen on the street moments after Murray was flattened had called the cops. But how had the heat traced them so quickly?

The two men took the cab back out and drove to the station house at 138th Street and Alexander. While Green went inside for his face-to-face with Detective Lloyd, Maglione waited in the car. The notes of the conversation Green had with Lloyd have been lost to time. What is known is that Lloyd told the cabbie a witness had reported seeing Green's cab run over a pedestrian on Austin Place. But Green was not taken into custody. Instead, he was allowed to leave and rejoined Maglione outside. The police were not yet aware of the bizarre conspiracy upon which they had stumbled. Green and Maglione immediately proceeded to Marino's house to clue him in. They dragged him out of bed and told him of the cops' involvement.

From Lloyd, Green had learned that Murray had survived his ordeal. Recalled Green: "I told [Marino] that in case Murray should die, not to collect the insurance on it because somebody had seen me run him over and that they might think—the law might think that there was something about the insurance, not to collect it. He said O.K."

Surprisingly, Marino remained calm.

"I heard Green say that he had to see Detective Lloyd down at the station house," Maglione said, "then I didn't hear no more after that." That was not quite true, though, because he also heard Marino telling Green, "Don't worry."

Marino's serenity is commendable. The plan was crumbling ever more rapidly. The gang was pretty much back to where it had started—one could even say they were worse off. They had no body—no proof that Michael Malloy had ever actually existed—nor did they have a victim to take the place of the mysteriously vanished Irishman. Had Marino finally come to accept the futility of it all, or was he just tired and eager to get back to bed? Whatever the reasoning, he sent Maglione and Green on their way with another assurance not to worry. Things, he said, would be taken care of.

CHAPTER 9
Have a Drink

Even in death, Malloy was a worthy adversary. The gang remained most flummoxed by the bizarre disappearance of his body. It simply had to be found. As Murphy had been cast to play Mellory's grieving brother, it was Murphy who Marino decided should start making phone calls. They were sure Malloy was dead. Only death could have prevented him from making his way to the bar and delving fearlessly into the depths of another bottle. Even if he had survived the accident and was now a drooling cripple, the gang was sure Malloy would have found some way to haul his broken body in and mount his bar stool. He was that determined to drink. Murphy was determined to drink, too, but he was told the bottle would have to wait until he had completed his task. So Murphy began calling—but he had to do it at the cigar and candy store on 167th Street.

He called morgues and hospitals throughout the five boroughs. He said he was trying to locate his missing brother, a gentleman by the name of Nicholas Mellory. No corpse identified as such had made its way into any morgue, nor had hospitals admitted any patients under that name. Maglione and Marino drank while Murphy worked the phone. Pasqua, who had exercised a wily awareness of when to make himself scarce, was now back on the scene. He had not been present the night the gang ran over Malloy, staying clear of the speakeasy and the other gang members. Nor had he shown himself during the Joseph Murray affair. On both those occasions he had been at home with his wife. It gave him a solid alibi. Compared to his fellow conspirators, Pasqua was a man of rather sharp intellect. He was the individual who knew how to get things done. Was he not the one who had successfully deceived New York's insurance industry? It was time for Pasqua to flex his mental muscle again and figure out a way to assemble the shattered remnants of what had once been a decent plan.

It occurred to him that their problems throughout this entire debacle were not so much rooted in Malloy's refusal to die—and now his disappearance—but in something more fundamentally human: greed. It was greed that had set this wild enterprise in motion. Sitting at the bar, contemplating the bottom of a glass, Pasqua decided it was time the gang shifted tactics yet again. They had run over two men, lost the body of one and failed to kill the other, all because they were desperately trying to make the death appear accidental. This would ensure double indemnity. They were miserable at it. Pasqua said as much to Maglione, who was sitting on the stool next to him.

"I got something different," Pasqua said. "Never mind that double indemnity, those guys don't know nothing about how to go about this double indemnity business. I got a different plan." The fact is, the gang knew nothing "about this double indemnity business" from the get-go. Death by automobile qualifies for double indemnity, death by tainted sardine sandwich and wood alcohol does not. From day one, the gang had blundered in one attempt after another. Pasqua had had enough. Like Marino, he was anxious to get this thing over with. The longer it went on, the greater the chance word would spread of what was happening.

Pasqua's business often brought him into contact with a physician named Dr. Frank A. Manzella, a former Republican alderman from Harlem. The good doctor's offices were at 249 East 116th Street, right across the street from Pasqua's undertaking business. It was Manzella whom Pasqua often got to sign the death certificates of those he was burying. Consequently, he'd gotten to know the doctor quite well and felt comfortable approaching him on certain things. In the age of the Depression, it was easy appealing to a man's wallet. Going behind the backs of the others, Pasqua had taken it upon himself to tell Manzella of the plot against Malloy.

Manzella was a burly individual. His jawline was hidden behind great mounds of flesh, and he had no visible chin. He wore nicely cut suits and certainly didn't look hungry, but what the hell? Whatever one's circumstances, $150 was still $150. That's how much Pasqua offered Manzella for his shady services. They met one afternoon at Pasqua's place of business. There, Pasqua put his plan forward. Once the gang killed whoever it was they were going to kill, Pasqua would call Manzella to the scene. The physician would confirm the poor slob's death and sign a death certificate listing a phony cause of death and identifying the victim as Nicholas Mellory. Once the guy was stuck in the ground, all incriminating evidence would be gone, Pasqua said. Everyone would be home free and a few bucks richer. The undertaker put forward a convincing case. Manzella agreed to render his services for the betterment of the Murder Trust's coldhearted plan.

With Manzella on board, Pasqua set about devising a scheme that was guaranteed to be a killer. Eager to hear

Pasqua's idea, Maglione leaned in closer on his bar stool. Talking was thirsty work, and Pasqua asked Murphy for a refill. He remained silent as Murphy topped his glass off with whiskey. He poured the drink down his throat and dragged his sleeve across his mouth. Satisfied, he was ready to share his master plan. He motioned to Marino, who was sitting at the other end of the bar, and called him over. The three men huddled in close. The plan was this: Marino would search the newspapers and find a furnished room to let. The prerequisite was that the room had to have a gas jet installed in the wall. Once the room was rented, they would lure their prey there and gas him to death. "Once we got him in the room, then we would give him the gas pipe and then Pasqua said he would get the doctor up," Maglione said. It was pretty cut-and-dried.

The plan seemed brilliant in its simplicity. It required them to stay near the victim until they knew for sure he was dead. There would be no escape this time. Marino and Maglione exchanged a quick glance and nodded their approval. The gas plan was a go. All they needed now was somebody to kill. This would not prove to be a problem.

Life is rife with special moments, episodes in the eternal continuum of time that cannot be truly appreciated unless one experiences them firsthand. There is a charge to the surroundings, a raw emotive power that can only be appreciated and understood if it is felt. Five days after Malloy was hit, such an occurrence took place at Marino's speakeasy: Michael Malloy returned—not from the other side, but from Fordham Hospital. Hobbling through the speakeasy's door, Malloy—"a bandaged, limping figure"—announced his triumphant return with the following declaration: "I sure am dying for a drink!"

The irony in his choice of words was staggering. Long before this point, the gang had almost grown accustomed to Malloy's ignoble returns. But this, somehow, was different—almost unsettling. Like a persistent patch of crabgrass on an otherwise spotless lawn, Malloy was back. The gang was shocked. They watched as the bane of their existence hobbled up to his bar stool, took a seat and asked Murphy for a drink. He looked a bit battered but really no worse off than normal. Murphy reached behind the bar and pulled out the jug of wood alcohol. By now, it was a reaction born out of habit. Within seconds, the sickening odor was drifting through the speakeasy. Having comfortably adjusted himself on his stool, Malloy took a long, satisfied gulp of drink. Yes, it was good to be back. The *Times* dryly summed Malloy's survival up in three words: "Gin resists motorcar."

Marino veiled his features behind a mask of warm welcome and relief. With the others watching, he slowly approached Malloy and took a seat on the stool next to him. The stench of smoke made his stomach tighten. Mustering the skills of a decent thespian, Marino began probing Malloy for information, acting politely curious as to the man's whereabouts over the last week or so. Everybody, Marino told Malloy, was wondering what had happened. It was unlike him to stay away from the bar for so long.

Malloy had quite a story to tell, though he was not entirely sure of all the details. The memory of events was scattered and convoluted, made hazy by too much booze. He remembered sitting at the bar, partaking in his usual pleasure and drinking himself into a deep, black void. From there, it was not clear what had happened. He assumed that at some point he must have staggered outside, for his next recollection was one he would have rather forgotten. He came to lying in the dirt and grit of a gutter. His body was bloodied and battered, and he began screaming for help. Was there a vague memory of headlights bearing down on him, or the vice-like grip of strong hands holding him in place? Did he have any memory of leaping out the way of the oncoming car at the very last moment? No one can say. But Marino was content to let Malloy ponder the events of that evening without Marino offering his own explanation.

This episode illustrates again the great mystery of Malloy's character. There is no indication that Malloy was suspicious of his drinking mates, nor does he seem to have asked them to fill in the blanks as to what happened that night. It didn't strike him as odd that in a two-week period he'd emerged from drunken oblivion to find himself half-naked and exposed to the elements on one occasion, and lying in a gutter and beat to all hell on another. Perhaps such episodes were reminiscent of his alcoholic past. He had been a drinker long before he first stepped foot in Marino's. Whatever the case may be, Malloy would have surely died that night in the gutter had he not been discovered by one of New York's finest.

Police Officer Herman W. H. Lampe—badge number 13956—of the 47th Precinct was on patrol duty the night the gang made road sausage of Malloy. Lampe was working the graveyard shift from 12:01 A.M. to 8:00 A.M. It was only a few minutes after he had signed on for his shift that a call came in from someone who said they had found a man lying in the gutter on Baychester Avenue, somewhere between Gun Hill and Boston roads. Lampe was immediately dispatched to the area. When he arrived on the scene, the street was quiet. Whoever had made the call had long since gone, perhaps not wanting to get involved. Lampe began his exploration of the street and looked for the outline of a huddled mass lying in the darkness. His search proved fruitless.

There was nothing in the gutter except the usual dirt and debris one would expect to find. Lampe glanced up and down the street. Thinking he might have missed something, he retraced his steps and kept his eyes to the ground. "I went over that course twice," he said. "I found nobody." Annoyed for being called out on what seemed to be an obvious prank, Lampe reported to the nearby Boston-Westchester station and placed a call to his home precinct. He informed the desk sergeant that despite his having searched the area twice, there was no body to be found. The sergeant, deciding it was better to err on the side of over-caution, told Lampe to make one more search of the area.

"The third time, I went back on Baychester Avenue near Gun Hill Road on the north side of the street," Lampe said. "I seen a man standing there with his hands upraised, and when he seen me coming down the road he cried, 'Oh, my God! Save me, or I will die.'" Lampe approached the man and was shocked by what he saw. Malloy, the officer said, was in terrible shape: "He was covered with blood. His head was all cut. His clothes, face, shirt and everything he had on was covered with blood. I asked him for his name. He told me his name was Michael Malloy." The fact that Malloy was able to stand and raise his arms was a miracle unto itself. In an ironic twist, Malloy's intoxication may have been what saved him from catastrophic injury, seeing as how his body was free of any rigidity when he was hit.

Lampe took Malloy by the arm and gently helped him up on the sidewalk. The two men walked to the Boston-Westchester station, where Lampe called for an ambu-lance. It was not long before an ambulance from Fordham Hospital pulled up in front of the station house. Malloy was loaded onto a stretcher and put in the back of the am-bulance. He was taken to Fordham Hospital and admitted by Nurse Marion Reilly. An examination revealed he had suffered "a fractured skull, a fractured shoulder, concus-sion of the brain—and alcoholism." That was in addition to numerous scrapes, cuts and bruises. He remained in the hospital for five days. When he was admitted, he was checked in under his real name and registered as such. Hence, when Joseph Murphy called the hospital in search of his "brother," Nicholas Mellory, there were no records of any such individual having been admitted. And why

Malloy was carrying a card identifying himself as Nicholas Mellory was something he could not explain to hospital staff.

Now everyone was back to square one.

The Murder Trust did not take any immediate action in the wake of Malloy's return. Instead, they let him get comfortable and settle back into his old routine. He showed up each afternoon and drank his wood alcohol, none the wiser or just not caring. But he should have. The day Malloy returned, Murphy—even while he poured Malloy poison—clued him in to what was happening. After everything Murphy had done to assist in Malloy's demise, it was a strange time for his conscience to kick in. There was, however, something sorry in the sight of Malloy hunched over the bar, bearing the physical manifestations of the Murder Trust's greed and brutality. Before all this happened, Murphy and Malloy had found solace together in the bottle. Malloy was really the one person who treated Murphy like an equal, for it was easy to see eye to eye when you were both lying drunk on the floor. Murphy decided it was time to come clean: "I told him that he better keep away from here otherwise that he was going to get fixed, what the bunch was going to do to him."

Malloy listened to what Murphy said and, as if seeking clarity, stared thoughtfully into his glass. He looked at Murphy and nodded. Things were suddenly cast in a harsh new light. In its unflattering glare, the warmth and hospitality with which Marino had treated him suddenly lost its luster. It may have also explained the episodes in the park and on the street. For at least a moment, Murphy was convinced Malloy would heed his warnings and flee the speakeasy never to return again. But another sip of drink sorted the matter out. "If they do anything to me," Malloy reportedly told him, "they will suffer for it themselves." He had withstood the gang's impressive slapstick arsenal of cunning and deviousness. Who was to say he wouldn't survive the next harebrained scheme they concocted?

Sitting at a table nearby, Tough Tony Bastone looked up from his game of pinochle and saw Murphy and Malloy in close conference. Murphy's voice was low, his expression conspiratorial. Bastone did not like the look of it. He could have leapt out of his chair and knocked their heads together, but instead he played his hand and waited for them to finish talking. Murphy eventually left Malloy alone and walked to the other end of the bar to pour a drink. An hour ticked by and no one said anything. It seemed that Murphy was in the clear. He was running a dirty rag over the bar when he saw Bastone get up from his card game and walk toward him. He leaned across the bar and fixed Murphy with a cold stare. He asked Murphy what the topic of conversation had been with Malloy. Murphy stammered, unsure how to answer. He would have to choose his next few words very carefully. He panicked and denied he had discussed anything. Bastone saw right through him.

"He told me I better keep my mouth shut or he would fix me," Murphy said. "Naturally, I kept my mouth shout. I didn't say nothing to him." Subsequently, Murphy cared for Malloy's life only when his own existence wasn't threatened. He quickly rejoined the ranks of the others and—along with the thus far inactive Kriesberg—would play a pivotal role in the final showdown.

The search for a room-cum–death chamber got under way on February 21. It was Murphy who was assigned to the streets, classifieds in hand, to find a room in which the gang could finally rid itself of Malloy. "Marino gave Murphy the money to rent a room," Maglione said. Marino received the money from Bastone, who contributed a counterfeit bill for the venture.

"Tough Tony gave me the money," Marino said. "There was a few counterfeit twenty dollar bills passed. He gave one counterfeit twenty dollar bill to James Salone, which was passed at Tinton Avenue at the Furniture Apartment house. There are two houses there. The good money—the next day he gave me—he sent five dollars down to be paid on some insurance, and the rest of the money went to Joseph Murphy to go and rent the room."

This was nothing more than a snide attempt by Marino to dirty Salone's otherwise clean record by associating him with the gang's sordid scheme. Murphy would follow in Marino's tracks, claiming Salone took a lead role in searching for a suitable room. Together, the two men pounded the pavement, stopping at a number of tenements and inquiring as to their available accommodations. For one reason or another, the rooms didn't pass muster. "We went to three or four places, and [Salone] did not take those," Murphy said. They were not looking for anything to parallel a room at the Ritz, just something with a bed and a gas jet in the wall. The man who actually did assist Murphy in his search was Daniel Kriesberg. Together, the men found what they were looking for at 1210 Fulton Avenue.

The building was a four-storey affair near 168th Street and less than a mile from the speakeasy. The landlord was a lady named Delia Murphy. On the afternoon of February 21, two men came knocking on her door. One of them introduced himself as Joseph Mellory and told her he was looking for a room to rent. Mrs. Murphy said she had a room for rent, and if the gentleman so wished, they could come in and take a look at it. She led them upstairs to the top floor, and took them down a narrow hallway. She stopped in front of a door, unlocked it and motioned for them to walk in and have a look around. The room was a squalid affair, boasting only the bare essentials in comfort. There was a bed against one wall with a small table next to it. There was a set of drawers and, in the wall opposite the bed, a nozzle to feed gas to the room's lighting fixture.

Murphy and Kriesberg went through the motions, walking around the room as if pondering its potential. "There was two young fellows," Mrs. Murphy said. "One of them took the room and the other young man didn't. We asked him how he liked the room." Joseph Murphy liked the room just fine. It was exactly what the gang was looking for. Murphy paid the landlady for the room and sent her on her way, thanking her for her time. Mrs. Murphy left them to their own devices. She assumed her new tenant would be spending the night. But when she awoke the next morning, there was no sign of him or his friend. "They were gone . . . I went upstairs and the room door was open," she said. "I looked in and I saw nobody in it."

Upon renting the room, Murphy and Kriesberg had returned to the speakeasy, where Marino and Bastone were anxiously awaiting a progress report. Malloy was sitting at the bar doing his usual thing. Pasqua was not present. When Murphy and Kriesberg entered the speakeasy, Marino looked up from the bar. "Everything O.K.?" he asked.

Murphy answered in the affirmative.

Everything was going according to plan, but this, of course, meant nothing. Like military commanders in times of conflict, the gang had learned that no plan survives initial contact with the enemy. The true test would come when they once again brought Malloy into the fray. First, they had to physically get him to the room in a manner that would not arouse suspicion. Next, they had to gas him in a way that would not cause a ruckus or draw the attention of the building's landlady and its tenants. It was Bastone who devised the plan. Tough Tony was not a man of verbal eloquence or revolutionary thought, but now his hour had come. According to those involved, it was at this moment that Bastone assumed true control of things.

* * *

Tough Tony's participation in the killing of Michael Malloy is indisputable. The mystery surrounding his involvement, however, is the extent to which he actually called the shots. His life cut short by a bullet, Bastone's side of the story was told by men trying to save their own skin. Recounting the final hours of Malloy's life, everyone cast Bastone as the chief organizer, forcing his will upon the others and flashing his pistols whenever he sensed a flagging of commitment on the part of someone else. "Bastone Called Stage Manager in Malloy Death," *The New York Herald Tribune* would later declare. "Tough Tony Flourished His Gun as They Killed Insured Man." Both Kriesberg and Murphy weaved duplicitous tales concerning Bastone and the events that transpired in the rented room at 1210 Fulton Avenue.

And while their stories were somewhat similar, they were also very different.

CHAPTER 10

His Final Stand

The afternoon of February 22, 1933, was much like any other at Tony Marino's speakeasy. Murphy stood behind the bar and helped himself to the inventory, while Marino sat in a corner and watched over things with an indifferent eye. Tough Tony was present and so was James Salone, who was nursing a drink at one of the tables. Malloy was firmly planted on his bar stool. He was drinking regular whiskey on this particular afternoon, and the place was free of the wood alcohol's obnoxious scent. In front of him was a bottle to which he helped himself with his usual vigor. Since Murphy's vain attempt to warn Malloy of the destructive forces plotting against him, there had been no further discussion on the subject. Malloy's courage was either born of drink, or the product of sheer Irish stubbornness. Where else could he have gone? He would have been hard-pressed to find another establishment that tended to his thirsts for free.

Malloy had more than overstayed his welcome. For the Murder Trust, frustration had evolved into steeled determination. Everything that had happened before was merely a prologue to this evening, for tonight the gang would shrug off previous failures and embrace victory. Present on that fateful afternoon was Daniel Kriesberg, who said he showed up to partake in a little drink. "As I was walking in the speakeasy, I sat down," Kriesberg said. "Tough Tony, Michael Malloy were by the bar, and behind the bar was Murphy. They were giving Malloy drinks."

Kriesberg ordered a whiskey. He took a seat at one of the tables and, minding his own business, sought a little solitude in his glass. At the bar, Bastone and Malloy were chatting amicably about nothing of any importance, when Bastone suddenly threw down the gauntlet. "Come on," he said to Malloy, "I have a challenge to see who can drink the most." He might as well have slapped Malloy across the face with a leather glove. Already quite inebriated, Malloy heartily accepted the invitation. Murphy knew his cue when he heard it. Under Tough Tony's menacing gaze, Murphy replaced Malloy's bottle of whiskey with a jug of wood alcohol.

The top came off the container and released the sickly stench. A clean glass was placed in front of each man. In front of Tough Tony was also placed a bottle of untainted whiskey. Each man filled his glass to the brim. Bastone gave a nod of his head, and both he and Malloy quickly drained the drinks in front of them. With the first shots successfully downed, the men reached for their bottles, refilled their glasses and threw back the contents in one fluid motion. The battle was joined. All attention in the speakeasy quickly focused on the duel. This was more than a bout, it was a contest for the ultimate prize—and everyone except Malloy knew it. Never mind the fact that Tough Tony had an unfair advantage; this was Bastone's moment, a chance to prove his superiority against a worthy opponent. But, Malloy was a heavy slugger who had proven time and again that he could take a hit.

For every shot Bastone took, Malloy responded in kind, each man a guzzling gladiator in top form. Shot after shot, neither man showed any signs of backing down. And then, suddenly, like the fighter who relaxes his guard and takes a hard right flush on the jaw, Malloy wobbled. But he didn't hit the canvas. He steeled himself for the next shot and took it with the gusto of a seasoned professional—but the crack in his defenses was widening. He was growing increasingly unsteady. The gang looked on as the dueling drinkers continued to slug it out. "They drank there about 15 or 20 minutes," Kriesberg recalled. In that short span of time, Malloy had drunk more than enough smoke to not only blind a man, but kill him as well. Kriesberg estimated that Malloy downed nearly two quarts of the vile brew. But, as in the past, the "Iron Man" proved he was made of tougher stuff, though he was now against the ropes.

And slowly he began to go down, drooping on his stool, clutching at the bar to keep himself upright. Perhaps Tough Tony, too, would have found himself sinking to the floor had he been consuming pure methanol. The gang watched as consciousness slipped away from Malloy, leaving him—once again—at their mercy. Malloy finally collapsed. Tough Tony raised his arms like a victorious heavyweight. Now the real work began. Marino ordered Murphy out from behind the bar and told him to pick Malloy up. Murphy bent down and managed to pull Malloy onto his feet, but Malloy's legs were gone. "The man had to be dragged home," Kriesberg said. "He was unconscious." Murphy slung one of his arms around Malloy's waist and wrapped one of Malloy's arms behind his neck. Marino told Murphy to take Malloy to the room at Fulton Avenue. This entailed dragging Malloy's dead weight about a mile. If the gang was trying to be inconspicuous, it was not going about it the right way. There was no time for Murphy to concoct an excuse to placate the inquiries of any curious passersby he might come across.

But Murphy need not have worried. No one bothered him on his strange trek. If the people Murphy passed on the street showed little concern, Delia Murphy, the Fulton Avenue landlady, was a little more wary. At about half-past nine that evening, there was a knock at her front door. She put her newspaper down and shuffled down the hallway to see who it was. When she opened the door, she was shocked by what she saw. "The young fellow," she said, describing Murphy, "had brought in this other man. He was like as if he was beastly drunk." Oh, how little did she know. She assailed Murphy with an inquisitive look, prompting "the young man" to explain to her that the unconscious form was his brother.

According to Mrs. Murphy, Malloy was more than just unconscious, "he was frothing out of the mouth." It was an unpleasant scene—not the sort of thing you wish to open your front door to late at night. Murphy told the landlady he was going to put his brother—who was feeling a tad under the weather—to bed for the evening. Mrs. Murphy nodded and followed him up the stairs. She propped the door open as Murphy helped "his brother" into the room. Murphy, his lungs burning, chest heaving and legs shaking, dumped Malloy on the bed with one final heave and took a seat to catch his breath. He told Mrs. Murphy her help was no longer required. She left the room, leaving her new tenant alone with his sickly brother.

It was not long before Malloy was groaning softly as consciousness slowly worked its way back into his body. Marino had actually planned for such a contingency. Before Murphy left the speakeasy, Marino had given him a bottle of smoke to leave near the bed. Murphy pulled the bottle from inside his jacket. He removed the top and left it on the bedside table before returning to the others. Murphy was gone from the speakeasy for about half an hour. As

Kriesberg recalled, "I saw Murphy take Malloy home. About 30 or 35 minutes later, Murphy came back, so Tough Tony sent him out—that is, Murphy—and Murphy came back with something under his coat."

Before Tough Tony sent Murphy out on his little errand, Marino asked Murphy if Malloy was secure in the room. Murphy said he was. He told the others that Malloy had regained consciousness, but was still pretty woozy. By the time Murphy left the room, Malloy had managed to sit up, prop himself against the wall and was sipping sluggishly from the bottle Murphy had left him. There was no chance of him going anywhere. The object Murphy came back with under his coat was a lengthy piece of rubber tubing. Where he managed to scrounge up such a thing at ten in the evening is anyone's guess. But everyone seemed pleased with his industrious nature. Satisfied, Marino approached Salone, who had remained sitting quietly at his table.

"Say, Jimmy, go ahead and take a walk with Murphy," Marino said.

There was something in Marino's voice that made Salone uneasy. He knew of the gang's secret councils and their nefarious plot to run Malloy over, but he had successfully kept himself out of that business. He had no intention of getting involved now. Salone took a sip of his drink and simply told Marino, "No."

Shunned, Marino turned to Kriesberg. "Go ahead, Dan," Marino said, "take a walk with Murphy."

"Where?" Kriesberg asked.

Tough Tony was immediately on top of him, his fists clenched. "You Jew son of a bitch," Bastone reportedly snarled. "Don't ask no questions and do as we tell you."

Of course, Kriesberg was not ignorant of all that had transpired beforehand, but he had sought to maintain a certain distance from it all. True, he had been the one to suggest feeding Malloy tainted sardine sandwiches. But had Malloy died, Kriesberg could have taken false comfort in the fact that he was not directly responsible. The sandwich had not been prepared by Kriesberg's hand—and it's not like he was pulling a trigger. The unsavory delicacy was a buffer zone between killer and victim. If he was involved in murder, it was at least a watered-down version. Kriesberg said unconvincingly that assuming an actual physical role in the taking of a life did not sit well with him. "All the rest of them knew what was going to happen and I didn't," Kriesberg said, "and they all refused to go up there, and they picked on a slob."

Kriesberg looked up into Tough Tony's blazing eyes. He knew saying no would result in levels of pain he never thought possible. "Well, I realized I had a wife and three children and I can't afford to be put away," Kriesberg said. "I know Tough Tony's reputation." And so Daniel Kriesberg, greengrocer and assistant to the Pants Bandit, acquiesced and agreed to play his part. Propelled by Tough Tony's fiery gaze, Kriesberg followed Murphy to the door. "As I started walking with Murphy, he walked about a block," Kriesberg said. "As I turned around, I saw that Tough Tony was following us, so Murphy told me what they were going to do. I said 'What's the idea?'"

Murphy told Kriesberg that the plan was to gas Malloy. They would connect one end of the rubber hose to the gas fixture in the room, then place the other end in Malloy's mouth. After that, it was just a matter of twisting the gas valve. "It is Tough Tony's, you know, orders," Murphy said, his words punctuated by Tough Tony's ominous footfalls behind them.

The men continued their walk in silence. Kriesberg's family weighed heavily on his mind. It was too painful a concept to even contemplate the idea that he would never see them again. He later claimed that it was for them that he followed through with this insidious act. It seemed like an eternity before they reached the Fulton Avenue address. Tough Tony remained on the sidewalk and goaded Kriesberg and Murphy into the building with murmured threats. The two men entered the boardinghouse and shut the door behind them before ascending the stairs to Malloy's room. "As we got up in the room, that is Murphy and I, the windows were closed and Malloy was laying on the bed," Kriesberg said. The bottle of booze Murphy had left with Malloy was nearly empty. Murphy and Kriesberg stood over the bed and stared at their sleeping prey. Murphy had the rubber hose in his hand, but neither man moved.

Tough Tony stood sentry on the street and made sure the spineless little bastards didn't try to double-back. Once satisfied they were staying put, Tough Tony returned to the speakeasy. Inside the room, Murphy and Kriesberg pondered their desperate situation. "If we don't do what Tough Tony tells us, the both of us are going to get it," Murphy said.

Kriesberg resigned himself to the fact that this was true. He stood there glumly as Murphy walked over to the wall and set about connecting the rubber tube to the gas fixture. Murphy got to his feet with one end of the tubing in his hand. He walked across the room to the bed, but stopped six inches shy of where Malloy lay. The tubing was too short. It wasn't going to reach. Murphy and Kriesberg stared stupidly at each other and then at the hose. Couldn't anything go according to plan? Murphy dropped the tube and, with Kriesberg's help, dragged Malloy off the bed and onto the floor. Malloy, out cold, didn't stir. The tube reached. Murphy bent down by Malloy's head and stuck the tube in his mouth. He pulled an old towel out from his coat pocket and wrapped it tightly around Malloy's face, securing the tube in place and blocking off Malloy's nasal passages.

Kriesberg stood there and watched until Murphy told him to take up a position by the gas fixture. Kriesberg did as he was told. Murphy checked the tubing one last time, making sure it was firmly planted in Malloy's mouth. Satisfied, he gave Kriesberg a nod and told him to turn the gas on. "I got kind of scared and put the gas on and off and made some sounds like s-s-s-s," Kriesberg said. The gas hissed and whistled through the tube, like some deadly vaporous snake, filling Malloy's mouth and lungs. Murphy remained crouched over Malloy's head, holding the tube in place in case Malloy began jerking spasmodically, or came too and tried to resist. Kriesberg kept working the fixture, turning the gas on and off—making hissing sounds with his mouth to hide the fact he was turning the gas off—until he couldn't take it anymore: "As the gas was escaping, I did that continually, at the same time pulling out the tube."

He turned off the gas and yanked the tube hard. He pulled it free of Murphy's grip and disconnected it from the fixture. Murphy jumped to his feet and demanded an explanation. "We were up there about two or three minutes," Kriesberg said. "I said, 'Well,' I says, 'I am not going to go through with it.'"

Murphy appealed to Kriesberg's sense of personal safety. "You might as well, because if we don't, we will get ours anyway," he said.

Kriesberg's fear of Tough Tony was absolute, and again he caved in. "We attached the tube again to the jet and I went through the same procedure as before," Kriesberg said. And so the gas snaked its way through the tube and back into Malloy, his chest rising and falling as his body absorbed the noxious fumes. Suddenly Murphy let out a cry of disgust. "Christ, the son of a bitch pissed all over me," Murphy said and told Kriesberg to turn the gas off. He removed the towel from Malloy's head and pocketed the tube, all the while cursing his damp clothing. "About another minute later," Kriesberg recalled, "we put Malloy back on the bed and I walked down first." Kriesberg scurried from the building and walked back to the speakeasy.

He left Murphy in the room to handle any final details that needed attending to.

When Kriesberg entered the speakeasy, Marino and Bastone were sitting at the bar, but said nothing to him. The silence was heavy and disconcerting. They eyed him suspiciously as he walked quickly to a table and took a seat. He wondered what Murphy was up to back in the room. Was Malloy dead? "I don't know if I murdered him or not, because the way I explained it, I turned the gas off and made a hissing sound with my mouth," Kriesberg said.

What if Murphy walked through the door and said Malloy was still alive? Tough Tony would march Kriesberg back to the room with a gun in his back to make sure he finished the job. After that, there would be no need to keep Danny Boy around. "I was scared. I was threatened with death . . . by that gang," Kriesberg said. "If anybody talks up, I have three children I love very much. They threatened whoever opens up will be killed on the outside by the gang."

Murphy showed up five minutes after Kriesberg. There was nothing in his demeanor that betrayed any hint that he had just partaken in another man's demise. He strolled to his place behind the bar and poured himself a drink.

"Well, Red, how was it?" Tough Tony asked

"I think it is all right," Murphy said.

Bastone and Marino exchanged an eager glance. Had they actually accomplished the impossible? It was too early to celebrate. Murphy had said he simply thought Malloy was dead. He couldn't say for sure and offered no concrete affirmative. For all they knew, Malloy was stumbling along the sidewalk at that very moment, heading in their direction like some unavoidable nightmare. The speakeasy's entrance suddenly loomed large and threatening. Any minute, Malloy—ravaged by an unquenchable thirst— would rip the door from its hinges. Baying like a frenzied beast, he would demand drink after drink and a sardine sandwich with each. Failure after painful, humiliating failure had made them all a bit paranoid.

Tough Tony asked Murphy for the rubber tube. Recalled Kriesberg: "Murphy gave Tough Tony the gas tube and Tough Tony went out, and where he went, I don't know, but he came back a half an hour later." During the half hour Tough Tony was gone, little was said. Malloy was not mentioned, perhaps out of fear the utterance of his name would draw him back into their world. When Tough Tony returned, he no longer had the length of rubber hose. The physical evidence had been disposed of. There was still no sign of Malloy. Of course, all this was according to Kriesberg.

The tale Murphy had to tell was somewhat different.

Murphy, a vagrant for the better part of his twenty-six years, wound up ensnared in the Malloy debacle as a direct result of his circumstances. Living in the speakeasy and sleeping on its floor was preferable to the New York City subway and the sleazy quarter-a-night Harlem hotels he was accustomed to. Later, he would freely admit to his participation in the Murder Trust's scheme. He said it was all a matter of proximity. How could he not be involved when the plan was hatched in the place he lived and worked, and when the chief conspirator was the very man he worked for? He certainly wasn't going to leave the speakeasy and go back to sleeping near the train tracks. "I had no where else to go," he said.

The free booze kept Murphy anchored to the place—just as it kept Malloy returning again and again. As heartless as the gang's actions were, there is something particularly cruel about Murphy's behavior. If anyone in Marino's was ever considered a friend of Malloy's, it was Murphy. The two had been comrades in the bottle. Had

Murphy developed no sense of loyalty toward the man? To Marino and the others, Malloy was nothing more than a way to make a buck. To Murphy, Malloy had been a companion. They had talked and shared hangovers. Now Murphy was playing his part in the man's undoing.

When he rented the room at 1210 Fulton Avenue, he had done so under the name of Joseph Mellory—just as Marino had instructed him to. When he brought the inebriated Malloy to Delia Murphy's doorstep, he told her Malloy was his sick brother, Nick Mellory. To all this, Murphy would freely admit playing his part. But in regard to Kriesberg's version of events as to what happened in the room that fateful evening, Murphy was extraordinarily blunt in his assessment; "That's a lot of hot air."

After bringing Malloy to Fulton Avenue, Murphy left him sitting up on the bed drinking from a bottle of whiskey. By Murphy's account, Malloy was able to walk from the speakeasy following the drinking contest, though he did lean on Murphy for support. "He was feeling good, but he was not drunk," Murphy said. "He had a bottle of this stuff with him and he took some drinks over there. By the time we got there, he was pretty good and drunk." Murphy admitted that he himself was not entirely sober that evening. "I had a few drinks in me," he said. And although he would later say his memory of events was somewhat hazy, he recalled enough to sabotage Kriesberg's efforts to portray himself as an unwilling participant. Having dropped Malloy off, Murphy returned to the speakeasy, where Marino and Tough Tony were waiting.

"Well," Marino said when Murphy entered, "did you take Malloy over to the room?"

"Yes, he is over there," Murphy said.

The hour was late when Murphy walked back into the speakeasy. Kriesberg was sitting at a table shuffling a pack of cards. He had previously made arrangements to play pinochle with Tough Tony that evening. After Murphy told

Marino that Malloy was properly situated, Marino approached Kriesberg. The game of cards would have to wait. Marino told Kriesberg: "Make sure he's gone, Danny." Kriesberg, Murphy said, simply responded with "Okay." There were no inquisitive looks, nor did Tough Tony have to strong-arm him. Kriesberg put down the cards and got up from the table. Walking to the door, he motioned for Murphy to come with him. Murphy followed him outside and the two men walked—without comment— to Fulton Avenue. They reached the building without the benefit of Tough Tony's escort and walked up the stairs to Malloy's room. Once inside, Kriesberg was all business. Taking his cue from Tough Tony, Kriesberg brushed back his jacket to reveal a gun tucked into his waistband.

He drew the pistol and ordered Murphy to close and lock the bedroom door. Kriesberg kept the gun trained on Malloy. With his free hand, he reached into his jacket pocket and withdrew a length of rubber hose. "Wherever he got the rubber pipe, I don't know," Murphy said. "He made me lock the door. Danny had a gun on [Malloy] and he said, 'Don't open the door.' And he pulls Malloy over on the floor." Kriesberg attached one end of hose to the gas fixture and stuck the other end in Malloy's mouth. From another pocket, he pulled out a towel and draped it over Malloy's face. Then he turned on the gas.

Kriesberg let it flow until Malloy was dead. "It was not even five minutes that that took," Murphy said. Kriesberg turned off the gas, and the two men stood silently over Malloy's lifeless form. Somewhere on the street below, a dog barked. Then the room was silent save for the duo's excited breathing. Their foul deed left an unpleasant odor in the air—one that smelled faintly of gas and wreaked of urine. In his final undignified moments, Malloy had pissed all over himself. But what did Kriesberg and Murphy care? Pasqua would be the one who cleaned it up. It was just as well, for had this not been Pasqua's idea? Thus far, he had successfully avoided taking part in any of the dirty work. But, oh yeah, this would certainly make up for that! "[Kriesberg] stood there for about five minutes after, and [Malloy] was not breathing," Murphy said. "Kriesberg said he was dead."

It was hard to believe that the deed was finally done, after so much trial and trauma. Kriesberg shoved the gun back in the waistband of his pants and knelt beside the body. He placed a hand on Malloy's chest, an ear to his lips, and listened attentively. There was nothing. Under his hand Kriesberg felt only the dirty cotton of Malloy's shirt. The man's chest was still. Beneath the skin and bone there was no detectable heartbeat. Kriesberg pocketed the towel and pulled the pipe from Malloy's mouth. He yanked the other end of the tube from the gas fixture and coiled it up in his hand. He stood up and gave Malloy one last looking over—just to be sure. Then he turned to Murphy. "He said he was dead and we went out and locked the door," Murphy said.

The men descended the stairs—leaving their vanquished adversary on the floor—and returned to the speakeasy. In the place were "Marino, Bastone and a few drinking fellows," Murphy said. Marino stepped out from behind the bar and approached Kriesberg. He was anxious to hear their news. "[Marino] asked Danny first, 'How is it?' in Italian, and Danny said it was O.K. in English," Murphy said. "What they said after that, I don't know." The Italian chatter lasted several minutes as Kriesberg presumably shared the details of Malloy's passing with Marino.

After all that had transpired, it had come to this: Ignominious defeat for a man who had unknowingly waged a ferocious yet valiant battle against those who sought to capitalize on his undoing. Despite the difference in Murphy and Kriesberg's stories, the outcome remained the same.

Michael Malloy was dead.

* * *

When Kriesberg and Marino finished talking, Marino told
Murphy to head back to the room and spend the night with
Malloy's corpse. "They wanted me to stay the night with
the body so the landlady would not know about it until the
morning," Murphy said. But there was more to it than that.
Marino was not going to take chances with a man who had
repeatedly shown himself to be impervious to death. It was
a grim task, but one Murphy did not mind doing. It was
not every day he had the chance to sleep in a proper bed.
He readily accepted and returned to the room and its grim
occupant.

That night, Joseph Murphy slept comfortably.

CHAPTER 11

The Morning After

The serenity of early morning came to an end for Mrs. Delia Murphy with word of a death in her house. Apparently, the sick fellow who had been brought in the night before had succumbed to whatever it was that was ailing him. In hindsight, the man had looked quite ghastly. While her knowledge of health and medicine was limited, Mrs. Murphy knew it was not normal for one to froth at the mouth. So her morning took a mournful turn. Before news of Malloy's passing was actually announced, however, an elaborate production was staged for the benefit of the landlady and other possible witnesses. And the director was none other than Frank Pasqua.

For Mrs. Murphy, the day began shortly after eight with some light housework. She was on the ground floor sweeping the hallway when she heard footsteps on the stairs. Looking up, she saw the man she knew as Joseph Mellory approaching her. They bid each other good morning and

Mrs. Murphy asked how Mellory's brother was feeling. "Don't go into my brother's room today," Mellory replied, "because he is very ill."

"All right," Mrs. Murphy said.

Mellory walked past her toward the front door. "I won't be long," Mellory said. "Wait until I come back."

And with that, Joseph Murphy slipped out of the building and out of character. After spending the night with a corpse, the chilled morning air was vibrant and refreshing. Upon waking that morning, Murphy had hauled Malloy up onto the bed and made sure the bottle of wood alcohol—now depleted—was prominently displayed on the bedside table. He had done everything he was told to do. All that remained was to play the role of Joseph Mellory until the insurance checks were safely in hand. As he strolled back to the speakeasy, Murphy wondered what his cut of the profits would be. More importantly, what would he buy? How long had it been since he'd felt a wad of cash in his pocket? Providing everything went smoothly from here on out, the future was looking grand.

At the speakeasy, Marino and Pasqua—their emotions a roiling cauldron of exhilaration and anxiety—sat at the bar waiting for Murphy. That initial evening when Pasqua had uttered those fateful words—"Why don't you take out insurance on Malloy? I can take care of the rest"—now seemed an eternity ago. The venture had brought them all to the brink of insanity, but their perseverance had paid off. Word of Malloy's death had reached Pasqua the night before. Tough Tony had called him from the cigar and candy shop. "Come down and be in no hurry," Tough Tony had said. "Come over to Marino's place." In turn, Pasqua had promptly contacted his physician friend, and the framework was laid for the plan that was now about to get under way.

*   *   *

At 1210 Fulton Avenue, Delia Murphy continued with her housework. She was still making her first-floor rounds with a broom when she heard two men conversing on her doorstep. Their voices were somewhat lowered, but nevertheless urgent. At first she was curious, but then she just became annoyed that two men were in conference on her stoop. "They had been outside my door for some time," she said. "I asked them what they were hanging around there for. They said they were waiting for a doctor. I said 'What for?'"

She recognized one of the men. It was Joseph Mellory, the brother of her sick tenant—but the other man she didn't know. Of course, Mellory made an impression the moment you saw him. "He had dirty old clothes," Mrs. Murphy said. "His face was filthy. His hands were filthy. Everything else was filthy." Through the grime, the look on Mellory's face was one of concern. It was obvious this other man was trying to comfort him. "This is my friend," the stranger said, patting Mellory on the back. "His brother is very, very low." The man told Mrs. Murphy they were waiting for a doctor to arrive to see if there was anything he could do.

"Who are you?" Mrs. Murphy asked, pointing at the man with the handle of her broomstick.

"I am the undertaker," the man replied.

Well, they certainly had all their bases covered. It seemed to Mrs. Murphy that the situation must have been truly dire for a man to contact an undertaker before his brother was even dead. As Pasqua recalled: "I spoke to a woman downstairs. She told me he came in very sick. You could see that he wasn't going to last long. I said, 'What makes you say so?' She said, 'He looked terrible when he came in, sickly looking and everything.'" With that, the two men went upstairs and disappeared into the bedroom. They were up there, out of sight, for the better part of an hour before the doctor arrived, shortly after nine. He knocked on the door and was let in by Mrs. Murphy. He introduced himself as Dr. Manzella and asked where the patient was.

The doctor had neither a discernible jawline nor a chin, and his face showed no laugh lines that might indicate a tender bedside manner. Huffing and puffing, he followed the landlady up the stairs to the door of Mellory's room. He nodded his thanks, opened the door just wide enough for him to squeeze in and disappeared inside. Not thinking any more about it, Mrs. Murphy went back downstairs to continue her housework. She was not used to such commotion and just hoped non of the other tenants had been disturbed.

Inside the room, Pasqua, Murphy and Manzella went through the motions. The doctor and undertaker, both smiling broadly, exchanged greetings then turned their attention—albeit briefly—to Malloy. "They had a little of this wood alcohol in the room on the table so the doctor could see it and claim [Malloy] died of that," Murphy said. Dr. Manzella's examination could hardly be called thorough. He walked over to the bed and stared down at the body. Still smiling, he brought his hand up to his mouth and dragged his lower lip down in a gesture of mock contemplation, then did the same to Malloy. "The doctor looked him over then pronounced him dead," Murphy said. So that was that. The pronouncement was official! It was time for Pasqua to get to work.

Downstairs, Mrs. Murphy was still sweeping what by now was the cleanest floor in the Bronx. Satisfied with the results of her labor, she decided to check on the Mellory fellow and see how his brother was doing. There had been no noise from upstairs for quite some time, and she was growing mildly concerned. She climbed the stairs and waited for the doctor to come out of the room with his prognosis. "I stood outside the door with the broom in my hand," she said, "and I said to the doctor, 'What's the matter with the man?'"

Technically speaking, it could be said there was nothing the matter with Michael Malloy anymore. The cause of death, according to Dr. Manzella, was lobar pneumonia. Looking back over his shoulder, he told the undertaker to swing by his office later that morning for a death certificate. Bidding Mrs. Murphy a good morning, the doctor waddled down the stairs and out of the building. It was now ten in the morning and time for Pasqua to do his thing. He draped one of the bedsheets over Malloy's lifeless form and told Murphy he was going to the Health Department to request a body removal. From here on out, things moved with an alacrity and smoothness that must have surely taken the Murder Trust by surprise.

CHAPTER 12

Frank's Story

Among those who comprised the Murder Trust, it could be said Francis Pasqua was a rarity. He was, by most outward appearances, the co-proprietor of a legitimate business and exercised a cerebral panache superior to his fellow conspirators. After all, it was his cunning and guile that had secured the insurance policies. So, too, had it been a plan of his devising that brought about Michael Malloy's ultimate demise. All the while, he maintained a certain distance from the gang's violent activities. But following Malloy's death, he crafted a version of events that sought to remove himself completely from the shady goings-on at 3775 Third Avenue. Even before Dr. Manzella had signed his name to Malloy's death certificate, Pasqua was working on his tale. In the event the plot was blown wide open, he had too much going for him—he couldn't be taken down with the others. He had the undertaking business to run. On top of that, he and his father had recently opened a beer garden behind the funeral parlor. One could have a drink while their loved one was embalmed.

Pasqua sought to portray himself as a man of quiet means, humbly carrying on the family trade. After all, one expected a man who dealt with the dead in the manner such as Pasqua did to possess a firm moral grounding. Indeed, Father Nicholas Paglia—a Catholic priest teaching at the Academy of the Sacred Heart of Mary, who had known Pasqua going on six years—said the undertaker's reputation for "truthfulness, honesty, veracity and law-abidingness" was "very good." And so Pasqua went about his business, taking care of the deceased, attending church and abiding by the law. He was home early each evening to spend time with his wife, Elvira, and their young child. Occasionally, when the odd thirst hit him, he would venture to Marino's speakeasy for a drink or two after work. Although he would chat amicably with others at the bar, he never took active steps to initiate friendships with the clientele—or so he would claim. They were merely casual acquaintances, fellows with whom he could idly pass the time over a glass of whiskey. He was, after all, a legitimate businessman, while those who frequented Marino's simply weren't.

And so Pasqua's version of events went like this:

It was on one particular evening in either September or October 1932 that he entered Marino's and saw a man he knew as Nicholas Mellory behind the bar, pouring drinks. Pasqua knew him as a neighborhood vagrant who spent much of his time hanging out on Third Avenue and 130th Street. He was a friendly enough fellow, chatting with others in his slurred Irish brogue. The tale he was telling Marino's patrons was one of woe. He was out of luck, out of work and out of money. He was squatting in slovenly tenement rooms and worked odd jobs where he could find them. Thankfully, the speakeasy's proprietor had taken pity on him and was letting him work the occasional shift behind the bar. When things were particularly rough, he was allowed to sleep on the speakeasy's floor.

It seemed to Pasqua that this Mellory fellow was somewhat of a loner, for he never spoke of family or friends. It was a mystery to Pasqua where Mellory came from. He just seemed to materialize out of thin air. Some days, Mellory would visit local businesses and see if there was any work to be had. He claimed to have been employed as a fireman at one point before life kicked him in the crotch. Pasqua recalled how Mellory frequently stopped by the undertaking business to see if he could lend a hand: "He just, you know, came around the place looking for something to do." Pasqua, like Marino, also felt charitable toward Mellory and employed him to do light work about the place. He also allowed Mellory to sleep in the back with the coffins. So Mellory yo-yoed back and forth between Marino's and Pasqua's, doing meager tasks for both men.

Although Pasqua only visited the speakeasy "about once a month or two," he was on good terms with Marino—good enough for Marino to approach him with a business opportunity. It happened one evening in September or October of 1932 when Pasqua was sitting at the bar having a drink. He was talking to Anthony Bastone, a gentleman for whom he did not care much. The man was, in Pasqua's words, "a bad character" who liked to boast of the frequent beatings he delivered in good measure to those who annoyed him. It had not been Pasqua's decision to converse with Bastone, but when Tough Tony spoke, you listened. Mercifully, Marino interrupted the conversation and pulled Pasqua off to the side. In a hushed tone, he told the undertaker that he wanted to insure Mellory.

Pasqua was indignant. "So, what do you want me to do?"

Marino looked over his shoulder to make sure Mellory could not hear the conversation. "Do you know anybody to insure him?"

"I don't know," Pasqua said. "I may be able to get somebody."

Marino seemed pleased. "You can have the funeral if you do so."

Pasqua did not like what he'd heard. It implied far too much, although no one had mentioned anything about death. He put his drink down and told Marino, "I don't do business that way." Besides, as he later claimed, "I figured someday the fellow would die and give me the funeral anyhow." But Marino was adamant, "so I was induced by Tony to get these policies out and he paid me. He paid me the premiums . . . Whatever intentions he had, I didn't know." And while Marino gave Pasqua the money to initially purchase the policies, it was Mellory who paid the weekly premium of 65 cents—supposedly from money he got working at Marino's—on policies obtained from Prudential and Metropolitan. Every Friday, Mellory would stop by the funeral parlor with cash in hand. As Pasqua noted: "[Marino] said, 'I will pay the agent and I will give you the money to pay it.' I had to call him up a couple of times and he said [Mellory] will bring the money down to me, and he would send the money down to me and that is how I used to pay it.'"

The only occasion Mellory ever failed to deliver the money was that time he was in the hospital for an oozing leg wound.

The story was pretty flimsy, but Pasqua believed it would serve his purpose should the plot ever be exposed. Of course, there was another angle—probably the most important one—to cover: Who to blame for hatching the murder plot in the first place? Again Pasqua decided that, if worse came to worst, he would point the finger at Marino. Yes, it was Marino who first suggested doing Mellory in and approached Pasqua with the idea. Just as he had with the insurance, Marino brought up the possibility of killing

Mellory on one of those rare occasions when Pasqua stopped by for a drink.

In Pasqua's mind, it went like this: "[Tony] came up to me one night with this [Green] and he says to me, 'Listen.' He said, 'What do you say we all do away with him?' "

Pasqua was not accustomed to such cryptic inquiries. If he wanted puzzles, he could do the crossword in the *Times*. "Do away with what?"

"Oh, I got some friends of mine got a car," Marino said. "I will give you a split."

A split for what? This was an affront to the ethics of the undertaking profession. Pasqua let Marino know as much, telling him, "I don't want a split. I want a legitimate funeral." It seemed to Pasqua that he would not have to wait long to bury Mellory on legitimate grounds. Wrecked by booze and harsh living, the man was a physical shambles. Every gurgled breath sounded as if it were his last. The bottle would do the guy in soon enough. But that wasn't fast enough for Marino, who looked disparagingly at Harry Green. Pasqua didn't know much about this "Hershey" character other than he sometimes drove a taxi. It was just as well Pasqua only frequented Marino's sporadically, for there certainly seemed to be a lot of shady activity going on around the place. Pasqua did, however, agree to Marino's request to keep the insurance policies at his house for "safekeeping." Marino didn't feel safe keeping them at the speakeasy, and his own house was in a constant state of turmoil thanks to his marital discord.

It was not long before word got out that Mellory was insured. This was a source of considerable interest among those who frequented Marino's, particularly Edward Smith and John McNally. Pasqua knew both men to be petty career criminals, and he didn't like either one of them—so he was quite surprised to open his front door one evening and find the two of them, along with Marino, standing on his doorstep. He didn't much care for these three men stepping foot into his home. Adding to his displeasure was the fact he knew Smith and McNally were the friends Marino had referred to days before who owned the car. Pasqua asked what the men wanted, making no effort to hide the disdain in his voice. Marino told him they had to talk.

As far as Pasqua was concerned, there was nothing to discuss. In no way was he involved in Marino's malevolent scheme. Yes, if word ever did reach the authorities, he would have to admit to having at least a limited knowledge of what was being planned within the speakeasy's dreary walls. But this story he was crafting would portray him as the voice of reason and righteousness—one that sought to thwart Marino's proposed injustices. Yes, he would say McNally and Smith came to his house, but it was not to offer them the job of running Malloy over. Pasqua reluctantly invited them into his home. He ushered McNally and Smith into the bedroom but grabbed Marino by the arm and kept him in the hallway. He wanted to know why Marino had brought these men to his house. "He had already made arrangements with these fellows down at his place and then brought them up to my place. They didn't believe he had the insurance policy and in order to prove it, he brought them to my house. He knew I had the policies and [was] holding them for him, and he took them up there to verify there was an insurance policy," Pasqua said. "Tony wanted to make them understand that the policies belonged to me. As a matter of fact, they belonged to him. He didn't want them to know."

Elvira could be heard in the kitchen preparing dinner. She would be most displeased if she came out and found this rabble in her home. Desperate, Pasqua asked Marino what he wanted from him. Marino kept his voice low: "Don't let these fellows know what the amount is."

"Why?"

"Because I don't want them to know," Marino said.

According to Pasqua, he knew Marino had his own corrupt reasons for wanting this, and he knew better than to ask what they were. "Well, that is your business," Pasqua said. "It is your policy and you are taking care of it. You are paying for it. It is your business, if you want to make a price with them, it is not my business. All I am here for, I am just holding your policies."

Marino nodded, and the two men went into the bedroom. McNally and Smith were sitting on the edge of the small bed. Pasqua lurked silently in the corner of the room. There was something exceedingly creepy about that fellow Smith's artificial ear. His nickname at the speakeasy was "Tin Ear," but the ear certainly didn't look like it was made of tin. Pasqua had heard it was made of wax. While Pasqua pondered the fake appendage, Smith and Marino engaged in animated conversation. They were discussing money—specifically, how the money would be divvied up once the policies were cashed in. Marino was telling Smith he had no control over the policies, as they were in Pasqua's name. The undertaker didn't like the conversation. Breaking his silence, he wondered aloud why the matter was even being discussed. It was then he learned that Marino had gone ahead and offered Smith and McNally the job of running Mellory over. Pasqua was shocked, absolutely shocked. He couldn't believe Marino had actually been serious about doing such a thing. Smith, it turned out, was not happy with the amount of money Marino had offered him.

"Tony wanted to give [Smith] $200 and they kicked and Tony pulled me aside again and he said, 'Oh, I will give them half,'" Pasqua said. "That is because he thought he was going to collect double indemnity." So Pasqua watched in horror as Marino offered Smith $400 to run Mellory over. Smith did not accept the offer, and the grotesque negotiations continued. It became apparent that the two men were at an impasse. Smith wanted more. Marino wouldn't pay it. Much to Pasqua's relief, it seemed that Marino's plan had been foiled. Anxious to have his dinner and cleanse his home of this riffraff, Pasqua hurried the men out of his house and into the night. He shut the door on Marino and the man's diabolical scheming. "I was never the type of fellow doing anything like that or let things like that be carried on in my home," Pasqua later claimed.

For a man who only stopped by the speakeasy "once or twice a month," Pasqua seemed to know a lot about those who frequented it on a more regular basis. It was not long after the meeting at his house that Pasqua again swung by Marino's to quench one of his rare thirsts. But if Pasqua was expecting to wash away the day's worries with a little whiskey, he had another thing coming.

Pasqua was sitting by himself at one of the tables. Marino's few regulars were present, including Tough Tony who, as usual, was spouting his violent rhetoric. One person, however, was not there—that person being the unfortunate Nicholas Mellory. Pasqua chose not to burden himself with wondering why. From the corner of his eye, Pasqua watched Marino approach him from behind the bar. He pulled up a chair and got comfortable at Pasqua's side. "He told me he ran him over," Pasqua said. "I said, 'Where is he at?' He said, 'I don't know.' And finally they somehow or other got in touch with Fordham Hospital and after that he said he wanted to try again. I said, 'You are crazy. What do you think you are doing?' I said, 'What have you got, a child's mind?' He said, 'Oh, I am doing this.' I said, 'I don't want to have nothing to do with it whasover.'"

That was all Pasqua could stand. Disgusted, he got up and left the premises.

Even by Pasqua's own account, he was now deeply mired in the plot—even if it was merely by association. And why didn't he, a respectable businessman, choose to

sever ties with Marino's surly lot? Like everyone else associated with the scheme, he would claim that a deep-rooted
fear of Tough Tony Bastone propelled him to keep his ob-
jections to himself. He had no desire to have Bastone pay
him a midnight visit. Even after Marino told him he'd run
Mellory over, Pasqua refused to stay away. It seemed these
thirsts of his were recurring with increasing frequency.

Against his better judgment, Pasqua stopped by the
speakeasy for a drink one night in February. Upon entering, he noticed that Mellory had been replaced by another
gentleman behind the bar. "I don't know whether he was an
employee," Pasqua said. "He was just behind the bar." And
he was also pouring drinks—not to mention helping himself to a few slugs. As Pasqua ordered his whiskey, he heard
someone at the end of the bar refer to the new bartender as
"Red." Pasqua said the bartender never bothered introduc-
ing himself; he simply handed Pasqua his drink and went
back to his own bottle. Seeking solitude, Pasqua took a
lone seat at one of the tables. It was not long before Marino
came out of the back room and approached him with another disturbing tale of criminality. This time, Marino
mentioned a plan to run over someone who looked like
Mellory. Well, that finally did it. Flabbergasted by his associate's macabre determination, Pasqua removed himself
from the speakeasy with the intention never to return again.
According to Pasqua, "The last thing I heard was that [Mel-
lory] was found dead in this room here. That is all."

Upon reaching this point in his carefully crafted fiction,
Pasqua realized he had to invent some backstory to intro-
duce Dr. Manzella, the man who signed the death certificate. He did this quickly enough. He would say that
Marino at one point asked him if he knew a doctor who
might provide a death certificate. The doctor, of course,
would be paid for his services. Naively, Pasqua asked
who the certificate was for. Marino told him it was for
Mellory. Not asking why—or exercising even a casual

inquisitiveness—Pasqua paid a visit to Manzella. "I went down there and I said, 'Some fellow wants to give you $150 for making a certificate for him,' " Pasqua said. "He said, 'Well, what kind of man is he?' I said, 'He is an alcoholic man, always drinks that wood alcohol all of the time, liable to go any day if he continues that drinking.' "

"Well," Manzella said, "let me know when the man goes."

Pasqua was up late the night of February 22. Come midnight, he was pondering the tangled web of crime and conspiracy into which—he would claim—he had been helplessly drawn. His dark meditations were rudely interrupted by a knock on the door. Who would be calling at such an ungodly hour? He half-expected to find Marino on the doorstep with another ghastly tale to tell. Instead, he found a young boy standing there—a boy he had never seen before. The lad told Pasqua there was a phone call for him at Marino's house. It was all very strange and Pasqua—who did not have a phone—was curious.

He grabbed his coat and walked the short distance to Marino's house. When he got there, he found a guy he recognized from the speakeasy—but whose name he could not recall—waiting for him. The man handed Pasqua the phone. Marino was on the other end of the line. "[Marino] on the phone told me to come down," Pasqua said. "I didn't get there until half-past seven, between seven and eight. They just told me, 'Come down and be in no hurry, come over to my place.' . . . I said, 'What is it?' He said, 'You come on over, there is no hurry.' I was at ease, and I said, 'All right, I will be over in the morning. You will tell me tomorrow morning.' "

Allegedly thinking nothing of the strange conversation, Pasqua returned home and went to bed. When he arrived at the speakeasy early the next morning, Harry Green, Tough Tony and Joseph Maglione were waiting for him. Marino was noticeably absent. Pasqua recalled that Green "told me

Mellory passed away and he brought me over to where he was living." Before making the short trip to Fulton Avenue, however, Pasqua went to the cigar and candy shop on 167th Street, phoned Dr. Manzella and broke the news: "I says that Mellory passed away. I told him, I told him a fellow by the name of Mellory. He asked me his name, I told him the name. When I called up and told him Mellory, he knew who I was talking about."

Pasqua asked Manzella how long it would take him to reach the Fulton address.

"I will be there in an hour," the doctor replied.

Not once, Pasqua would say, did he even ponder the possibility that Marino had finally succeeded in murdering Mellory. His moral conscience refused to let such a consideration enter his mind. Instead, he believed Mellory had succumbed to his own vices. Anyone who drank as much as Mellory did was destined for an early demise. "I thought they were going to let him stay in the [speakeasy] and drink himself to death," he said. "I didn't know they were going to carry on that way." And so Pasqua, accompanied by Harry Green, went to Fulton Avenue to see the body for himself. He was let in by the landlady. Waiting for the undertaker on the first floor was a man Pasqua recognized as "Red," the bartender he'd seen the last time he was at the speakeasy. Red introduced himself as Joseph Mellory, brother of the deceased Nicholas. Pasqua said it was the first time he had heard that Nicholas Mellory even had any family. Pasqua asked Red where his brother was, and was led up the stairs to the dead man's bedroom.

The first thing Pasqua noticed when he entered the room was the bottle of booze on the bedside table. Yes, it was just as he'd thought: The man's liver had finally called it quits. As the undertaker, there was not much he could do until after the physician had examined the body. He wiled away the time, waiting for Manzella, chatting with "Joseph Mellory"—although he said he found it strange that Mellory should have a brother after originally saying he had no family. Eventually, Manzella showed up. He poked and prodded Mellory's body, rolling it over on one side and then another. He applied his stethoscope to the man's back and chest, and checked for a pulse in the wrist and neck. Manzella pronounced the wretch dead. He shook Pasqua's hand, told him the death certificate would be ready that afternoon and returned to his office.

Later that morning, after the body was removed, Pasqua returned to the speakeasy to tell Marino that everything was taken care of. Instead, it was Marino who had something to tell Pasqua. And it was now he learned the horrible truth. "They told me one of them had done the job," Pasqua said. "He said, 'One of the boys done the job to him.' "

"What is the reason for that?" Pasqua asked.

Marino just laughed.

"Who is the wise guy who done it?" asked Pasqua.

"Danny is the fellow that put the pipe in his mouth and gave him gas."

"I thought he would drink himself to death," Pasqua said.

"No," replied Marino. "Danny put the pipe in his mouth."

On that anticlimactic note, Pasqua concluded his story. He felt confident he had covered all his bases. The story's purpose was to illustrate that while he knew to a certain extent what was happening, he refused to play any physical part in such violent debauchery. Pasqua said that when he learned the true extent of Marino's cunning, it was by then too late. Unfortunately, his tale was a tapestry weaved with so many lies, he would have trouble keeping it straight. Under the questioning of a determined district attorney, his story would collapse under the immense weight of its many untruths.

CHAPTER 13

Payday

On the morning of February 24, 1933, Alex J. Medovich, the grave superintendent at Ferncliff Cemetery in the town of Greenburgh, received a business order from the home office of the Ferncliff Cemetery Association. It was a burial order for one Nicholas Mellory. The requesting undertaker was Frank Pasqua. The order stated that the deceased was a charity case. Medovich consulted the cemetery map and selected a suitable plot: "Location, single grave, 2070, St. Francis section." It was, Medovich said, "a special grave picked out for poor people." Medovich confirmed the order with the association's home office then asked two of the groundskeepers to prepare the plot for a burial. He made a note in the cemetery ledger, recording the $12 fee Pasqua would have to pay for the opening of the grave. Medovich knew Pasqua purely on a business level, for he had ordered "several" burials at the cemetery before.

That afternoon, Pasqua arrived at the cemetery in a

rented hearse, with a coffin in the back. Noted Medovich: "Why, according to the way we term it, [the casket] was a cheap proposition, sort of darkish color."

Pasqua paid Medovich the $12 burial fee and watched as the casket was lowered into the ground. He stood silently and listened to the scrape of the shovels and the melancholy sound of sod landing on cheap wood. Pasqua pondered the box's dreadful secret. Soon it wood be lost forever beneath eight feet of dirt.

Not even the planning of Malloy's burial was free of corruption.

Dr. Manzella worked leisurely hours. His office was open five days a week from 9 A.M. to 10 A.M. There followed a two-hour lunch period until noon, then Manzella returned to the office for one final hour of business before closing shop for the day. Several hours after Manzella pronounced Malloy dead, Pasqua paid a visit to the physician's office to collect the death certificate. "That was just about the time he was in the office, 12 to 1," Pasqua said. "I found him there." Perhaps in a conscious effort to further distance themselves from the evil they knew they had perpetrated, the two men briefly discussed Malloy's shoddy health and ferocious appetite for the drink. It was bound to have killed him sooner or later. Pasqua had merely leant a hand in speeding up the process. Manzella handed Pasqua the death certificate.

Pasqua gave it a quick read. It stated: "I certify that I attended the deceased from Feb. 18, 1933 to Feb. 23, 1933, that I last saw him alive on the 23rd day of February and that death occurred on Feb. 23, 1933 at 11:30 a.m., and that the cause of death was as follows: Lobar Pneumonia." Beneath this, Manzella had signed his name in scrappy cursive. The remaining particulars as filled in by Manzella were just as false. The certificate listed Nicholas Mellory as being forty years old at the time of his death and working as a laborer and florist. The United States was given as his place of birth. It noted that both his parents were born in Ireland. The fictitious Anna Kenny was listed as the fictitious Nicholas Mellory's mother. It all looked good to Pasqua.

Manzella had done his part. Now he was anxious for the $150 that had been promised him. Pasqua assured Manzella that once the policies had been cashed, the doctor would receive his payment. First, there was more immediate business to attend to.

The man charged with removing Malloy's body from the Fulton Avenue tenement was Salvatore Cordovani. He was a chauffeur for his brother's firm, the Cordovani Undertaking Company, at 2083 Second Avenue. Pasqua's Burial Services contracted with the Cordovani brothers for all its body removal needs. It was late in the morning when Cordovani received word from Pasqua that his services were required at 1210 Fulton Avenue. When Cordovani pulled the hearse up in front of the building, he found Pasqua waiting for him. The undertaker was in no mood for casual conversation. "All he said to me was to get the body," Cordovani said, noting a sense of urgency in Pasqua's voice. Cordovani hurried upstairs to have a look at the deceased.

The body was sprawled across the bed. Whoever he was, he "had a pair of pants on, he had a shirt on, he had one shoe on." Asking Pasqua's father—who had arrived shortly after Manzella—for a hand, Cordovani went back downstairs to the hearse and retrieved the "body removal basket." The two men lugged it back to the room, placed it on the floor and approached the bed. Ralph Pasqua took Malloy by the hands and Cordovani grabbed the feet. They heaved him off the bed, put him in the basket, and down the stairs they went with their cumbersome load.

Cordovani was there for no more than ten minutes. He loaded Malloy into the back of the wagon and transported the body to Pasqua's funeral parlor. Malloy was placed on a slab in the parlor's mortuary, where he would be prepped for burial.

As far as Pasqua was concerned, Malloy could wait. The guy certainly wasn't going anywhere. Before attending to his undertaking duties, Pasqua returned to the speakeasy to show off the death certificate. There was much cajolery and backslapping, and a few drinks downed. As Pasqua basked in the glow of the Murder Trust's victory, it occurred to him there was still money to be made from this little venture.

In the normal course of business, after a body arrived at Pasqua's mortuary, an embalmer would prep the body for its final resting place. It was a rather messy process. An incision was made in the femoral artery to allow the blood to drain from the body. Further incisions would be made, in the carotid or femoral artery, through which the embalming fluid would be injected. The body would be cleaned and attired in elegant dress. Hair would be combed; perhaps makeup would be applied. Generally, a family member would purchase the casket and the grave, and the deed was done. With Malloy, of course, there would be no grieving family to view his body prior to burial, nor would there be anyone to select and pay for a high-quality casket and grave. That did not mean, however, that Pasqua couldn't charge the insurance companies for such things.

Pasqua quickly ran some numbers through his head. Indeed, he could make a tidy sum. He ordered one more drink then made his way back to the funeral parlor, death certificate in hand, and set himself to work.

Malloy was waiting on a cold slab. The clothes in which he died were mere threads. The white shirt had long since turned gray, and his toes protruded from holes in his socks. His underwear was soiled. Pasqua went through Malloy's pockets in the vain hope there might be something in them worth keeping. All he found was half a cube of chewing tobacco. Having no need for it, he slipped it back into Malloy's trouser pocket. There would be no embalming for Malloy, and Pasqua certainly wasn't going to waste a good casket on such a derelict. In the words of the Bronx district attorney, Pasqua did nothing but simply "throw Malloy in a box." The casket Pasqua selected was made of gray-painted pine. There was no lavish cushioning or wood-lacquer finish. There was nothing to it at all, and that included the price: $18. Pasqua wheeled it from the casket display room into the morgue. He placed it beside the slab on which Malloy lay and simply rolled the deceased into it. He closed the lid and wheeled the casket into the chapel, where it remained until burial. Economy was the name of the game.

Now he went to his office. He sat down at his desk and drew up an itemized bill—something he could send to Metropolitan and Prudential. Pasqua knew it would only cost $119 to bury Malloy. That included the $18 for the casket, $24 to hire a wagon to transport Malloy to the cemetery and $65 for body removal from Fulton Avenue. He already knew the charity grave would cost a mere $12, but the bill he drafted was slightly inflated. Going from what Pasqua put on paper, Malloy received a royal sendoff.

In his deceit, Pasqua spared no expense. According to his bill, there was a funeral procession consisting of three cars—at $25 each—to take Malloy to his $60 grave. There were floral arrangements and wreaths, as well as the $15 suit in which Malloy was buried. By the time Pasqua had finished adding his many extravagances, the bill had reached a hefty $460. He stood to make a $341 profit in addition to the cut he was due on the insurance policies. Unlike the others in the gang, Pasqua always had a contingency plan in place. He believed in thinking ahead; such was the reasoning behind the elaborate tale he crafted for use in the event anything went wrong. Now he devised another story to cover him should his treachery with numbers come to light.

His excuse would be: "I was told to do that."

Should he have to resort to such measures, he would blame pistol-wielding Anthony "Tough Tony" Bastone. He would say the man suggested—in conjunction with intimidating gestures—that Pasqua pad the funeral expenses. Pasqua would say it happened at the speakeasy as the others sat at the bar celebrating procurement of the death certificate. Tough Tony, provocatively stroking the protruding grip of his pistol, hinted that perhaps Pasqua should beef up the numbers. Pasqua would say he took it for what it was: not a suggestion, but a gently worded order. Such were the benefits of associating with a murderous thug. If—through some breach of secrecy—the authorities discovered the plot and came crashing down on Pasqua, he could simply point his finger to the fellow with the treacherous reputation and say, "He made me do it."

Pasqua hid the bill in his desk drawer. The next morning he went to the New York City Department of Health and filed the death certificate. That same afternoon Malloy was stuck in the ground.

It was the afternoon of February 25 when Pasqua and Murphy ventured into Harlem and visited the offices of the Metropolitan Life Insurance Company on 125th Street. Murphy was afraid to go on his own as he was unsure how to file a claim. "[Murphy] wanted me to go down and fill out the death claim," Pasqua said. "He said he knew nothing about it." And so, with Pasqua's assistance, Murphy—posing as the deceased's brother, Joseph Mellory—filled out the Proof of Death Claimant's Statement for policy number 1536363M for the amount of $800. On the application, Murphy listed the occupation of his pseudonymous identity as "fireman"—a career Malloy once had. He gave his place of residence as 1210 Fulton Avenue. He had told the landlady he would still be using Fulton Avenue as a mailing address.

The claim was filed and made its way without a hitch through the various processes of the Metropolitan machinery. On March 1, the insurance company issued check number B 1145978 for $800 to Joseph Mellory and stuck it in the mail. It arrived at Fulton Avenue the next day. When Murphy swung by that morning to check the mail, he found the envelope waiting for him at the foot of the stairs. There was a feeling of euphoria as he ripped it open to reveal its precious content. He shoved the check into his pocket and ran back to the speakeasy, where Marino was waiting. When Murphy entered Marino's place, he held the envelope aloft like some trophy won after a bitter contest. Marino ran from behind the bar and snatched it from him.

After all the trials and tribulations, the sweat and toil, their perseverance had been duly rewarded. Marino and Murphy naturally celebrated with a drink. They clinked glasses and thought expensive thoughts. Then Marino dispatched Murphy to the candy and cigar shop with orders to telephone Pasqua with the news. The undertaker chuckled over the phone and told Murphy he would be right over. According to Murphy, once Pasqua arrived, the three of them piled into the car and sped off to Metropolitan's Harlem offices to cash the check.

Marino and Pasqua had already discussed the distribution of funds. As Marino recalled: "[Murphy] was supposed to get a few hundred, because Frankie says he is entitled to more than anyone else in the crowd. Furthermore, he says outside of Danny and Murphy, no one is entitled to it. They are the only ones that done the work." Indeed, Murphy had done much of the dirty work: spiking

Malloy's drinks, tainting his food and placing himself in front of a moving vehicle while holding Malloy in place for Harry Green. The man deserved a large cut.

Pasqua and Marino waited in the car while Murphy went in with the check. He was directed in the lobby to a cashier's window on one of the upper floors. He slid the check across the counter. He was a trembling live wire of nervous energy as he watched the cashier count out the bills. As he reached for the cash, Murphy fought hard to maintain his composure. He stuffed the bills in to his pocket.

Afraid to let it go, he kept his hand wrapped around the bundle as he scurried toward the elevator. In the car, Pasqua nervously drummed his fingers against the steering wheel. Marino sat silently—his eyes fixed on the building's exit—and waited for Murphy to emerge with the goods. There was much excitement when Murphy's scraggly form eventually hit the street. Murphy—thrilled with his accomplishment—scrambled into the car's backseat and handed the damp wad of bills to Marino, who immediately started counting. Pasqua stomped on the accelerator and peeled the car away from the curb. Already, Marino was divvying up the spoils. To Pasqua he gave $400. He kept the other half for himself, slipping Murphy a paltry $65 instead of the previously planned "few hundred." To Murphy, however, it was an absolute fortune.

The bartender promptly put the money to good use. "I ate," Murphy said. "I bought shirts, and I bought Marino a suit, and this suit I got, and shirts and stockings and a hat." Later that afternoon, back at the speakeasy, they slipped money to the other participants. For his part, Bastone received $65—a pathetic amount for the plot's alleged "mastermind." Kriesberg pocketed $50. Money was also put aside for Harry Green and Joe Maglione. Pasqua, meanwhile, drove to Dr. Manzella's office and paid him $50. He said the remaining $100 would be delivered once they had collected on the Prudential policies. Manzella said that would be fine.

On February 25, Pasqua showed up at the Prudential offices to file a claim on the two policies. He spoke with Frederick Freyeisen, who asked if he could view the body to verify Pasqua's claim. "I wanted to see the body to verify whether that person was the person insured, which is customary." Freyeisen noted. "I asked Mr. Pasqua when I could see the body. He told me he was already buried."

The red flag immediately went up, and the real problems began.

Adolph Koldewey worked for Prudential. A loyal employee, he had served the company for forty-one years as a claims inspector out of the home office in Newark. His duties included the investigation of claims on policies less than a year old, disappearance cases and disability claims. So it was that in the early days of March 1933, Koldewey was assigned to investigate claims made upon two policies taken out only three months prior. A folder was placed on his desk with the pertinent documents and information. With copies of the insurance applications and the death certificate pertaining to one Nicholas Mellory in hand, the seasoned insurance man began his investigation.

"First of all, I went to the neighborhood and place that the application had the address of, which was 1959 Hobart Avenue, I believe, in the Bronx," Koldewey said. "I made inquiries there of the neighbors as to the insured." His inquiries were met with quizzical expressions and shrugged shoulders. No one he spoke with had ever heard of Mr. Nicholas Mellory. "I could get no information," Koldewey said. Immediately, he sensed that something was not right.

He decided to approach the case from a different angle, choosing to work backward starting with Mellory's death.

"I next went to No. 1210 Fulton Ave., in the Bronx, to the place where the insured died, according to the death certificate," he said. "I inquired of the housekeeper or landlady." Mrs. Delia Murphy had an interesting story to tell. It was one of slovenly drunks and strange men congregating on her doorstep. She told Koldewey of the two men who had come to her building to rent a room. One of them had said it was for his brother. Koldewey listened with increasing interest as Mrs. Murphy told him of the man that was brought to the room, a man foaming at the mouth and sick with drink. A man, she said, who was dead the next morning. Koldewey scribbled the particulars of the story in his notebook and thanked Mrs. Murphy for her time.

Next on Koldewey's list of people to visit was Mellory's employer, the florist Michael Del Gaudio. Ever since Pasqua approached him with his ominous request to vouch for a man he never employed, Del Gaudio had wondered what the undertaker was up to. Now, on that early March morning when the well-dressed man entered his shop and began asking questions concerning Nicholas Mellory, Del Gaudio wondered what he had gotten himself into. The man introduced himself as an investigator for the Prudential Insurance Company and fired off a number of questions to which there were no easy answers. Del Gaudio quickly discovered that it was hard to vouch for a man you had never met. But he stammered his way through the interrogation as best he could, hoping that what he said confirmed whatever information the insurance man had thus far ascertained. It was a relief when Koldewey thanked him for his time and turned to leave.

That evening back at his office, Koldewey reviewed what he had learned so far. The interviewing of residents on Hobart Avenue, Mrs. Murphy and Del Gaudio had been spread out over a one-week period. Over those few days, the mystery surrounding Nicholas Mellory had deepened. Koldewey's interviews had done little more than reveal a series of conflicting stories. Residents of Hobart Street had never heard of Nicholas Mellory, yet Mrs. Murphy claimed to have met a man whom she was told was Mellory. And Del Gaudio claimed to have employed Mellory but could offer nothing to substantiate his claim, such as a physical description or payroll receipts. After more than four decades in the business, Koldewey knew he had heard enough to be certain something was afoot—but what, exactly, he couldn't say. He checked his list of people to talk to and saw he had yet to call Francis Pasqua, the man who had insured Mellory.

On the morning of March 10, Koldewey dropped by Pasqua's Burial Service on 116th Street. Frank Pasqua looked even younger than Koldewey expected, and carried himself with an air of quiet confidence. The undertaker gently shook Koldewey's hand, perhaps mistaking him for one who had come seeking funeral arrangements for a dead loved one. Koldewey introduced himself and stated his business. Pasqua was immediately on his guard. The other insurance company hadn't sent anyone sniffing around.

Pasqua suggested they retire to his office off the main room. Koldewey, not one for pleasantries where insurance was concerned, immediately got to the point. "I inquired of him how long he had known the insured; how long the insured had lived with him," Koldewey said. "He told me that he had known the insured about two years; that the insured had lived with him at 1959 Hobart Ave., in the Bronx, about five months; that he had left there on December 27. He further said that the insured had worked for him at times off and on for about a year."

As Pasqua spoke, Koldewey scribbled feverishly in his little notebook. The incessant scratching of pen on paper made Pasqua shift uncomfortably in his seat. The undertaker casually wiped his sleeve across his brow and fixed Koldewey with a reassuring smile. The murder ring had come too far to let everything fall apart now. Koldewey, for his part, was unsure what to make of Pasqua. While he had an answer for everything, Pasqua's quiet air of confidence had staled to one of desperation. Referring to his notes, Koldewey asked Pasqua about the claimant, Joseph Mellory. Pasqua said that was the deceased's brother, who lived in Mrs. Murphy's building at 1210 Fulton Avenue. Koldewey did not believe him. During Koldewey's conversation with Mrs. Murphy, she told him that the surviving Mellory had stopped by on several occasions since his brother's death to check on the mail. And although she said the brother maintained Fulton Avenue as his mailing address, he had not slept there in several nights. Since then, Koldewey had stopped by Fulton Avenue several times in the hopes of catching the elusive Josephy Mellory. He had been unsuccessful in his attempts.

Koldewey now believed he was on to something. He explained to Pasqua that before Prudential could issue payment on the policies, he had to interview the surviving Mr. Mellory. This was merely a formality to ensure that Prudential had all its facts straight. Pasqua told Koldewey it was perfectly understandable. If need be, he would bring Joseph Mellory to Prudential's Bronx district office to sort out whatever matters remained. Koldewey said that would be more than adequate. Rising from his chair, Koldewey shook Pasqua's hand, eager to face him on his home turf.

Throughout his inquiry, Koldewey worked out of Prudential's Bronx district offices in the Kaplan Building on 177th Street, right next door to the Bronx County courthouse. The day after meeting Pasqua, the undertaker called Koldewey and said he and Mr. Mellory would be available

the following day to come and address whatever concerns
Prudential had regarding the policies. Koldewey said that
would be fine. On March 13, Pasqua arrived at the Kaplan
Building with Joseph Mellory in tow. Present at the meet-
ing in Koldewey's office were Koldewey; Frederick
Freyeisen, the agent who had sold the policies; and one Mr.
Nuer, an assistant superintendent.

The Prudential men comprised a formidable corporate
brain trust—one that would easily bury Pasqua and Murphy if they blundered on their story. Pasqua had reassured
Murphy before entering the building that everything would
be fine. Now he wasn't so sure. Nevertheless, he maintained an outward appearance of self-assurance as he
shook hands with each of the men. He introduced the Prudential gang to Joseph Mellory—a man who seemed rather
ill at ease with the formal setting. Koldewey was impressed
that Pasqua had produced the claimant, but was curious as
to why Pasqua felt it necessary to attend the meeting.

"First of all, I inquired of Mr. Pasqua what interest he
had in the insurance that he should be there at the time,"
Koldewey said. "He told me that his sole interest was the
collection of his funeral bill. He said that he was there with
Mr. Mellory because Mr. Mellory was not versed in business matters; he was there to help him out."

Even before Pasqua and Murphy were comfortable in
their seats, the questioning had taken a severe tone. Pasqua
only hoped Murphy could withstand the investigator's
heavy barrage. It was Murphy that Koldewey now set his
sights on. Rifling through a stack of papers for reference,
Koldewey asked the man he knew as Mellory to describe
his brother's general health prior to the issuance of the
policies. Murphy stammered for an answer in the harsh
spotlight of Koldewey's stare. He told the insurance man
he wasn't sure if his "brother" was sick or not prior to the
insurance being issued. As Koldewey later recalled: "He
said that he had heard that his brother was working for a

friend of his, Mr. Pasqua, and that he had gotten in touch with him because he heard that his brother was drinking quite a lot and was sleeping in alleys and other places like that. He thought that he would have to get a room for him to try and straighten his brother out."

Murphy weaved a morbid tale of a man down on his luck. It was a story of sloth and inebriation, of a man beaten by the hand life had dealt him. One could almost hear the razor-thin strains of a violin underscoring this depressing exposition. Murphy said he was not sure whether his "brother" had ever been hospitalized or spent time languishing in any institution. Koldewey nodded throughout Murphy's dissertation and scribbled in his notebook. When Murphy was done, Koldewey produced one of the insurance applications and placed it in front of Pasqua. He pointed to the signature supposedly applied by Nicholas Mellory and asked if in fact it had been scrawled by Nicholas Mellory's own hand. Pasqua did not like the question. It implied too much. Just how much did this insurance man suspect? Despite his apprehension, Pasqua said the signature was most definitely that of Nicholas Mellory.

Koldewey's face was a blank page. It betrayed nothing, yet seemed to speak volumes. He returned the application to the pile of paper on his desk and resumed asking his questions. "I inquired of Mr. Frank Pasqua as to the insured's signature, authentic signature," Koldewey said. "He said although [Mellory] had worked for him and had lived in the back of his undertaking establishment, he had no authentic signatures. He told me that he knew of no lodges he could have belonged to. He said he did not drive a car. He had no license. I asked him then who had paid the premiums on the policies and he told me that he had paid the premiums, but that the insured had always given it to him to pay for him."

Koldewey was begrudgingly impressed. The undertaker had an answer for everything—but Koldewey was convinced the guy was crooked. He duly made note of the fact that "Pasqua did most of the talking." For a man who had supposedly just lost his brother, Joseph Mellory seemed to have very little to say. Koldewey would have expected the deceased's next of kin to express some consternation over Prudential's refusal to make good on the claim. Whatever was going on, Koldewey realized that Joseph Mellory's involvement was secondary to Pasqua's role. The crux of the matter lay in determining who signed the name Nicholas Mellory to the insurance forms. Koldewey had an idea: "I requested then an itemized undertaker's bill, thinking perhaps I might get Mr. Pasqua's signature."

Pasqua maintained his outward composure. There had never been any intention on the part of Prudential to make this an amicable affair. It was instead an ad-hoc tribunal. Pasqua told Koldewey he could provide a bill, but he would have to send it to him as he hadn't brought it with him. Koldewey said that would be fine and rose from his chair to indicate the meeting was over. All five men exchanged handshakes and forced smiles before Pasqua and Murphy scurried from the office. Koldewey watched them leave. He had little intention of recommending that the company approve payment on the policies.

Out on the street Pasqua took a breath and tried to calm his frazzled nerves. He looked at Murphy, who—because of his lack of understanding in such matters—did not appear the slightest bit fazed. Pasqua was somewhat envious of his colleague's mentally detached approach to everything. Pasqua thought things would be easier for him, too, if he could stumble through life drunk and stupid.

On March 25, Koldewey received a letter from Frank Pasqua. It was the itemized undertaker's bill he had requested, but Koldewey still did not have the writing sample he desired. Everything on the bill, including Pasqua's name at the bottom, had been typed.

CHAPTER 14

Don't Call the Man "Yellow"

Anthony Marino liked the feel of his new suit. He was not accustomed to such fashionable fare. A suit meant respectability and signified some degree of success. It spoke of evenings on the town and celebratory dinners commemorating some happy event. All these were concepts foreign to him. There was not much to celebrate when your balls throbbed all the time. Nevertheless, the gang's recent success did justify a certain amount of frivolity. Standing behind the bar with a drink in hand, Marino allowed himself a smile. He had recently confided to Murphy that had Malloy survived the gassing, the whole plan would have been scrapped. There was only so much failure a man could handle before he had to admit defeat. But it was funny how things always seemed to work out in the end.

The process of killing Malloy had been nothing short of a full-time job. The planning and implementation of the gang's various schemes had become as much a part of

Marino's daily routine as opening the speakeasy each morning and locking it up at closing time. Now there was a strange calm about the place. Gone were the hushed murmurings of covert planning and the initial excitement of those back-room meetings. It was all done with. What was there to aspire to now? The $800 from Metropolitan was as good as gone. After being divvied up and spent on various luxuries, the cash had been as fleeting as the gang's glee with Malloy's death. And now some insurance claims guy was investigating the matter.

Pasqua had told Marino about this fellow Koldewey. He was snooping around, asking questions that shouldn't be asked. Pasqua feared that the insurance man was on to them. Why else would he try to secure a writing sample? "Don't be surprised," Pasqua had warned Marino, "if the man comes knocking on your door."

Marino swallowed the contents of his glass and poured himself another. What if the insurance man went to the police? Marino's mind harkened back to the night Green knocked on his door and told him the cops had questioned him regarding a hit-and-run accident. The insurance man's investigation was far removed from any inquiry the police might make into a seemingly unrelated traffic accident. Was there any loose thread that if pulled would bring the two investigations together and unravel the murder ring's activities? Marino wasn't sure. For all he knew, the police had dropped their inquiry. For neither he, nor anyone else, had heard anything more about it.

Marino looked at his watch.

The hour was late and he was tired. His head hurt from thinking too much. It was time to go home. He finished his drink and headed for the door. Save for Maglione and Bastone—who were sitting at a table and arguing— business was dead. Murphy, teetering on the other side of sobriety behind the bar, was left in charge. He raised an unsteady glass to show Marino all was under control. It was nothing he hadn't handled before.

The date was Sunday, March 19.

The enjoyment Murphy generally derived from robbing Marino of his liquor was being hampered by the increasingly bad vibe emanating from Maglione and Bastone's table. The two men had discarded any hint of the civility or friendliness with which they usually addressed each other. The topic was insurance money. Bastone—who had received $65 for his part—wanted the lion's share of the Prudential policies once they were cashed. He had spent the better part of the past week bitching about it. By now, Maglione's simmering temper was reaching a fast boil, and he told Bastone to go to hell. There was no reason Bastone was entitled to more than the others. But just when it seemed things were about to get ugly, Maglione—who had received only a fraction of his promised share—excused himself from the table to use the lavatory in the back. Bastone stayed put and grumbled in Italian as he refilled his glass. With the sound of the toilet flushing behind him, Maglione emerged from the restroom minutes later with a pistol in his hand. He strode toward Bastone and fired one shot. The blast roared like thunder in the confines of the cramped speakeasy. Bastone, groaning, staggered from his chair and clutched his shoulder. He walked a few unsteady paces before Maglione fired again. Bastone screamed and fell to the floor.

Keeping his head low, Murphy watched the horror unfold from behind the bar. Maglione bent over Bastone's unconscious form and relinquished him of his .45- and .25-caliber handguns. Suddenly, Bastone leapt to his feet in a surprising fit of vitality. None of Maglione's shots had found their mark. Taking advantage of his assailant's surprise, Bastone ran out the speakeasy door. But Maglione was quick to regain his senses and give chase with a gun in each hand. Out on the street, he fired four shots at Bastone's fleeing silhouette. Two of the bullets struck home. One tore through Bastone's left thigh. The other pierced his heart and killed him instantly. Maglione turned to run and left his former friend's body in a spreading pool of blood. Unfortunately for Maglione, Policeman Larkin of the Bathgate Avenue station was patrolling his beat nearby and heard the shots. He ran toward the commotion and arrived in time to see Maglione fleeing in the opposite direction.

Larkin immediately gave chase. He yelled at Maglione to halt. Out of shape and out of breath, Maglione was hard-pressed to show his heels and increase the distance between himself and the cop. With smoking guns still in hand, he was arrested and taken to the Bathgate Avenue station. Back at the speakeasy, Murphy had emerged from the safety of the bar. He moved slowly to the front door with a bottle still clasped firmly in his hand and peered into the street. There was Bastone, a lifeless lump, center stage in the pallid glow of a streetlight. Even through the haze of intoxication, Murphy knew things had taken a severe turn for the worse. Poured straight from the bottle, the shit was about to hit the fan.

A number of police units arrived on the scene, along with Dr. Miller of Morrianhills Hospital. Miller examined Bastone. He casually explored the wounds, pronounced him dead and ordered that the body be removed to Ford-ham Hospital. Meanwhile, several detectives inside the speakeasy got down to the business of interrogating Murphy. The hapless bartender could offer little insight into what the two men had said prior to the shooting. Their verbal exchange had been in Italian. But this was of little hindrance to the police, as they had in Murphy an eyewitness to the calamity. So it came to be that Joseph Murphy—much to his chagrin—was taken into custody as a material witness in the murder of Anthony "Tough Tony" Bastone.

While Murphy had little to say regarding the altercation, Maglione—undergoing his own interrogation at the Bathgate Avenue station—had a very interesting tale to tell. Not until after the cuffs were slapped on his wrists did Maglione realize the catastrophic potential of his actions. Now he found himself being grilled by Bronx Assistant District Attorney Tilzer, Detective Lieutenant McLaughlin and a number of other detectives as to his motive. Thinking quickly, Maglione told his inquisitors he simply lost control after Bastone challenged his manhood.

The story Maglione told went like this:

A week earlier, Tough Tony had introduced a friend of his to a policy slip collector in Harlem. Deciding to try his hand, the nameless friend placed a bet with the collector on his lucky numbers and wound up winning $96. The trouble began when the friend tracked Tough Tony down at a bar and told him the collector had refused to pay out the winnings. Tough Tony "became incensed that the collector had welched on payment to a man he had introduced to him." Hence, Tough Tony took it upon himself to collect his friend's winnings and use whatever force he deemed necessary to remedy the situation. He tapped Maglione for backup and told him he could keep half of whatever money they were able to collect. Bastone and Maglione ventured into Harlem one evening in search of the rogue collector. The two men beat the pavement for the better part of an evening and "visited the usual haunts of the policy slip collector but were unable to find him." It was not long before their legs grew tired and their throats dry. Opting to forfeit the search in favor of grander pursuits, they retired to the Bronx and their regular table at Marino's, where they saw out the remainder of the evening from inside a bottle.

The two men reconvened at Marino's the following night. Tough Tony suggested that he and Maglione continue their search for "the welcher." Maglione refused, saying he'd rather spend his evening drinking. It was then that the two men had their first significant argument. According to Maglione, Tough Tony's attitude became condescending. He pointed an accusatory finger at Maglione's chest and said, "You're yellow. You're afraid." Maglione chose to ignore Tough Tony's childish insult and moved to the bar in search of friendlier conversation. At a loss to explain his buddy's behavior, Maglione gave Tough Tony a wide berth over the next several days. During that time, Tough Tony made the rounds at various drinking establishments and whispered in the ears of some of his associates that Joseph Maglione was suffering from a lack of spine. Tough Tony's comments inevitably made their way back to Maglione, who "decided to talk the matter over with Bastone." This brought him to the early morning hours of March 19.

By the time Maglione reached the speakeasy, Bastone had already been there for quite some time, going several rounds with a bottle and winding up unconscious on the sofa that doubled as Murphy's bed. When Maglione entered the premises, Bastone woke up and joined him at the bar. There, the two men "talked angrily for a moment" before Bastone ordered drinks for himself and his "former pal." The two men retired to their usual table and continued their argument over two glasses of whiskey. It was at this point that Maglione excused himself to use the restroom. Despite the stone-cold facts of the case, Maglione insisted he blew Bastone away in self-defense, out of fear for his life. But pulling the trigger had done more than kill Bastone, it had cracked a fragile facade and exposed an insidious plot to anyone who dared look close enough.

On the morning of March 19, 1933, Joseph Murphy was booked into the Bronx County Jail. One of the jail's "residents" who witnessed the arrival of the new inmate was Dr.

Mayer Bernstein, a physician serving a three-month sentence for an alimony violation. "I was in bed at the time," Bernstein said. "When a prisoner was usually brought in there was a commotion attached to it . . . So a commotion was caused that morning. A new man was brought in, and on such occasion it was the anxiety of most of us to know why a man was brought in, his welfare and so on."

The commotion woke Bernstein up. The time was 6 A.M.—far too early to be social. "I did not get out of my bed until eight, and the room where the material witnesses were confined was on the way to the water closet or to the bathroom there, and for curiosity and other reasons I stepped in to see who our new man was."

The man Bernstein saw was a physical wreck, dirty and half-conscious, sprawled out on a small cot. Bernstein tried to rouse the fellow out of what he perceived to be a "semi-comatose condition." Murphy did not stir. His breath came and went in heavy rasps and "was very foul." Bernstein said it smelled of "urine." The doctor was concerned and took Murphy's pulse, which was "full and slow." He lifted Murphy's eyelids and noted that the man had contracted pupils. In his medical opinion, Bernstein decided Murphy was under the influence of "either a narcotic, a hypnotic or from bad alcohol." Bernstein left Murphy to sleep it off. When Murphy finally did emerge from his cell, five days had passed.

Murphy was not sure what to make of his new surroundings. He loathed the sense of enclosure, for it reminded him of his younger years spent in various foster homes and institutions. On the flip side, it was nice to have a proper bed and three meals a day—but of primary concern was his reason for being incarcerated. What would he tell the authorities when they came to him with their questions? Murphy was not even sure if Maglione had been captured. If, however, he had had the chance to flip through *The New York Times* the day after he was booked, he would have seen the headline: "Jobless Bartender Dies in a Quarrel." The last paragraph of the article read: "Maglione is a stationary fireman out of work. He was arrested near the [speakeasy] and held on charges of homicide and violation of the Sullivan law."

The strain Murphy found himself under was apparent to all who looked at him. Recalled Bernstein: "Murphy began to leave his room. He looked very haggard, his eyes were deep-set, his head was still drooping and walking very uncertain, with uncertainty." Initially, Murphy kept to himself. He would come into the cafeteria at mealtimes and collect his food, but refuse to sit or talk with the other men. He chose to eat in solitude. But slowly he emerged from his shell and took a liking to the kind doctor who made repeated attempts to befriend him. "I made an effort to speak to the man and elicit from him, not from the medical point of view, but from a sociological point of view, being human beings, his life history, his associations, his education, his life, as well as the cause that brought him to the jail," Bernstein said. "And I spent with him on the whole quite a few hours in private so as to get all this information from him."

While Murphy was making friends and growing accustomed to his new accommodations, Marino and Pasqua were struggling to maintain control of a situation they feared was now out of hand. On the morning of Monday, March 20, both men had opened the morning edition of *The Home News* to find the stunning front-page announcement:

TWO-GUN GANGSTER IS MURDERED FOR INSULT IN SPEAKEASY DISPUTE

Central figure in at least two previous shooting affrays of a spectacular nature, in the first of which he battled four armed bandits after they had shot and seriously wounded a policeman, Anthony Bastone, better known as " 'Tough

Tony,' the two-gun man," lies dead in the Fordham Morgue today, victim of a man he had described as "yellow."

The killer, who calmly recounted to police the indignities heaped upon him by Bastone, which finally resulted in the killing, is Joseph Maglione, 30, 861 Forest Ave., near E. 160th St., an unemployed stationary engineer who is the father of four children.

Maglione was to be arraigned in Bronx Homicide Court this morning, while the bartender in Tony Marino's alleged speakeasy at 3775 Third Ave., near 171st St., who witnessed the bitter dispute which preceded the shooting, is being held as a material witness. He is Joseph Murphy . . . recently serving as bartender in Marino's. He makes his living quarters there.

Marino stared helplessly at the paper. He looked at the floor, hoping the earth beneath him would open up and swallow him whole. To the left of the article was a picture of a sleeping Maglione slumped in a chair at the station house, his head resting in an open palm. The caption underneath the picture read: "Giving every indication of boredom as he recounted details of an argument which finally caused him to shoot and kill his one-time pal, Joseph Maglione, 30, enjoys a brief respite from questioning at Bathgate Ave. station."

Reading the article again, Marino found himself torn by conflicting emotions. He was thrilled to be free of Tough Tony, but the possible consequences of Maglione's actions terrified him. Not only had his speakeasy become a crime scene, but he was now without a bartender. And what of Murphy? What tale would he tell? The man was going to be called before the grand jury and forced to testify!

Marino met with Pasqua later that day to brainstorm a new strategy. There was nothing, however, they could do. They had no way of knowing what Murphy was going to say on the stand. The other great unknown, of course, was whether Maglione would strike a deal with prosecutors and blow the whistle on the rest of the gang. Everything was falling apart. And just when it seemed things couldn't get any worse, Adolph Koldewey started asking questions again.

Pasqua had stonewalled Koldewey, and the investigator didn't like it. Koldewey took the itemized funeral bill—typed instead of handwritten—for what it was: a delaying tactic. Pasqua was buying time and fortifying his cover story. Following the meeting with Pasqua and Joseph Mellory in his Harlem office, Koldewey knew the two men were blowing smoke up his shorts. After more than four decades on the job, gut instinct counted for something. What he'd seen that afternoon was nothing more than a ventriloquist act—and Mellory was the dummy. The man had looked disheveled and—if the truth be known—somewhat hungover. Furthermore, there had been no discernible reason for Pasqua to attend that meeting. Now, having failed in his attempt to procure a writing sample from the undertaker, Koldewey set his sites on Mellory. If he could get Mellory alone, he was sure he would uncover the truth. But as with everything else associated with the case, it was easier said than done.

Koldewey conversed with Frederick Freyeisen, the original Prudential agent, who told him that Joseph Mellory was working behind the bar at a speakeasy on Third Avenue. And so Koldewey embarked on a new investigation. But instead of clearing a straight path through the smoke and mirrors so elaborately deployed against him, Koldewey would wind up walking in circles. "The investigator could not find Murphy [Mellory]," records said. "[Mellory] was not around for some unknown reason, and his repeated attempts to locate him were naturally unsuccessful." As he had done when trying to ascertain some knowledge of

Nicholas Mellory's life, Koldewey was merely chasing the product of a wicked imagination. And it began when he entered the speakeasy that afternoon in late March and confronted the lone barman. The establishment, void of customers, had an air of lonesome desperation about it. There was a grimy quality to the overall atmosphere of the place. It was one Koldewey doubted would benefit from the bartender's mindless wiping of the bar.

Dirty rag in hand, Anthony Marino looked up from his work when Koldewey entered the premises. He knew instantly that this man was not a customer, for none of his clientele carried themselves with such authority. Besides, few customers had stopped by for a drink in the wake of Maglione's violent episode. As it was, Marino was expecting to eventually cross paths with Koldewey. He had already told his sister, Rose, that "if anybody comes here you know nothing; the party is out of town, if they come looking for me, or anybody." She thought it was a mysterious comment for him to make, but believed it was merely a result of his brain being addled by venereal disease.

Arriving home one night, Marino was met at the door by his wife. She told him a man from the insurance company had stopped by the house that afternoon looking for him. "She said he was an insurance agent, but didn't know what kind of agent." Unfortunately for Marino, he had not offered the same admonishment to his wife as he had to his sister. And now, on this afternoon in late March, the two men finally came face to face. Their encounter was brief. Koldewey explained that he was looking for Joseph Mellory, a man he heard had once been in Marino's employ.

Marino told Koldewey he had not seen Mellory for some time. He told the investigator Mellory had left town, venturing to Philadelphia to visit family on what promised to be an extended stay. Where exactly in Philadelphia Mellory was staying Marino could not say—but he assured Koldewey that he would contact him once Mellory returned. According to case files, "Wherever Murphy [Mellory] was, [Koldewey] went to the different people with whom he thought Murphy might have contacts of one kind or another." Koldewey's search took him all over the Bronx and even brought him into contact once again with the wily Pasqua. Not surprisingly, Pasqua related the same story to Koldewey that Marino had—a version exact in all its details. This only served to further rile Koldewey's suspicions. There was something else, too. Other than Pasqua and Marino, no one had heard of Joseph Mellory—just as no one had heard of Nicholas Mellory. His inquiries were met with puzzled stares and shaking heads. Residents and business owners along Third Avenue had never made Joseph Mellory's acquaintance. Likewise, neighbors of Pasqua's and Marino's were unfamiliar with the name.

What had happened to the Brothers Mellory?

Koldewey was perplexed. Frustrated, he returned to his Harlem office and reviewed the facts: One man was dead; another had simply vanished. There was no conclusive proof establishing a blood relation between the two aside from Joseph Mellory's assertion that they were indeed brothers. He flipped through his notes, hoping to find that one core piece of puzzle around which the other scattered remnants would fall into place. As hard as he tried, he couldn't find it. Regardless of the angle from which he explored the perplexity before him, his thoughts always returned to Pasqua. The undertaker was the common link between the two. He retrieved from his desk drawer the itemized bill Pasqua had sent him.

For a man nobody seemed to know, Nicholas Mellory had sure had one big funeral.

The Bronx Grand Jury convened the first week in April to determine if there was sufficient evidence to indict Joseph Maglione on charges of first-degree murder. Subpoenas were issued and witnesses testified. On the morning of April 3, Joseph Murphy found himself standing in the witness box, left hand raised, his right hand on the Bible, swearing to tell the truth. As Maglione sat bristling with anger at the defense table, Murphy told the grand jury that he had seen Maglione and Bastone verbally lashing each other moments before the shooting. No, he didn't know what it was they were fighting about.

Tony Marino—much to his chargin—was also subpoenaed to testify as to the nature of Maglione's relationship with Bastone. It was at times, Marino said, a little acrimonious.

On April 3, the grand jury indicted Maglione on a charge of first-degree murder. He was arraigned four days later and pleaded not guilty.

CHAPTER 15

The Unraveling

By now, the greatest liability to the Murder Trust and its dark secrets was the members of the Trust itself. Even after Malloy's demise, they were not content to abide by civilized law.

Harry "Hershey" Green received only $20 of his promised $150. Marino assured the cabbie that the remainder would be paid once the gang had collected on the Prudential policies. Murphy's detention and the suspicions of Adolph Koldewey, of course, threw everything into disarray—but it hardly mattered. In early April, Green was arrested in New York City for carrying a concealed handgun. He was dumped in the Bronx County Jail along with Maglione and Murphy. Daniel Kriesberg was apprehended that same month after depriving several individuals of their trousers in another Pants Bandit robbery. As was noted in May: "Kriesberg is being held on a charge of having participated in a hold-up at the Heaton Spring Works Co. plant at 140th St. and Wales Ave. said to have been engineered by Marie Baker." The arrests of Green and Kriesberg on charges unrelated to Malloy's death were nothing more than dumb luck on the part of the police. Investigators had little inkling of the convoluted conspiracy in which the men had participated.

Marino was now staying away from the speakeasy. He took false comfort in the belief that maintaining his distance lessened his guilt. He hired James Salone to tend bar and look after the place. Salone received a dollar a day for his services. Pasqua, meanwhile, clung to the belief that should Murphy or the others in jail talk and the plot be exposed, his carefully crafted story would bail him out. It brought him little comfort.

Meanwhile, throughout the Bronx, in smoky dens of iniquity and shady back alleys, a story began making the rounds. It was passed on via the hushed tones of men huddled at bars and repeated over games of cards. It was the tale of a man who refused to die—a man so virulent with life, not even the weight of an automobile could rob him of his vitality. Even Mother Nature proved powerless against him. It was a story of greed and desperation. It was only a matter of time before the story made its way to the lips of those who passed things on to the police. Patrolmen working the beat and detectives scouring the borough's seedy underside began returning to their station houses with a bizarre tale. One man who sat up and took notice was Inspector Henry Bruckman of the New York Police Department's Homicide Squad. He, in turn, brought the story to the office of Bronx County District Attorney Samuel J. Foley.

Born on the Lower East Side of Manhattan in 1891, Foley was the son of former New York Senator Samuel Foley, who represented the Twelfth District in the Bronx from

1896 to 1906. The father's political career got under way in 1890 when he was elected by Tammany to the state assembly, where he served for five years. In his later career, the elder Foley spent several years as the secretary for the Tammany General Committee and was chief disbursing officer of the House of Representatives. He died in a New York City sanitarium on June 26, 1922, at the age of fifty-nine—not living long enough to see his son's entry into public life two years later at the age of thirty-three. The younger Foley was educated in the city's public schools and graduated from Manual Training High School in Brooklyn. A robust young man who excelled on the athletic field as well as in the classroom, Foley went to George Washington University. There, he was quarterback for the school's football team and captain of the basketball team. He graduated in 1913 with a degree in law.

During the First World War, Foley fought overseas with Company M of the Seventh Regiment. He served with distinction, suffering a severe leg wound in combat. He entered the army as a private and was discharged as a captain. Following the end of hostilities, he returned to the States and pursued his career as an officer of the court. He was eventually named assistant district attorney on August 1, 1924, by prosecutor Edward J. Glennon, who would eventually go on to become a justice of New York State's Appellate Division. In March 1933, Governor Herbert Lehman named Foley district attorney for the County of the Bronx. He succeeded Charles McLaughlin, who vacated the job when he was appointed to the state supreme court. Foley loved his work, and went after those he prosecuted in the courtroom with aggressive enthusiasm. When the first faint whispers of the Malloy killing reached Foley, he had barely finished moving into his new office.

He immediately ordered an investigation.

It was the last week in April when Bruckman and Captain John J. McIlhargy "started an investigation with the aid of Detectives Byrnes and Carroll of the Homicide Squad." For the police, it was a different kind of inquiry. Detectives were being dispatched to solve a killing of which there was no physical evidence to prove it actually happened. Bruckman was asking his men to hit the streets and verify the authenticity of the strange rumors swirling around. According to Bruckman, the case would be built on information filtered through "the grapevine." As one Bronx reporter noted: "The killers and their accomplices took elaborate precautions to prevent detection and they would have been successful had it not been for the fact that 'someone talked' and gave officials the clue which ultimately caused District Attorney Foley and Inspector Henry Bruckman to detail almost every available detective in the borough to the task of unraveling all the ramifications of the fiendish plot."

The "someone" was John McNally. Sitting in his cell in the Bronx County Jail—after being busted in April for carrying a concealed weapon—McNally realized that his previous criminal career made him a prime candidate for a lengthy prison stay. Looking to secure a sweet deal for himself, he requested a visit with the district attorney. There, in Foley's fifth-floor office, he told an interesting tale of a meeting at a certain undertaker's house regarding the planned killing of a lowly drunk. The authorities accepted the story with a hearty air of skepticism.

"The authorities faced a difficult case . . . Mr. Foley and Inspector Henry Bruckman and a score of detectives worked day and night," noted one scribe for the *Times*. The detectives worked the beat, paying visits to speakeasies throughout the borough. They hunched over bars and kept their ears open. They pulled informants into the shadows of back alleys and asked what they knew of this strange killing. Was it true? Who was involved? It was not an easy task sorting through the half-truths and blatant lies. And even when the truth was spoken, it was so outrageous de-

tectives scoffed at its likelihood. Bruckman instructed his
men to track down the sources behind the various tales and
reconstruct the events of the purported crime. Each story
lead detectives to another source, and it was not long before investigators noted that different people were dropping the same names into their stories, thus corroborating
McNally's tale. The detectives' endless questioning eventually began to yield some dividends. A reporter following
the story wrote that detectives found "their difficulties
somewhat lessened by the fact that three of the men they
wanted for murder were already in jail."

They were, of course, Murphy, Green and Kriesberg—
none of whom realized what was transpiring in the world
beyond their cells. The investigation also uncovered the
name of the deceased. Further inquiry revealed the place
where he was buried. As each new piece of information
was gathered, it was sent back to Foley's office. There, Foley and Bruckman worked in close concert, assembling the
scattered pieces of a very complex puzzle. Foley, however,
was not yet ready to question the men already in custody,
for he did not want to play his hand too soon. When he
confronted the conspirators, he wanted to do it armed with
more than mere supposition. He wanted concrete proof of
their savage intentions and sought a court order authorizing Mellory's exhumation. Another name mentioned was
that of Anthony Marino. This piqued the interest of one of
the lead investigators, Lieutenant George Winters of the
Motor Vehicle Homicide Squad, number 3, who had
known Marino for the past ten years as a casual acquaintance from the neighborhood. Marino's name had been
mentioned in connection with Pasqua's and the acquisition
of several life insurance policies. This brought authorities
into contact with Adolph Koldewey, who had his own tale
to tell. The seasoned insurance man was by now sure the
death of Nicholas Mellory was a sham. His search for the
man he knew as Joseph Mellory had produced zero results.

"Well, from wherever [Joseph Mellory] was, he never returned," case files state. "So, of course, the policies are still unpaid."

Bruckman was eager to have Marino and Pasqua hauled in for questioning, but Foley still urged patience. The case was staggering in its complexity and sheer heartlessness. It was, Foley said, "the most brutal murder" ever to come before him, and he was leaving nothing to chance.

Despite what little information they had to go on when they began their inquiry, detectives advanced the investigation at a stunning rate. Weeding their way through "the grapevine," they learned that Mellory's real name was Malloy. They went to Fulton Avenue and spoke with Mrs. Murphy, who told them of her encounter with the Mellory brothers. On the morning of May 11, Justice Callahan granted Foley permission to exhume Malloy/Mellory's body. Now Bruckman could pursue his other leads. That same day Lieutenant Winters and Inspector Bruckman visited Marino at his home. The conversation the three men had was cordial, but it accomplished little. Marino confessed to nothing. As Winters recalled: "I talked to Marino and I asked him if he had anything to say, to say it, to come out with the truth. He said he had nothing to say to me; that he wanted to see Mr. Foley. I asked him if he insured the fellow and he said, 'No.' He said he received a little of the money. I asked him how much and he said, 'A little.' He said he was not there when the insurance was collected— that he was waiting outside. I said, 'Who went down there to collect the insurance?' and he said, 'Murphy and Danny.' He said he didn't know Danny's name."

Winters asked Marino if he was telling the truth. Marino assured the lieutenant he was. Winters didn't believe him. Bruckman leaned forward in his chair. "Where is Michael Malloy?" he asked.

"The last time I saw him he was in Fordham Hospital," Marino said, explaining that Malloy had gone there to seek treatment for a "running sore" on his leg. That was back in January, Marino explained, and Malloy hadn't been seen or heard from since. Marino displayed no outward sign of emotion as he answered the question, but the inquiry rattled him. Winters had limited his questions to the disappearance of Nicholas Mellory. There had been no mention of Malloy until Bruckman brought him up. Did this mean they knew Mellory and Malloy were the same person?

"This is the truth?" Bruckman asked.

When Marino told him it was, Bruckman countered by saying Malloy was dead and that detectives were at Ferncliff Cemetery digging up the body. Marino again said there was nothing new he could tell them and that the information he provided was "nothing but the truth."

Highly skeptical, the two investigators drove to Foley's office and debriefed the prosecutor, who ordered that Murphy be brought up from the county jail for questioning. "On May 11th, the District Attorney's office of this County went to the cemetery where we went to the grave in which Nicholas Mellory had been interred and we disinterred the body," Foley noted. "He was brought to Bronx County Morgue where the autopsy was performed on him, where various people were called who identified this Nicholas Mellory that we dug out of the pauper's grave as Michael Malloy. On that same day, I got Mr. Murphy, whose whereabouts were known to me, brought up out of the jail and talked to him. He told me that he had been in the car when Mike Malloy was run over."

But Murphy revealed much more than that when he was brought to Foley's office at 4:20 P.M. that afternoon. He spilled names, substantiating information gathered by detectives on the street and supplied by McNally. He implicated Maglione, saying Bastone was murdered because of a dispute over the insurance money. Revealing all the intricacies of the scheme, Murphy told Foley, "The plan was for me to be Malloy's brother, and that he had no mother and father. I was supposed to be his brother . . . and my name was supposed to Joseph Mellory." He started at the beginning and wound his way through the whole sordid exercise. He shared with Foley the story of the gang's botched attempts on Malloy's life, and told the prosecutor they even went so far as to try and kill another man in Malloy's place. This was news to Foley, as well as Bruckman and McIlhargy, who were both present.

While Foley questioned Murphy, Detective Eddie Byrnes went to pick up Marino. Elsewhere, McNally was hauled into the morgue, where he identified the body of Nicholas Mellory as being that of Michael Malloy. Frank Pasqua was approached by two detectives at the funeral parlor. "The District Attorney would like to talk to you," one of them said as he flashed Pasqua his badge.

The plot's unraveling was well under way.

CHAPTER 16
The Third Degree

Anthony Marino sat slumped in a chair in his small living room and stared into an empty glass. He reached for a bottle and poured himself another stiff one, contemplating the quagmire of complexities that was his life. In another room, his wife tended to their crying baby. Husband, father, business owner—it was really all too much. Generally, he was not prone to inner reflection, but recent events were forcing him to consider the big picture. It was just a matter of time before everything came crashing down on him.

In the hall, the phone jangled on the hook and shook Marino free of his reverie. It was just shy of four-thirty in the afternoon, and Marino wondered whether it might not be Frank ringing to discuss shared concerns. When he answered the phone, however, the voice on the line was one he didn't recognize

"Anthony Marino?"

"Yeah, who's this?"

"Mr. Marino, my name is Detective Eddie Byrnes. I was wondering if you might have time to talk." The tone of voice suggested that Marino was to make time now.

"I know what this is about," Marino replied. "I'll meet you at the station house."

"Don't you trouble yourself," Byrnes said. "I'll come and pick you up."

Byrnes's car pulled up in front of Marino's house only a few minutes later. Marino stepped outside before the detective could knock on the door.

"Mr. Marino."

"That's me."

"The district attorney would like to talk to you."

"Well, I guess I don't have no choice in the matter," Marino replied and yelled to his wife that he was stepping out for a while. The two men said nothing as they walked side by side down the garden path to Detective Byrne's Buick. As the car pulled away from the curb, Marino wondered if he would ever set foot in his house again.

Murphy's questioning was a cordial affair. He hemorrhaged information of his own free will. Marino and Pasqua's encounters with the district attorney were not as civil. Both men ducked and weaved, and worked tirelessly to shift the blame to other people.

Marino was brought into Foley's office at 5:15 P.M. after Murphy had been escorted back to his cell. Three men—all of whom were wearing badges—sat in close conference around the district attorney's desk. Foley motioned for Marino to take a seat and introduced the small congregation. There was Acting Captain McIlhargy of the 7th Division, Lieutenant Winters and Inspector Bruckman. Off to the side, typing away on his little machine, was Thomas J. Riordan, a grand jury stenographer for Bronx County.

The customary pleasantries of introduction were brief

and quickly swept aside by the business at hand. Foley asked Marino to confirm his name, address and profession—then the grilling began.

"When," Foley asked, "did you first hear Malloy was dead?"

"Just now I heard he was dead."

"You mean in the office here?"

"Yes."

"Today, May 11th?"

"That's it," Marino replied, feigning shock.

"When did you last see Malloy alive?"

"Well," said Marino, "what month is this?"

"May."

"About seven or eight months ago."

Foley was incredulous. "You have not seen him in all that time?"

Marino was adamant. "No."

"What you are telling us now, Marino, is the truth?"

"Yes," Marino said, "the truth."

"You are not giving me false answers?"

"No."

"You are not giving me false answers because you are conscious of being guilty in this matter?"

"I am not guilty in this matter."

Marino studied the clock on the wall and wondered how long this would last. Could he maintain this false front under such brutal inquisition? Cracking under pressure was not a viable option. This was murder they were talking about, and looming large over every word was the morbid premise of being zapped in the state's hot seat. So, for the next couple of hours, Marino didn't necessarily lie, he simply omitted certain truths and answered Foley's questions with "I don't know" and "I refuse to answer."

"Are you afraid that answering these questions might incriminate you?" Foley asked.

"I have no lawyer."

"Do you need a lawyer to help you to tell the truth?"

"All I want is to tell the truth."

Marino continued to tackle Foley's questions as best he could and failed miserably in the process. His selective memory on some and refusal to answer others spoke volumes. It was clear, however, to all present that he had no intention of voluntarily surrendering details. Marino knew he was in it deep. He was playing against a team with a definite home-field advantage.

Foley did not like Marino. He found the young man slovenly and contemptible. He would later add "stupid" to that short list. "This statement that you make here is made without any promise by me?" Foley asked.

"That's right."

"Is there anything else you want to add to it?"

"I don't want to say no more."

The interrogation lasted nearly two hours. Having weaned little information from the suspect, Foley decided to let Marino ponder things in the solitude of a holding cell. Marino was led from the room. Alone with his thoughts—without the comforts of a bottle to cushion the hard truth of his circumstance—Marino's defenses slowly began to crumble. The next time he faced Foley, Marino—for his own self-preservation—would look the man in the eye and tell his story, manipulating the more unseemly details to divert attention from his own involvement in the wicked scheme.

Like Murphy, Daniel Kriesberg offered little resistance to Foley's questions when was brought up for questioning at 7:00 P.M. Instead, he made a futile attempt at appealing to Foley's sense of mercy.

"I was scared," Kriesberg said. "I was threatened with death."

"By whom?" Foley asked.

"By that gang, if anybody talks up," Kriesberg said. "I have three children I love very much. They threatened whoever opens up will be killed on the outside by the gang. I don't know nothing about the law. It happened on the outside, you understand. They threatened, and I can't afford to be put away. I'll give you the whole story from the beginning."

And that's what he did, detailing how he and Murphy gassed Malloy. "Mr. Foley, tomorrow morning there is another story I'll tell you personally," Kriesberg said. "All I'm asking of you is a little leniency."

"Dan," Foley said, "I'm not making any promise to any man."

"Mr. Foley, I would like to have a little talk with you," Kriesberg said, desperately maneuvering to put himself in the prosecutor's favor. "There is something that will interest you very much."

Foley failed to take the bait: "What is going to happen to you, Danny, I don't know. I give you no promise. You have been made no promise of any kind."

And with that, Kriesberg was escorted back to his cell.

At 7:20 P.M., Pasqua was brought into Foley's office. For the past several weeks, the undertaker had psychologically prepped himself for such a confrontation. He had gone over his story many times. Key to its success was maintaining the fact that he never knew Michael Malloy, only a gentleman named Nicholas Mellory.

Pasqua made himself comfortable as Foley shuffled through some notes.

After having Pasqua state his name and address for the stenographer, Foley launched his offensive.

"Do you know Tony Marino?"

"Tony Marino, yes."

"How long have you known him?" Foley asked.

"Oh, about seven years."

"Did you visit his place on Third Avenue?"

"Yes," said Pasqua. "About four months ago was the last time I was there."

Foley asked Pasqua if he knew Joseph Murphy.

"Who is that?"

"Joe Murphy," said Foley, "Red?"

"Oh, Red, that is fellow who used to work for Marino," Pasqua said.

Foley scribbled some notes.

"Do you know Mike Malloy?"

"Malloy?"

"Yes," said Foley, "the one who hung around Marino's speakeasy the same as Joe Murphy."

"No," Pasqua said.

"He is the man you buried under the name Mellory."

"I know Mellory," Pasqua said, "but I don't know Mike Malloy."

Pasqua told Foley he had met Nicholas Mellory about three or four years prior, on the corner of Third Avenue and 130th Street. He was loitering, looking for the odd job to line his pockets with a few bucks. Pasqua offered him a job cleaning up around the funeral parlor. "He used to sleep back there a few nights," said Pasqua, adding that Mellory last slept on the premises back in December.

Foley asked if Mellory had a brother. "Well, that is Red," Pasqua said.

"Joe Murphy?"

"Yes," said Pasqua, "that is the one I knew as his brother."

"Who introduced him to you as Mellory's brother?" asked Foley.

"When I took charge of the body they called me and told me to go up there and told me his brother was taking charge," Pasqua said. "This is the fellow I met."

"You know he is not Malloy's brother, don't you?" the prosecutor said.

Pasqua feigned disbelief. "No, I don't know that."

Foley felt his patience ebbing away. "Let's be frank about it," he said. "Don't you recall an occasion when there was a conversation at your home concerning the method of killing Malloy? You don't wish to make any statement about this?"

"In what manner?" asked Pasqua, incredulous.

"Do you wish to make a confession about your participation in the killing of Michael Malloy?"

"I have no confession to make."

And so the questioning continued, as Foley scraped together facts—gathered by the detectives and secured by Foley from McNally, Murphy and Kriesberg—and presented them to Pasqua, who vigorously denied any implication in the killing. He stuck by the story that he had never heard of Mike Malloy. Then he screwed up. It was a simple slip of the tongue, but it was enough to do him in. It happened when Foley was questioning Pasqua about the doctor who signed "Mellory's" death certificate. Pasqua told Foley that "Mellory" had been a patient of Dr. Manzella. Mellory had been visited by the physician twice before he died. It was for this reason that Pasqua called Manzella out to examine Mellory's body and to write the death certificate.

"[Mellory] was visited by Manzella?" Foley asked.

"Yes, twice."

"Tell me about it," Foley said.

Pasqua was growing weary. "He was visited twice by the doctor, which I don't know anything about. I don't know what it was for; being he had this same case that is why I called him up when anything happened."

"Who told you Manzella had the case?"

"I knew it for a fact," Pasqua said.

"How did you know it?"

"Because Malloy told me."

Foley raised an eyebrow, "You mean Mike?"

"Yes," said Pasqua. And in that moment, he was fried.

"You called him Mike?"

Pasqua, realizing what he had done, searched frantically for the words to put this incredible blunder right. "I used to call him Malloy because I knew him as the name Malloy—then they told me his real name was Mellory." He was against the ropes swinging wildly, hoping for that one lucky punch.

"Didn't you tell me a minute ago that you didn't know him as Malloy, that you knew him as Mellory?" asked Foley, smelling blood.

"Mellory, yes," Pasqua stammered. "I asked him one time, 'What is your right name?' and he said, 'Mellory.' Whether they were kidding or not I don't know, because I never implicated myself with any of these fellows before."

"He was known to you as Malloy?"

"No."

"What was he known to you as?"

"The name I knew first was Mellory."

"You never heard Malloy used?" Foley asked.

"No."

"But you just said you did."

This wasn't going the way Pasqua had planned. He was starting to feel overwhelmed. Foley was steering the narrative, denying Pasqua a chance to tell his side of things—to recite the story he had spent so much time crafting. Foley, meanwhile, was becoming increasingly annoyed with the slimy character before him. Going on what Joseph Murphy had told him, Foley knew Pasqua was lying about everything. Instead of trying to retrieve information piecemeal from Pasqua, Foley decided to give the undertaker a chance to open up and present the whole story as he saw fit. Once the story was on the record, Foley could take his time in deconstructing it lie by sordid lie, all the while watching the conniving little creep squirm in his seat.

"Tell me," Foley said, "what you know about this case from your first being drawn into it."

Pasqua straightened in his chair. "Mr. Marino came over to me one day and says that he had a fellow by the name of

Mellory to be insured. So I said, 'What do you want me to do?' " He wound his way through the whole nefarious plot, placing all the blame on Marino and Tough Tony—both of whom, Pasqua said, strong-armed him into securing insurance policies for Mellory. That, however, was the extent of his participation in the overall scheme. It took no more than a few minutes for Pasqua to finish his story. "If that is going to help," he told Foley, "I don't know."

And now it was Foley's turn. From the pile of paper in front of him, he pulled out a copy of the itemized funeral bill Pasqua had sent Koldewey. "You put a bill to the Prudential for $400 although you were already paid by the Metropolitan. When you buried this man, all you did was just throw him in a box, wasn't it?"

"Put him in a casket," Pasqua corrected.

"You buried him in a plain, black box didn't you?"

"It was gray."

"And these items you charged in the bill of March 25, 1933, are not items of actual expense to you, are they? You didn't have any three cars at $25 each?"

"No."

"You didn't even have the embalming, did you?"

Again, Pasqua answered in the negative.

"This bill," Foley said, making a statement more than a question, "for $460 is a complete fraud."

"I was told to do that," Pasqua said, explaining that he had feared angering Tough Tony. "I was threatened by Tough Tony and I heard he came up to my house one night, that they were going to knock me off, and there was a little fear in me. I was forced, otherwise I would never have done these things willingly." Pasqua told Foley that Tough Tony did not want to blow the insurance money on the trivialities of a funeral.

Foley asked Pasqua why he didn't come forward to report the crime after Tough Tony was killed. Pasqua said two associates of Tough Tony's swung by the funeral parlor not long after Bastone's death. They told Pasqua to keep his mouth shut about everything. If he didn't, the consequences would be dire. Even by Pasqua's own questionable standards, it was a pathetic excuse—but he refused to yield and admit any blatant wrongdoing. The questioning continued well into the night. During the proceedings, Foley had Daniel Kriesberg and Delia Murphy marched through the office. It was a crafty psychological ploy just to let Pasqua know that officials had access to other sides of the story. The interrogation finally ended after midnight with Pasqua insisting that the entire diabolical scheme was the product of Tough Tony and Anthony Marino.

It was just shy of 10 P.M. when the phone on Foley's desk rang. It was Hochman, the assistant medical examiner, calling to tell Foley that tests had proved that Michael Malloy died of carbon-monoxide poisoning.

It was 1:10 A.M. on the morning of May 12 when Marino was brought back into Foley's office for round two. Inspector Bruckman and Captain McIlhargy were still present. Detective Byrnes leaned against a bookcase stacked with heavy volumes. New to the proceedings were Assistant District Attorneys Breslin, Flynn and Carney. Having spoken with the medical examiner several hours prior, Foley now had a cause of death in the matter of Michael Malloy.

The conversation immediately got off to an ominous start.

"Tony," Foley said. "You're in the hot seat."

Foley was a robust-looking individual, well fed, with a burgeoning second chin and a thick, well-combed crop of gray hair. Despite the late hour, he looked amazingly unruffled. "Tony, do you want to tell me all about this thing?" he asked. "Start at the beginning, when it was first talked about, knocking this fellow, Malloy, off for insurance. Tell me all about it."

Marino stammered, unsure how to respond. Foley suggested that perhaps Marino needed a little help. He nodded to one of the detectives, who briefly stepped out of the office and returned with Joseph Murphy. Murphy took a seat next to his onetime boss and spoke freely of how it was Marino who instructed him to rent a furnished room with a gas fixture. There was talk of wood alcohol and futile attempts on Malloy's life. Unfazed by Marino's piercing stare, Murphy again detailed for Foley the night they tried to run Malloy over. Then he spoke of collecting the insurance money and how he gave it to Marino so it could be split among the rest of the gang. Marino interjected here, insisting that Murphy must be mistaken, but Murphy stood his ground—sobriety having induced a new clarity of mind.

"I gave you $800," Murphy said to Marino.

"You did not," Marino insisted. "You gave it to Pasqua. Don't you remember that?"

"No, I do not," Murphy shot back. "I gave it to you!"

Foley took great pleasure in this display of bickering. "I was delighted to have them question each other," Foley said. "I felt, naturally, that they might elicit far more information than I could groping in the dark."

When Murphy was done, he was escorted back to his cell.

"Well, Marino," Foley said, "what do you have to say for yourself?"

Realizing his situation was hopeless, Marino acquiesced. "I want to tell the truth and nothing but the truth," he said. "I am ready to open up and talk, but I want a break."

"Well," Foley said, "I'm not promising anything, Tony."

Marino cleared his throat and made himself comfortable. "Well," he said, "it was Frankie's idea . . ." He spilled everything, but he continued to maintain that Tough Tony was the stage manager behind it all. Although Maglione had been the one to secure the services of Harry "Hershey" Green, Marino—not wanting to further implicate his childhood friend—said that it was Kriesberg. He also said it was Kriesberg's idea to run over a vagrant and substitute the body for that of Malloy's: "Danny got a car. He was a hack driver, and then Danny took some other guy over to near the Ward's Bakery over towards, over that way there, towards Port Morris. They took him and they put a card in this guy's pocket, supposed to be Mike Malloy, but it wasn't Mike Malloy and he got some broken ribs."

It was nearly two in the morning by the time Marino exhausted his story. It was an impressive tale. It was also disturbing. Foley sat and stared at him. The prosecutor's gaze pierced Marino and tunneled its way into his gut, where it became a cold, dead weight in the pit of his stomach.

"Well," Marino asked quietly, "what about a break?"

Joseph Maglione was pulled from his cell at 2:30 A.M. and hauled into Foley's office, where he was grilled for nearly two hours. Climbing back into his bunk, he cursed the day he ever met Michael Malloy and Anthony "Tough Tony" Bastone.

On the morning of May 12, Foley broke the news to the media, revealing what *The Home News* called "one of the most diabolical plots for profit in the annals of this city." The paper broadcast the news under a large front-page headline:

INSURANCE MURDER 'TRUST' SEEN IN ARREST OF FIVE FOR MAN'S DEATH

Baring the almost unbelievable details of an alleged "murder trust's" cold-blooded killing of at least one man

in a gruesome plot to defraud insurance companies, Dist.
Atty. Samuel Foley today announced the arrest of a Bronx
undertaker and four others for homicide and a former Republican Alderman from Harlem as an accessory . . .

The success of that investigation was attested by the appearance of the accused men in the line-up at Police Headquarters this morning and the fact that two others are being
detained as material witnesses.

On Saturday, May 13, the Office of the Bronx County
District Attorney revealed that "because of evidence pointing to an almost incredible conspiracy to murder a friendless 'down-and-outer' to collect insurance money, it was
believed that prosecutors in the other boroughs would co-
operate in a city-wide probe to determine whether a highly-
organized 'murder ring' was responsible for scores of
suspicious deaths in the past several months." The wording
was somewhat misleading, however, as "highly organized"
implied a slick killing machine. Nevertheless, Foley pondered "the existence of a widespread 'murder syndicate'
made up of professional dealers in death who picked victims at random from the ranks of the city's friendless and
obscure." Foley said he "would acquaint all metropolitan
prosecutors with the details" of the current investigation.

That investigation now included a city-wide search for
the vagrant the gang had tried to kill in place of Malloy.
And just when Foley and Bruckman thought nothing else
could surprise them, they received an anonymous tip regarding the death of Mabelle Carlson, the onetime girl-
friend of Anthony Marino. What struck Foley was the
similarity between the method employed to kill Mabelle
and the steps taken by the gang to rid themselves of Malloy
that winter's night in Crotona Park. Even so, Foley conceded that "no effort will be made to charge the man with
his sweetheart's death until after his trial, with at least four
others, on the original murder charge. Even then, it is

doubtful if sufficient evidence will have been obtained to warrant a first-degree murder charge."

So appalled was he by the tenacity of the culprits that Foley decided early on to prosecute the case himself. Once that decision was made, he sought to speed up the "legal machinery" and rush the indictments. Murphy, Marino, Pasqua, Kriesberg and Green were arraigned before Magistrate Klapp in Homicide Court on Friday, May 12. They were held without bail. Dr. Manzella—who also was apprehended—was released on $10,000 bail fronted by the Concord Surety Co. Meanwhile, word of the bizarre case traveled quickly and it traveled far. Within days, Foley's office was swamped with communiqués from anxious people all over the country who feared for loved ones in the New York area.

On Monday, May 15, 1933, Foley again held court with the media. Giving every angle of the story prominent play on its front page, *The Home News* reported: "The Malloy murder revelations have caused considerable uneasiness among persons throughout the United States, Foley revealed yesterday. The prosecuting official has received a large number of letters and telegrams concerning various persons who died in the Bronx under circumstances which now appear suspicious to relatives."

On the morning of Sunday, May 14, Maglione had gotten a chance to address Marino and Pasqua when he bumped into the two of them in the jail's visitors room. "I went down and I walked up to them. I says, 'Why did you fellows implicate me in this case?' I said, 'If I wanted to do the same to you, I could have went up to the District Attorney's Office the first day I got locked up myself.' So, Marino says to me, 'We thought it was you that squealed, but you have nothing to worry about.' So, Pasqua said to me, 'Your name was not mentioned at all. We will clear you out of it and we will go to the bat on the other rap. Just make out you don't know nothing at all about it, because we are going to try to put all the blame on Murphy and Kriesberg.'" Of course, by now it was too late—for even Maglione realized that "Mr. Foley has all the cards on the table."

On Tuesday, May 16—a mere four days after Marino and Pasqua's arrest—Foley convened the Bronx Grand Jury, parading before it twenty witnesses who presented a most unflattering picture. Although Foley was intent on investigating "whether the lethal tentacles of the Murder Trust may have been extended toward a dozen unsuspecting victims," he made the Malloy case his top priority, allocating all his time to it. He said there was evidence "strong enough to send the ring leaders to the electric chair." Their cohorts, he added, would be put away for a very long time. Although Foley considered all involved to be guilty, he named Murphy and Kriesberg as the actual killers, citing that they were the ones who took Malloy to the furnished room on Fulton Avenue and applied the gas. Nevertheless, the testimony offered was damaging to all five defendants, all but ensuring a shocking end to their young lives before the trial even commenced. Marino, Pasqua, Murphy, Kriesberg and Green relived one startling failure after another as Foley called witness after witness, each painting a sordid tale of human grist. Most damaging to the defendants was the testimony of Edward Smith and John McNally, both of whom recalled in explicit detail the negotiations at Pasqua's house.

The following day, Wednesday, May 17, *The Home News* reported: "The Bronx County Grand Jury acted promptly in returning indictments yesterday in connection with the gas murder of Michael Malloy . . . Within a short time after some 20 witnesses told their sordid stories of the murder, which is said to have proved successful only after repeated attempts, the charges upon which the prosecutor is expected to demand the death penalty were handed up in Supreme Court." Dr. Manzella was indicted on the lesser charges of being an accessory after the fact and failing to notify the medical examiner and police of Malloy's death.

While Foley presented his case to the grand jury, Homicide Squad detectives—sitting at desks piled high with paper—were reviewing the police department's murder files, on the lookout for any bizarre death that remained unexplained. On Sunday, May 21, the Bronx newspaper reported that claims suggesting "that the so-called 'murder trust,' which has already been accused in two insurance killings, caused the drowning of a third victim in Long Island Sound were being investigated . . . Every effort is being made to check a story that members of the alleged murder ring enticed a man into a boat in Long Island Sound after insuring his life some months ago and then pushed him into the water." And "while information about his supposed murder is by no means complete, police hope to collect enough evidence for use in case the charges now lodged against the indicted men fail to 'stand up' in court."

In the end, the allegation amounted to nothing, but it hardly mattered. Foley was more than confident that his case against the Murder Trust in the slaying of Michael Malloy was strong. His confidence was only bolstered three days later when detectives announced that they had found the vagrant the gang had hoped to substitute for Malloy. Finding Joseph Murray had been no easy task. Detectives had scoured the city, trudging from soup kitchen to soup kitchen. They queried people in breadlines and made the rounds in homeless shelters. They traipsed from one cheap speakeasy to another and canvassed the city's Depression colonies. These were aptly named, being glum refugee camps for unemployed men. It was in such a place known as "Camp T" that Detective Lloyd of the Alexander Avenue station—who originally talked with Green regarding the hit-and-run all those months ago—and Detective Carroll of the Bronx Homicide Squad found Murray, languishing in a ramshackle hut on the corner of Twelfth

Avenue and 133rd Street, near the Hudson River. Police said, "Murray readily agreed to become a material witness when he was told that District Attorney Samuel J. Foley of the Bronx did not believe he had met with an accident on the night of February 7, but that the gang had deliberately run over him with a taxicab." He was booked into the Bronx County Jail as a material witness in lieu of $20,000 bail. But when compared with his prior accommodations, Murray "expressed satisfaction with the comforts of his new quarters, the assured meals and the State's remuneration of $3 a day." So comfortable was Murray in his new abode, he referred to it as his "palatial home."

This, and the other wild elements of the case, all played out great in the press, which portrayed Malloy as an underdog who went down fighting all the way. So bizarre were the specifics of the crime that *The New York Times* pondered the spectacular details of it in an editorial dated May 27, 1933. Under the heading "Quite up to Fiction," the paper's editorial writer opined:

> The crime fiction industry must evidently be preparing for competition of the most formidable kind from the current police annals of New York City. There is the unsolved Ridley case with its thrills unnumbered. Less complicated and architecturally even more satisfying is an insurance murder conspiracy which the law authorities seem to be on the point of winding up.

After explaining the many facets of the case, the writer noted:

> Apparently, [the gang's] murder technique is far below their savage intentions.

In the Bronx County Jail, Marino and the gang pondered their uncertain future. Harry Green, who always exercised a blatant nonchalance about human life, suddenly found his attitude changing under the threat of the electric chair. Imbued with a newfound moral obligation, he took it upon himself to turn state's evidence and to share with Foley all he knew about the plot and his role as a failed killer hired for $150. Elsewhere, Maglione wondered what—if anything—Marino and Pasqua could do to help him beat the murder rap on the Bastone case. One morning in July, while he was getting a haircut in the jail barbershop, Maglione again encountered Marino. "I says, 'What are you fellows doing about my case?'"

There was now little civility between the two. Marino, angered by his own predicament, lashed out. "Listen, this is all your fault! If you did not get in this trouble, none of us would have been locked up. If you had done what Tough Tony wanted you to do and knocked McNally off, you wouldn't have nothing to worry about!"

"Listen," Maglione said, "you take care of your case and I will take care of mine!" After consulting with his court-appointed attorney, Maglione turned state's evidence against his onetime cohorts in the hopes of bettering his own situation.

CHAPTER 17
The Trial

Foley knew he had enough to try the case successfully. "The gang deprived Malloy of life, not through hatred, not through malice, not through fear of him, not for revenge, not for any understandable reason in God's world, but because they wanted money," Foley said. "Cruel, avaricious, greedy, remorseless, merciless, they never gave him a chance, and they have had no pity amongst themselves since. That derelict represented to them a golden opportunity." Reviewing each of the suspect's stories and the facts surrounding the murder, he refused to believe that Tough Tony exercised unimpeachable power over such coldhearted rabble. It was Foley's opinion that Marino gave the orders and Tough Tony carried them out. "Big Tough Tony, the big bad boy!" Foley mused. "He got $65. The man who could give orders, the man who had complete charge of this gang—the mastermind, the dominating force, the vicious personality, the fear-inspiring, two-gun gangster."

As far as Foley was concerned, Bastone was a two-gun thug who took orders and killed for a cheap buck. He was not someone who exerted control—just look at the evening they took Malloy out in the car to run him over. "Did the king tough-man sit in the car and say, 'You take this man out, you kill him'? No, Bastone was one of the ones that did the dirty work along with Mr. Murphy, the alleged mental defective and moral delinquent. Bastone had to get out in the road. He was not the boss of that outfit. If he was, what was he doing out there with Marino sitting in the car?"

On Tuesday, October 3, 1933, an all-male jury was seated for the trial of Marino, Pasqua, Kriesberg and Murphy. Although charged with the murder, Harry Green would be tried separately because of his turning state's evidence.

Edward Lowy, a dress manufacturer who lived at 1457 Bryant Avenue, was selected as jury foreman. It took two days to seat the jury. "For the first time in Bronx County," reported *The Home News,* "in accordance with a law which had been passed after a campaign by *The Home News* to avoid the frequency of mistrials due to incapacity of a juror, two extra jury-men were selected." The trial got under way on October 4, 1933, before a packed courtroom. The four defendants sat together at a long table; between each of them sat their respective attorneys. Representing Marino was Francis X. Mancuso, a former judge. While examining potential jurors, Mancuso suggested that Marino would be pleading innocent by reason of insanity. Kriesberg was represented by Robert A. Dillon and I. Julius Berg, while Luke LeRolle and Morris Permut defended Murphy. The task of defending Pasqua fell to Samuel S. Liebowitz. The presiding judge was the Honorable James Barrett.

The seating gallery was crammed with reporters and the mere curious as Foley commenced opening arguments: "May it please the Court, Mr. Foreman and gentlemen of the jury. We are proceeding to trial here under indictment number 462 of 1933, which charges Daniel Kriesberg,

Joseph Murphy, Anthony Marino, Frank Pasqua and Harry Green with the crime of murder in the first degree. Harry Green is not on trial here. The statements I make to you now are known as the People's opening of the case, and they contain the facts which I shall prove to you upon the trial, and upon which at the conclusion of the trial I shall ask you to convict these four defendants, now on trial, of the crime of murder in the first degree."

The trial began with Assistant Medical Examiner Charles Hochman and city toxicologist Dr. Alexander O. Gettler testifying that Michael Malloy died of monoxide gas poisoning, and not pneumonia as was listed on the death certificate. From there, the prosecution presented its compelling case, "wringing a sordid story of utter brutality from the lips of men." Insurance agents were called to the stand and detailed the gang's attempts to collect life insurance on Malloy. On Monday, October 9, the first full week of the trial got under way. It commenced with Edward Smith taking the stand and testifying that he had turned down an offer to run Malloy over. John McNally followed, and expounded on Malloy's treatment as a human speed bump. McNally's testimony "revealed the alleged murder plot in all its gruesome details," noted one reporter.

From his "seemingly unlimited supply of witnesses" Foley next called Maglione. On the stand, Maglione testified that it was Pasqua who hatched the plan to gas Malloy, and he said that he'd heard Kriesberg confess his role in the derelict's death. It was Robert Dillon, Kriesberg's attorney, who tackled the cross-examination.

"How many murders have you committed?"

"None," said Maglione."

"Well, you killed Bastone didn't you?"

"I sure did."

"It was a murder?" Dillon asked.

"No," Maglione exclaimed. "It was self-defense."

"I suppose you are too tenderhearted to kill a man?"

"Yes," Maglione.

The parade of human grist continued well into the next day—October 10—when Foley called to the stand Harry Green, "an unusually frank young man," according to *The New York Herald Tribune*. In a conversational manner, Green told how he was hired by Marino to run Malloy—and then Murray—over. Mancuso, Marino's attorney, sought to portray Green as a ruthless cutthroat.

"If you were freed in the morning, would you hesitate to kill for hire?" Mancuso asked.

"Well, I might," Green replied. "It depends on how much I need the money."

Like the other defendants, Green did not present a sympathetic character. Under questioning from Mancuso, Green admitted he would have been willing to kill Malloy for any price.

"You would have taken anything?" Mancuso demanded.

"I might have."

"To you, a human life had no value whatsoever?"

"Not at that time," Green said.

"Well, when did you first come to realize that a human life had some value, since you have been in jail, charged with murder in the first degree?"

"Yes."

"After the two attempts to kill Malloy had failed, although Malloy was struck by you, did you give it any thought that what you were doing was criminal?"

"I knew it was criminal," Green said. "But I didn't give it any thought."

"So that when Maglione again told you, or the others told you about scouting through the slums of the city to find a man who resembled Malloy, you most readily and willingly went along with them?"

"That is correct."

"And you took that as any other decent, honorable task?"

Green was unrepentant: "That is right."

It was Murray who next took the stand to recount his run-in with the now notorious "Murder Trust." Murray was followed by Ralph King, a stenographer with the District Attorney's Office, who read the statements made by the defendants on the night of May 11 and the morning of May 12 in Foley's office. King's testimony lasted well into the next day, Wednesday, October 11. The press, meanwhile, took great pleasure in reporting the news, noting "the never-dull proceedings." The in-court readings prompted *The Daily News* to pontificate on the deeper meaning of the trial when it reported on October 12:

INSURANCE DEATH TRIAL
TURNS INTO MURDER LECTURE

A seminar in murder, with theses by four unwilling candidates for a master's degree, edified the scholarly in Bronx County Court yesterday.

The subject, selected by the State, was: "How to Kill a Man—in Five Painful Lessons." The victim, Michael (Iron Man) Malloy, who ran the gamut of exhaustive laboratory experiments, could not, of course, be present.

Each thesis on the subject, displaying a knowledge of murder that bettered the best efforts of the Borgias [sic], was prosaically marked "Confession." But the clinical spirit was there.

Once the statements had been read into the record, Foley announced that the prosecution was resting its case. Court recessed for the day, thus granting the defendants "a day's respite from the ordeal of listening to the damning evidence" against them. The prosecution had presented so many witnesses, it prompted one courtroom observer to speculate that "everyone in the Bronx except the police must have known about this murder."

Rather ominously, the defense opened its case on Friday, October 13th. "Detectives were scattered through the courtroom as the defense opened its case before Judge Barrett and a jury," *The Home News* reported. "There were extra court attendants on duty to prevent any attempt at escape or the possibility of a break for freedom. The precautions, however, appeared to be unnecessary as the men faced their inquisitors."

Murphy was the first one to take the stand in his own defense. Under direct examination by his attorney Luke LeRolle, Murphy told the pathetic tale of his childhood and of a rough life on the streets. On the stand, the story he told differed considerably from the one he had told Foley back in May. He said that he hadn't known Malloy was insured until after the man's death, and further asserted that everything was done out of fear of Tough Tony. It was the first time he had resorted to the "Tough Tony defense." When Foley had questioned him several months prior, Murphy freely admitted that it was Marino who hatched the murder plot. The statement of Murphy's that had been read into evidence two days prior bore this point. Approaching the stand to cross-examine the defendant, Foley sought to set the record straight.

"Who was the first one to mention anything to you about killing this Malloy?"

"Tough Tony was."

"Well," Foley said, "you never told me that before, did you?"

"No. I didn't say or tell you that before."

"Were you afraid of Tough Tony?"

"I was," Murphy replied.

"Is that why you did not tell me?"

"Yes, sir, it is."

Foley screwed up his forehead in a look of mock puzzlement. "Well, you came to my office on the 11th day of May, didn't you?"

"I did."

"Tough Tony had been dead then a couple of months hadn't he?"

"According to my knowledge, yes."

"So it was not fear of Tough Tony that made you keep his name out of it when you gave me the statement, was it?"

"Just what do you mean?" Murphy asked.

"I mean this," Foley said. "You said a moment ago that you refrained from mentioning Tough Tony in some respect because you were afraid of him. You said that was the reason why you did not tell me about Tough Tony in the statement you gave me. You say, too, that you know that Tough Tony was dead for several months when you gave me the statement?"

"Right."

"Then, I say to you, it could not have been fear of Tough Tony that kept his name out of the statement that you gave me on May 11, could it?"

"But I didn't tell you then," Murphy exclaimed.

"You didn't tell me what?"

"What I am saying here."

"I know you did not," Foley said. "It was not fear of Tough Tony that kept his name out of the statement of May 11th, was it, when you were in my office upstairs?"

"I don't get you."

And so Foley went through the whole thing again, explaining it to Murphy as if the defendant were a mentally challenged child.

"I didn't tell you nothing about it," Murphy said. "I thought when I would get to the stand I would say that."

"Oh," said Foley. "You thought when you got here you would say it?"

"Yes," said Murphy. He told the prosecutor and jury that he had been saving the truth for the witness stand. He went on to say that he had been nothing more than a powerless "onlooker" in the killing of Malloy, adding that it was

Kriesberg who actually accomplished the nearly impossible feat by turning on the gas that evening at Fulton Avenue. This really riled up I. Julius Berg, Kriesberg's co-counsel.

"Do you want the court and jury to believe that Kriesberg turned on the gas?" Berg demanded.

"They can suit themselves," Murphy said.

"If Murphy's attitude had been belligerent during cross-examination, Marino's was more so," *The Home News* reported. "He swung his body so that he faced the jury, rather than his questioners, and stared straight at the members of the panel."

Questioned by his attorney, Francis X. Mancuso, Marino told the jury that he suffered from "several social diseases."

"You have been under medical treatment for some time, haven't you?" Mancuso asked.

"I was."

"For what?"

"For sif, clap, blue balls."

"When you say 'sif,'" Mancuso said, "you mean syphilis?"

"Syphilis is right."

"Pretty well advanced stage, wasn't it?"

"Well," said Marino, "I have the marks to prove it."

"No, steady, no," urged Mancuso. "Do not do anything unless asked."

It was Tough Tony who had concocted the scheme to kill Malloy, Marino testified—and it was Maglione "who said he had a man who would do the trick," referring to Harry Green. Tough Tony forced all of them to take part in the killing. "He was going to knock off everybody," Marino said.

Under cross-examination by Foley, Marino said he had no recollection of anything he might have previously told the prosecutor. "You don't remember anything about it?" Foley asked.

"That is right," Marino replied.

"Your recollection was fairly clear on May 11th when I talked to you, wasn't it?"

"I don't remember."

"You don't remember whether it was or not?"

"That is right."

Each of Foley's questions was met with Marino's standard answer of "I don't remember." Marino recalled nothing. He remembered no details pertaining to the collection of the insurance money. He could not remember anything about the rented room on Fulton Avenue. He harbored no memory of being a passenger in Green's cab the night they ran Malloy down. Asked by Foley if he could recall even the slightest detail, Marino responded, "No, but this is the time and place to tell the truth, before a jury. I am under oath now."

"That is all," the prosecutor said. As far as Foley was concerned, Marino's sudden bout of amnesia spoke volumes.

To bolster his client's plea of innocent by reason of insanity, Mancuso next called Dr. Alphonse Ziviello, the physician who had treated Marino for his "social diseases" from the beginning of August 1932 to September 9 of that year. These venereal issues, Ziviello said, were to blame for Marino's mental abnormalities. Although the good doctor conceded that he was not a psychiatrist, he was quick to assert, "I do think that the man was not normal mentally just from observations and his conduct."

And what, Mancuso wanted to know, were these observations?

"Well," Ziviello said, "he would come in and slam the door in my office, throw his hat on the chair or on the desk and when I called his attention to his behavior, he would always come back with a snappy answer."

Cross-examining the witness, the prosecution sought to explore the matter further.

"Have you given us the basis for your opinion as to Marino's abnormality?"

"Yes."

"Will you tell us the basis?"

"The basis of my opinion," Ziviello said, "is the observation of his conduct and behavior."

"Give us specific acts."

"Well, as I said, he would walk in my office, and would open and slam the door and throw his hat on my desk. Let the books fall down. Very frequently, as I stated before, I would ask him a perfectly good question and he might come back with a very snappy answer. 'How are you feeling?' for example. 'Well, all right,' something like that, of that sort. Those things to me are not normal."

Judge Barrett posed his own question to the witness: "You mean, Doctor, you asked him a question, 'How are you feeling?' and he says, 'All right,' and that means he is not normal?"

"No, it's the way he would answer," Ziviello said. "He would not answer in a sane fashion the way the average individual would." Ziviello continued, saying he further based his opinion of Marino's mental instability on the fact that the defendant once said he hoped to make something of his life. It was obvious, Ziviello said, that a man of Marino's stature and physical state would never amount to anything. As such, he concluded that Marino suffered from delusions of grandeur.

Pasqua's attorney sought to clarify the issue: "So, if a man said to you he hoped to make something of himself, and threw his hat on the desk and slammed the door and threw books on the floor, you would say he was insane?"

"Abnormal mentally," Ziviello said.

It was not an overly convincing argument.

* * *

On Sunday, October 15, *The Home News*—previewing the coming week's court proceedings—reported: "Tomorrow, Danny Kriesberg and Frank Pasqua, completing the quartet of accused murderers, will face the withering fire of Dist. Atty. Samuel J. Foley in his final effort to send them to the electric chair—the penalty which awaits them in the event of conviction. A survey of the testimony adduced during the past two weeks reveals the four men as their worst enemies."

Monday's court proceedings commenced with Frank Pasqua being called to the stand. Under direct examination, Pasqua said that everything was Tough Tony's idea. "It was in the month of either September or October," Pasqua said. "Tough Tony called me into the speakeasy at 3775 and he says to me that he wished to have someone insured, and I asked him who it was. He says the fellow behind the bar, meaning Mike Malloy." Pasqua denied ever taking part in the Murder Trust's brainstorming sessions. His role in the overall scheme was limited to that of an unwitting participant. He took possession of the body after Malloy died, only to discover days after burying him that he had been murdered. Furthermore, he rebuked the statement he had made to Foley in the prosecutor's office on May 11, and denied ever paying Dr. Manzella cash to fake a death certificate. Then it was Foley's turn. Wrote one reporter, "None of the men accused of participating in the crime were subjected to such grueling cross-examination as was accorded Pasqua."

Foley came out with all guns blazing—turning Pasqua's own words against him—utilizing the fact that Pasqua knew Malloy by his actual name and not that of Nicholas Mellory. It was painful to watch. He lured Pasqua into the trap by asking him about his relationship with Murphy: "When did you first meet Joseph Murphy?"

"I met Murphy about two weeks before Malloy's death," said Pasqua, lying.

"Before Malloy's death?"

"Yes."

"Did you ever know him before February of this present year?" Foley asked.

"No."

Foley, skeptical: "You never did?"

"No."

"Where was it that you met him?"

"In the speakeasy at No. 3775 Third Avenue"

"What was he doing there?" asked Foley. "Was he a customer or an employee?"

"An employee."

"By what name did you know him?"

"Red," said Pasqua, fidgeting in his seat.

"Well," said Foley as he paced up and down in front of the jury box, "when did you first find out what last name he was known by?"

"At the death of Malloy."

"What did you find out his name was then?"

"Mellory," Pasqua said. "Joseph Mellory."

"You believed that to be his true name at the time, didn't you?"

"I didn't know the man."

"Answer the question please," Foley demanded. "You believed that was Red's right name, Joseph Mellory?"

"Yes, sir."

"Did you believe that he was a brother of the deceased?"

"Yes, I did."

"Well," said Foley, "you knew the deceased's name was Michael Malloy."

"I did."

"So, you thought Joseph Mellory was Michael Malloy's brother?"

Pasqua knew his world had descended into another circle of hell. With the eyes of the jury upon him, the undertaker scrambled in his chair and tried to make something of his unfortunate situation. "No, I knew he was not his brother," he said. "That is the name he was supposed to use at the time that the death occurred."

"I asked you a moment ago, Pasqua, if at the time of the death, you believed Red to be Joseph Mellory and I think your answer was yes, is that correct?"

Pasqua was lost: "What, that I believed him to be the brother of Malloy?"

"No," Foley said. "The question that I first asked was what name did you first find out Red might be known by and your answer was Mellory, is that correct?"

"No, he was told to use the name Mellory."

Even the judge was starting to lose his patience. "Pay attention to the questions," Barrett demanded.

And then it was Foley again, riding Pasqua like a $10 whore. "Answer the question that is asked of you. Did you not say to me that Mellory was the first name by which you knew Red outside of the word 'Red' itself?"

Sinking in his chair, Pasqua said, "Yes."

"Did you not say that you believed him to be the brother of the deceased?"

"No, he was not the brother."

"Did you not say that you believed him to be the brother of the deceased?"

"Well," Pasqua said, the fight ebbing from him, "if I did say it, it was a mistake."

"Do you want to correct it?"

"Yes."

"Are you impelled to correct that statement now because I called your attention to the fact that you knew the deceased as Malloy? You knew that the name Mellory used for the deceased was a fictitious name, didn't you?"

"Yes," Pasqua sighed. And it only went downhill from there.

Foley presented to the court all the insurance applications Pasqua had filled out. "The witness seemed surprised that he had made four applications," *The Home News* reported. Foley asked Pasqua if he had tried to insure Malloy under his real name and, when that failed, tried again under the name Mellory. Pasqua said he had. "As he did so," the Bronx paper reported, Pasqua "drew a handkerchief from his pocket and dried his hands and then asked for a glass of water. It was evident that he was disturbed."

Pasqua "was almost limp and thoroughly nervous" when he left the stand. The defense next called Pasqua's wife, Elvira, to try and minimize some of the damage the undertaker had inflicted upon himself. She said Frank was a loving man who would never participate in such a vile scheme. She then turned to the judge's bench and said, "We were married five years ago next December by Judge Barrett, here." The ceremony had taken place in the very courtroom where her husband was now fighting for his life.

Several social and business acquaintances of Pasqua's were then called to the stand in rapid succession, each testifying they knew the undertaker to be a good and decent sort.

On these kind words, court recessed for the day.

When proceedings resumed on the morning of Tuesday, October 17, it was Daniel Kriesberg who took the stand. Under the direct examination of his attorney, Kriesberg gave a "rapid-fire" account of the Murder Trust's activities. Not once did he look up from his lap and make eye contact with the jury. He asserted that he was nothing more than a patsy—such was the reason the gang selected him to go to Fulton Avenue on the afternoon of February 22 and finish Malloy off. He said he was threatened with death. "I got a wife and three children" Kriesberg said. "I couldn't afford to be killed."

Under the nurturing guidance of his attorney, Kriesberg related the events as they played out in the room. He described how scared he was turning on the gas fixture as Murphy held the rubber tube in Malloy's mouth. Continuing to cast the trial as a clinical allegory, the *Daily News* reported that "Kriesberg's confession . . . marked him as No. 1 candidate for the State's highest degree (600 volts)."

Foley made mincemeat of Kriesberg on cross-examination.

"When you got to the room, you knew you were there to murder the man, didn't you?" Foley asked.

"That is right."

"Did you proceed to murder him as quietly as possible?"

"We were only up there for three minutes."

"Did you proceed to murder him as quietly as possible?" Foley repeated.

"I didn't want to murder him."

"Well," the judge interjected, "did you murder him?"

"I didn't know if he was dead or not when I left," Kriesberg said.

"Did you try to murder him?" Foley asked.

"Yes, I did."

"Did you try to murder him as quietly as possible?"

"Right."

"You did not want to be interrupted, did you?" Foley asked.

"I did want to be interrupted."

"So, that is why you made no noise at all, is that right?"

"We couldn't make any noise," Kriesberg said. "You can't make any noise."

"You were quiet because you wanted to be interrupted?"

"No, but I wish I was interrupted."

"Well, you didn't want to be interrupted then, did you?"

"Oh, yes, I did."

"February 22nd," said Foley, "is a day when many people do not have to work, is that correct?"

"I don't know."

"Well, don't you know that there are a great many people who do not have to work on Washington's Birthday?"

"A great many people do."

"Yes," conceded Foley, "but it is a holiday for some. You had a better chance of finding somebody home in the other rooms of that house on a holiday than on an ordinary working day."

"I don't know," said Kriesberg.

"But you did not try to find out if anyone was there, did you?"

"No."

"You never asked anybody in the house, say the landlady, to go and bring you a policeman, did you?"

"I didn't know the landlady."

"You never tried to find anybody in the house to help you by saying, 'I want to murder a man and I don't want to do it'?"

"I don't know."

"You don't know whether you did or not?" Foley asked. "Is that your answer?"

"Ask the question again, please."

And so Kriesberg dug a hole for himself. His testimony amounted to nothing more than a full admission of his participation in the plot and Malloy's murder. With Kriesberg having testified, all four defendants rested their cases. One could almost hear the crackling current surge through the dreaded wooden chair in the Sing Sing death house. Closing arguments got under way on Wednesday, October 18. The defense attorneys continued to argue that their clients were dominated by the fearful Tough Tony Bastone, who "packed a gat." Reported the Bronx newspaper, "The fact that Tough Tony was murdered in the same speakeasy, which served as headquarters for the 'mob,' made no difference."

Kriesberg's attorney stood before the jury first, arguing

that his client had no part in the conspiracy to kill Malloy. It was only because Kriesberg feared for his life that he went to the Fulton Avenue address with Murphy on the afternoon of February 22, Dillon said. Contrasting Kriesberg with the likes of Harry Green, Dillon sought to portray his client as a kind, gentle man lacking the coldblooded heartlessness so evident in the other conspirators.

Luke LeRolle, Murphy's attorney, placed the blame for Murphy's criminality on a childhood squandered away in unloving foster homes. A lifelong derelict, Murphy had been forced by circumstance into his current predicament. Marino's speakeasy offered the promise of warmth, drink and shelter. Lured by that promise, Murphy unfortunately "fell in with the most desperate mob of criminals I have ever seen," LeRolle said, referring to the actual speakeasy as "putrid." It was Murphy's chronic drinking that dimmed his wits and senses, blurring the stark reality of what was unfolding around him. Murphy was too drunk to realize what was going on the nights the gang went out in Green's cab and tried to kill Malloy and Murray. Murphy was simply not to blame for what happened. His voice cracking with emotion, LeRolle urged, "Free Murphy, the wandering boy from the sink hole of iniquity, in contact with the most desperate group of criminals ever to face a jury in this court . . . Put him behind prison walls where he will have a chance to redeem his soul."

Arguing for Pasqua and Marino, former judge Francis Mancuso approached the jury box. "Marino," he said, "is an imbecile incapable of plotting such a crime. Maglione was the arch-conspirator and Bastone his lieutenant. These four men were their puppets. Bastone double-crossed Maglione on the insurance split and, for that reason, was murdered." Mancuso urged that the jury hospitalize Marino for life and give the man a chance to seek treatment for his venereal and mental diseases. Pasqua, meanwhile, had done nothing more than fulfill his normal duties as undertaker, Mancuso said. He claimed the body and rendered funeral services, never knowing there was a conspiracy to kill Michael Malloy. As for the purchasing of insurance, Mancuso said it was not uncommon for undertakers to do such things for their clients. He sought to portray Pasqua as young and innocent. "Why, when Pasqua took the witness stand, he was tied up in a knot and didn't know what he was talking about," Mancuso said. "He showed the mentality of a 12-year-old boy, notwithstanding the fact that he is 24."

Foley, who had been sitting at his table scribbling notes, put his pen down and got to his feet. It was 2:45 P.M. "Malloy is dead," he said. "Let us not forget that. When you hear academic discussions about moral imbecility and faked insanity, this man said this, that man said another thing, men have records and men are accomplices and men have promised. Malloy is dead. Malloy has been murdered." Pointing to the four defendants, Foley asked: "Morally depraved? Of course, they are morally depraved, as low, vile and contemptible as the human tongue can describe."

He reviewed Pasqua's multiple attempts to secure insurance for Malloy under both real and fake names. Waving the death certificate in front of the jury, Foley blasted Dr. Manzella—who was awaiting trial—for agreeing to betray the ethics of his profession for a paltry sum. "The document signed by Dr. Manzella, the certificate of death. It might just as well be a death warrant signed by the Governor of the State because the promise of that document made by Manzella to Pasqua and relayed by him through Marino to the mob was the death knell for Malloy." The plot, Foley said, was nearly a perfect crime. Had not "Pasqua, the innocent, and Murphy, the stupid . . . the pair of them as greedy as ever lived" gone to Prudential to file a claim, perhaps their evil ways would not have come to light.

Foley took issue with the defense attorneys repeatedly

referring to Malloy as a "drunken sot, old in sin and vice."
Elaborating, he said: "Malloy was taken like a dog and
killed without any opportunity to make his peace with God,
if he believed in God. But I do have it sticking somewhat in
my throat to have this poor inoffensive old man described
as a drunken sot, old in vice and crime . . . So far as I know,
the only vice he had was that he was a drunkard; he drank
whenever the opportunity afforded. But if you can find in
that single vice anything so strongly condemnatory of him
that it deprives him of the same pity that you would give to
a dog, then perhaps you can justify what was done. How
many of you 12 men, seeing a dog lying in the street, could
run over it, and if you had run over the dog with your own
car, could you possibly turn around, go back and run over
that prostrate form again? You could not bring yourself to
do it. That is the man they tell you is a drunken sot. Well,
he had a right to live. He had a right to that same spark of
life that every one of us will instinctively fight for from the
day our mothers bore us."

Foley argued that the gang had taken Malloy's life "not
through hatred, not through malice, not through fear of
him, not for revenge, not for any understandable reason in
God's world, but because they wanted money. They sacri-
ficed him body and soul that they might have his blood
money." Foley urged no mercy. "It was the most cruel,
heartless crime. They showed no mercy to Malloy, and
they should receive none."

The courtroom was silent as Foley returned to his seat.
Addressing the jury, Judge Barrett informed the panel that
it could find the accused guilty of first- or second-degree
murder, first-degree manslaughter, or it could acquit them.
It took the judge nearly two hours to instruct the jury on
deliberations. If the jury did indeed find Marino to be insane, he could not be found guilty. Likewise, if the jury believed that Murphy's judgment was impaired by his
alcohol abuse, he, too, must be acquitted.

* * *

The jury was handed the case at 7:15 P.M. on Wednesday, October 18. "Judge Barrett announced that the members of the panel might begin deliberations immediately or go out to dinner," *The Home News* reported. "It was apparent, even then, that there was a minor difference of opinion because they could not decide for an hour to adjourn to a restaurant." At 9:15 P.M., the twelve men retired to the jury room and commenced deliberations. For more than five hours they remained behind closed doors, debating the evidence presented. In the early morning hours of Thursday, October 19, the jury requested portions of the court transcript be read to them. It took the better part of an hour for Louis Roos, the court clerk, to read the desired portions, before the jury once again retreated to its room at 4 A.M. Fifteen minutes later, word came that a verdict had been reached.

The four defendants were led back into the courtroom. On hand for the reading of the verdict and scattered throughout the courtroom were sixteen detectives, in addition to deputy sheriffs, uniformed police officers and court attendants. The atmosphere was tense as the defendants were asked to rise. One reporter noted that the four men's faces seemed to be drained of all blood, and Murphy's forehead was damp with perspiration. Edward Lowy, the jury foreman, seemed just as nervous with what he was about to do. Facing Lowy, the court clerk asked: "What is your verdict as to Daniel Kriesberg?"

The news was not good as Lowy announced that each man was guilty and must die in the electric chair. Kriesberg swayed unsteadily on his feet but managed to stay upright. Marino shot an angry glare in the jury's direction. Pasqua flinched. Murphy, however, betrayed no sense of emotion, his face a neutral landscape. The judge set formal sentencing for later that afternoon. Barrett thanked the jury for their service and for rendering a "fair and just" verdict. As officers approached the four men to take them back to jail, Bronx County Sheriff Robert L. Moran approached the judge to tell him that he wanted the convicted murderers out of the county jail as soon as possible.

Outside the courtroom, crowded by reporters, Foley was jubilant. "I don't want to give the impression of gloating over these convictions," he said. "But, once more, a Bronx jury has upheld the local reputation for common sense and courage. I think it was a proper verdict for a most cruel murder, which was inspired by nothing more than sordid greed."

Back in their cells, the condemned were in poor spirits. Murphy and Pasqua nervously paced back and fourth. Marino told one jailer who checked in on him to get lost. Kriesberg, overwhelmed by it all, lay curled on his bunk. Shivering, he asked a guard for an extra blanket.

At ten o'clock that morning, they were back in court— under heavy guard from twenty-four armed officers—for the formal sentencing. The judge said it was his understanding the men wanted to "get it over with." He sentenced Marino, Pasqua, Kriesberg and Murphy to die in Sing Sing's electric chair the week of November 20. As the judge made his pronouncement, Marino, in "a half-hearted show of bravado" turned and flashed a smile at the gathered reporters.

"Have you anything to say?" the judge asked, having passed sentence.

Speaking for all of them, it was Marino—his voice dripping with sarcasm—who answered. "We have nothing to say, Your Honor."

Guards surrounded the condemned as the proper paperwork was filled out for their transfer to Sing Sing, where, in the death house, their cells and the chair were waiting.

* * *

Early Saturday morning, the four were bundled into a large van behind the Bronx County Jail. Joining them for the ride to Sing Sing were seven deputy sheriffs and "a Negro convict sent up for five years." A reporter from United Press International tagged along. "The killers sang most of the way, their most popular song being 'My Gal, Sal,'" he wrote. "Once in a while the Negro joined in."

The van pulled up at the prison's gates, and the condemned—shackled at the wrists and ankles—were herded out of the vehicle. They had $16.05 between them. Kriesberg was the last one to enter the prison grounds. As the reality of his situation sunk in, he turned to the reporter.

"It's a fine day," Kriesberg said, "for some people."

EPILOGUE

The Final Toast

The (Ossining) *Citizen Record,* Thursday, June 7, 1934:

4 MEMBERS OF MURDER SYNDICATE WHO FINALLY KILLED 'DURABLE' MALLOY DIE IN CHAIR TONIGHT

At Sing Sing Prison tonight, in the little room with the horrible chair, the Bronx murder syndicate will sit down to death.

One by one the undertaker Frank Pasqua, the speakeasy operator Anthony Marino, the bartender Joseph Murphy, and the fruit dealer Daniel Kriesberg they will die and the state of New York will have avenged the strangest murder in its history.

After reviewing the case and Malloy's death by gas in a furnished room on Fulton Avenue, the article concluded:

The gas did it.

Tonight at Sing Sing, in another furnished room, electricity will do it.

The appeals process dragged on for five months before the day of execution arrived. On three separate occasions the condemned escaped the chair with only hours to spare. Then, one day, their luck ran out. "Four members of 'the murder trust' who were convicted of one of the most brutal murders in the history of the Bronx, are scheduled to die in the electric chair sometime after 11 o'clock tonight," *The Home News* reported on the morning of June 7. That same afternoon, the four condemned men were ushered from their cells on Sing Sing's death row and placed in pre-execution cells a dozen paces from the death chamber's door. Marino, Kriesberg and Murphy struggled to maintain their composure. Pasqua, however, was made of much softer stuff. Reported the Bronx paper: "In an effort to dodge the chair, Pasqua has hinted he is willing to 'squeal,' hinting that he had information linking the murder ring with several other insurance plots."

District Attorney Foley ultimately rejected the offer.

The execution was a big media event. In death, Malloy had become something of a grim celebrity, garnering the respect of those who covered his bizarre end. But there was a more gruesome reason for the intense interest. The state-sanctioned killing of Marino, Pasqua, Kriesberg and Murphy was to be New York's first "quartette execution" in fourteen years—the last one having taken place on December 9, 1920. On that occasion, Joseph Milano, Joseph Useoff, James Cassidy and Charles McLaughlin were electrocuted for murdering an employee while robbing an Interboro Transit station in the Bronx. But it was a crime that lacked the panache of Malloy's undoing.

* * *

Robert Campbell, a reporter with *The Daily Mirror,* spent
the afternoon hanging around the death cells, witnessing
the final hours of Marino and the lads. As the fateful strike
of the clock drew near, the men carried themselves with
decreasing dignity. They cried and pleaded for clemency,
Campbell noted. They begged Principal Keeper Sheehy for
word from Albany, but there was none to report. Campbell
recorded their final hours with dramatic flare:

> The heart-rending farewells of relatives. The visits of spir-
> itual counselors, Rev. Father John McCaffrey, Catholic
> chaplain, and Rabbi Jacob Katz. Now the final "head
> shave." Time races. It's getting dark. Outside the silver
> moonlight. A shriek of a New York Central train. Life.
> Happiness. New York.

The death house was "wet with their tears," Campbell
wrote. "No longer braggarts. Gone their Rebelaisian [sic]
banter. None of the swagger they aped when they first went
up the river. They were befuddled from fright." While
Marino, Pasqua and Kriesberg were bidding tearful
farewells to their families, Murphy sat in his cell alone. He
was the "forsaken." The only visitor he ever had was his
lawyer. Then, shortly after 8 P.M.—with just three hours to
go—the principal keeper entered Murphy's cell with word
from the governor's mansion. The bartender had been
granted a two-week reprieve.

The stay was granted by acting Governor Bray upon the
request of District Attorney Foley. The day before, Morris
Permut—one of Murphy's attorneys—had visited Foley at
his office. With him he brought Dr. Mayer Bernstein, the
physician who had befriended Murphy in the Bronx
County Jail. Bernstein told Foley that based on his own
thirty-day observation, he believed Murphy to be mentally
incompetent. This opinion was bolstered by evidence Permut presented to Foley that showed that Murphy, under his

real name of Archie Mott, had spent nearly a decade in a school for "feeble-minded boys at Mansfield, Connecticut."

When Murphy heard the news, he showed no outward sign of emotion. "Take me out of here," he said, and was removed to another cell in the death house. He would not be executed until the following month. Murphy's reprieve enlivened the others with a sense of false hope—especially Pasqua. The undertaker was not handling his predicament well. He had, it was noted, remained "dead on his feet all day. Broken through terror. A whining, nervous wreck." But there would be no exercise in mercy for Pasqua and the others. To Maglione and Green, the condemned cast bitter thoughts. For turning state's evidence against his co-conspirators, Maglione was spared a first-degree murder charge. Instead, he was sentenced on December 8, 1933, to five years in Sing Sing for manslaughter. Likewise, Green received a five- to ten-year sentence in Sing Sing for felonious assault.

Dr. Amos Baker, the prison physician, visited Marino, Pasqua and Kriesberg several hours before their execution. It was his job to assess the mental state of each prisoner and determine who would be the "lead-off" man, protocol calling for the weakest to die first. As Pasqua remained an emotional wreck, he was granted the dubious honor.

The hour finally arrived. Wrote the *The Daily Mirror*'s Campbell: "It's 11 o'clock. The crack of doom. Now the flic-flac of feet. The unlocking of the cell. 'Good-bye,' from the parched lips of the two that remain behind. The 'Last Mile.' Only a dozen steps."

Thirty witnesses sat in the death chamber's viewing gallery. Pasqua was ushered into the "silent, glaring" room at 11:01 P.M. He was accompanied by Reverend McCaffrey, "whose ministrations he appeared to accept with poor grace," *The Home News* reported. Pasqua looked nervously around the room as a team of guards strapped him into the nasty oak chair. His gaze was one of terror as the black death mask was pulled over his face. The room was silent. In his quiet protest against capital punishment, Sing Sing's Warden Lawes turned away and faced the wall. Then, at 11:02 P.M., the switch was pulled. Pasqua's body tensed. His fists clenched tightly, turning his knuckles white, and his toes curled in his prison slippers.

Again, Campbell recorded the scene in dramatic fashion: "Elliot, the official killer, twirls the wheel of death. The 'kwe-e-e-' of the dynamo. Two-thousand volts and 10 amperes. The rip-saw current that tears one apart. Three shocks." At 11:07 P.M., the current was cut. Pasqua's body went limp. He was examined by Drs. Charles Sweet and James Kearney of the prison staff. Both men pronounced him dead. As Pasqua's body was being wheeled out of the chamber on the "push buggy of death," Marino was led in. A reporter wrote that the onetime speakeasy owner "appeared small in his prison slippers and glanced nervously at Father McCaffrey as the straps were fastened into place."

The current went through Marino at 11:08 P.M. He was pronounced dead five minutes later and wheeled from the ghastly room. Last to die was Kriesberg, escorted to the chair by Rabbi Katz. He stared straight ahead as the straps were fastened across his chest, arms and legs, and the electrodes were applied to his scalp and left calf. "The tallest of the three, his jaws were set in a grim scowl" as the mask was pulled down over his face. The first of the three shocks went through Kriesberg's body at 11:14 P.M. He was pronounced dead four minutes later.

"In 17 minutes, the State has taken its toll on three lives," Campbell reported. "It's the State's toast to old 'Mike the Durable.'"

BIBLIOGRAPHY

The primary source material for *On the House* was the actual court records pertaining to the case. Archived at the Bronx County Courthouse under indictment number 462-33 and calendar number 382-33, the documents paint a sordid picture of criminal imbecility. It is these records the conversations quoted in this book come from.

ARTICLES

"The New York Speakeasy: Who Shall Close It?" *The New York Times,* Sunday, September 15, 1929.

"1932 is Booted Out, New Year Greeted with Noisy Revelry," *The New York Times,* January 1, 1933.

"Counterfeiters Active During the Depression," *The New York Times,* Sunday, March 12, 1933.

" 'Two-Gun' Gangster Is Murdered for Insult in Speakeasy Dispute," *The Home News,* Monday, March 20, 1933.

"Insurance Murder 'Trust' Seen In Arrest of Five for Man's Death," *The Home News,* Friday, May 12, 1933.

"6 Held in Insurance Death Plot, Gas Finally Kills Hardy Malloy Victim," *The New York Evening Post,* Friday, May 12, 1933.

"Insurance Murder Charged To Five," *The New York Times,* Saturday, May 13, 1933.

"Insurance Plot Inquiry Told of 2 More Victims," *The New York Herald Tribune,* Saturday, May 13, 1933.

"Seven Seized in Insurance Murder Trust," *The Daily Mirror,* Saturday, May 13, 1933.

"Strange Death of Woman Is Linked to 'Murder Trust' as Quiz Widens," *The Home News,* Saturday, May 13, 1933.

"Two More Deaths Linked to Plot," *The Sun,* Saturday, May 13, 1933.

"Blame Insurance Ring for Death of One's Sweetheart," *The New York Daily News,* Sunday, May 14, 1933.

"City-Wide 'Murder Trust' Inquiry Looms as Other Deaths Are Probed," *The Home News,* Sunday, May 14, 1933.

"Girl Identified In 'Murder Trust'," *The Daily Mirror,* Sunday, May 14, 1933.

"Girl's Murder By Pneumonia Duped Doctor," *The Home News,* Sunday, May 14, 1933.

"Murder Plot Seen In Another Death," *The New York Times,* Sunday, May 14, 1933.

"Murder Trust Witness Feared 'Ride' Victim," *The Daily Mirror,* Monday, May 15, 1933.

"Police Learn Name of 3d Marked for Death by Trust," *The New York Daily News*, Monday, May 15, 1933.

"First of 20 Witnesses Called Before Grand Jury in 'Murder Trust' Quiz," *The Home News*, Tuesday, May 16, 1933.

"5 Are Indicted As Murderers for Insurance," *The New York Herald Tribune*, Wednesday, May 17, 1933.

"5 Indicted as Murderers In Insurance Ring Probe," *The New York Daily News*, Wednesday, May 17, 1933.

"Indicted As Slayers In Insurance Plot," *The New York Times*, Wednesday, May 17, 1933.

" 'Murder Trust' Inquiry Is Pressed Following Indictment of Six Suspects," *The Home News*, Wednesday, May 17, 1933.

" 'Murder Trust' Suspects to Face Immediate Trial," *The Home News*, Thursday, May 18, 1933.

"Murder Trust Linked to Third Death as Police Launch Hunt for Girl Aide," *The Home News*, Sunday, May 21, 1933.

"Bronx Man Held As Murder Proxy," *The New York Evening Post*, Thursday, May 25, 1933.

" 'Murder Trust' Witness Found in River Camp," *The Home News*, Thursday, May 25, 1933.

"Substitute Victim In Murder Found," *The New York Times*, Friday, May 26, 1933.

"Vagrant Welcomes Stay in Jail Cell as Witness in 'Murder Trust' Case," *The Home News*, Friday, May 26, 1933.

"Witness Called Insurance Plot Substitute Held," *The New York Herald Tribune*, Friday, May 26, 1933.

"Six Chose For Jury In Insurance Murder," *The New York Times*, Tuesday, October 3, 1933.

"4 On Trial In Bronx In Insurance Slaying," *The New York Times,* Thursday, October 5, 1933.

"Murder Trial Is Told of Insurance Dummy," *The New York Times,* Friday, October 6, 1933.

"Jury Hears Gruesome Tale of Cold Brutality Charged to 'Death Trust,'" *The Home News,* Tuesday, October 10, 1933.

"Got $20 To Run Down Man With A Taxicab," *The New York Times,* Wednesday, October 11, 1933.

"Hired as Killer for $150, Taxi Driver Admits," *The New York Herald Tribune,* Wednesday, October 11, 1933.

"Taxi Driver Admits Two Attempts to Slay 'Insurance-Trust' Victim," *The Home News,* Wednesday, October 11, 1933.

"Confessions Bare A $50 Murder Fee," *The New York Times,* Thursday, October 12, 1933.

"Four on Trial in 'Insurance Slaying' Base Case on Fear of 'Tough Tony,'" *The Home News,* Thursday, October 12, 1933.

"Jury Told Gas Extinguished Durable Malloy," *The New York Herald Tribune,* Thursday, October 12, 1933.

"Bastone Called State Manager in Malloy Death," *The New York Herald Tribune,* Saturday, October 14, 1933.

"'Murder Trust' Defense, Fighting for Lives, Blames Slain Gangster," *The Home News,* Saturday, October 14, 1933.

"Two Shift Blame In Insurance Death," *The New York Times,* Saturday, October 14, 1933.

"Man Accused as Actual Killer Takes Stand Tomorrow in Insurance Death," *The Home News,* Sunday, October 15, 1933.

"Harlem Mortician Denies Knowledge of Murder Plot in Derelict's Death," *The Home News,* Monday, October 16, 1933.

"Dead Man Blamed In Insurance Murder," *The New York Times*, Tuesday, October 17, 1933.

"Four on Trial for Insurance Murder May Hear Verdict Tonight," *The Home News*, Wednesday, October 18, 1933.

"Malloy Murder Trial Near End," *The New York Evening Post*, Wednesday, October 18, 1933.

"Murder Testimony Ends," *The New York Times*, Wednesday, October 18, 1933.

"Plotter Relates Gas Tube Exit of Durable Malloy," *The New York Herald Tribune*, Wednesday, October 18, 1933.

"Four Found Guilty in Malloy Killing," *The New York Evening Post*, Thursday, October 19, 1933.

"Jury Holds Fate Of Four Men in Insurance Death," *The New York Daily News*, Thursday, October 19, 1933.

"Jury Weighs Fate Of Four In Killing," *The New York Times*, Thursday, October 19, 1933.

"Death Verdict Stuns 4 Who Gassed Malloy," *The New York Herald Tribune*, Friday, October 20, 1933.

"Four Convicted in Insurance Killing Sentenced to Die in Week of Nov. 20," *The Home News*, Friday, October 20, 1933.

"4 Doomed To Chair For Insurance Plot," *The New York Daily News*, Friday, October 20, 1933.

"4 Malloy Killers Sentenced to Die," *The New York Evening Post*, Friday, October 20, 1933.

"Four Men To Die For Bronx Killing," *The New York Times*, Friday, October 20, 1933.

" 'Murder Trust' Quartette Sings on Trip to Sing Sing," *The Home News*, Saturday, October 21, 1933.

"Admits Injuring Malloy," *The New York Times*, Tuesday, November 15, 1933.

"Appeal Delays Death Penalty," *The New York Times*, Sunday, November 20, 1933.

"Appeal Stays Slayer's Death," *The New York Times*, Monday, November 21, 1933.

"Fifth Member of 'Murder Trust' Is Given Five-to-Ten-Year Prison Term," *The Home News*, Monday, November 21, 1933.

"Murder Witness Jailed," *The New York Times*, Monday, November 21, 1933.

"Admits Insurance Killing," *The New York Times*, Monday, November 28, 1933.

"4 Scheduled to Die in Chair at Sing Sing," *The Citizen Record*, Wednesday, June 6, 1934.

"4 Members of Murder Syndicate Who Finally Killed 'Durable' Malloy Die in Chair Tonight," *The Citizen Record*, Thursday, June 7, 1934.

"Four of Bronx Murder Trust to Die Tonight," *The Home News*, Thursday, June 7, 1934.

"3 Die at Sing Sing Prison for Bronx Murder," *The New York Times*, Friday, June 8, 1934.

"Three Die In Chair For Barfly Murder," *The Daily Mirror*, Friday, June 8, 1934.

"Three of Murder Trust Die in Chair, Fourth is Reprieved for Sanity Test," *The Home News*, Friday, June 8, 1934.

"New Murphy Evidence Heard," *The New York Times*, Wednesday, June 20, 1934.

"Murphy Goes to the Chair," *The New York Times*, Friday, July 6, 1934.

"Judge S. J. Foley, 60, Of The Bronx Dies," *The New York Times,* Tuesday, May 15, 1951.

Aspects on the debauched history of drunkenness and prohibition were garnered from the following sources:

BOOKS

Behr, Edward. *Prohibition: 13 Years That Changed America.* Arcade Publishing, 1996.

Coffey, Thomas M. *The Long Thirst: Prohibition in America 1920–1933.* W. W. Norton & Co. Inc., 1975.

Sann, Paul. *Kill the Dutchman! The Story of Dutch Schltz.* Arlington House, New Rochelle, New York, 1971.

Hirschfeld, Al. *The Speakeasies of 1932.* Glenn Young Books, 2003.

Additional details on the strange case of Michael Malloy were found in:

Wallace, Irving, and David Wallechinsky. *The People's Almanac #2.* Bantam Books, 1978.

Simon Read lives in the San Francisco Bay Area, where he works as a newspaper reporter. He does not have a wife or a pet. He enjoys a drink and is currently working on his next book, *In the Dark: A True Tale of Murder in Wartime London,* which will be published by Berkley in 2006. You can reach him through his website at www.simon-read.com.

Penguin Group (USA) Online

What will you be reading tomorrow?

Tom Clancy, Patricia Cornwell, W.E.B. Griffin,
Nora Roberts, William Gibson, Robin Cook,
Brian Jacques, Catherine Coulter, Stephen King,
Dean Koontz, Ken Follett, Clive Cussler,
Eric Jerome Dickey, John Sandford,
Terry McMillan…

You'll find them all at
penguin.com

Read excerpts and newsletters,
find tour schedules and reading group guides,
and enter contests.

Subscribe to Penguin Group (USA) newsletters
and get an exclusive inside look
at exciting new titles and the authors you love
long before everyone else does.

PENGUIN GROUP (USA)
penguin.com/news